LISTENING DEEPLY

LISTENING DEEPLY

An Approach to Understanding and
Consulting in Organizational Culture

Second Edition

Howard F. Stein

UNIVERSITY OF MISSOURI PRESS
Columbia

ISBN: 978-0-8262-2124-7
LCCN: 2017932460

∞™ This paper meets the requirements of the
American National Standard for Permanence of Paper
for Printed Library Materials, Z39.48, 1984.

Typefaces: Frutiger and Garamond

Portions of Chapter 3 were previously published as "Enuresis and Its Contexts: From Organizational Crisis to Family Ghost," *Family System Medicine* 9 (1) (1991): 77-81. Copyright © 1991 by the American Psychological Association. Reproduced with Permission.

Letter of permission from Joanne Preston, Editor, *Organization Development Journal* to Howard F. Stein, May 10, 2016. Portions of Chapters 4 and 6 were previously published as "Metaphors of Organizational Trauma and Organizational Development: A Case Example," *Organization Development Journal* 9 (4) (Winter 1991): 22-30; portions of Chapter 5 were previously published as "Aggression, Grief-work, and Organizational Development: Theory and Case Example" and "Unconscious Factors in Organizational Decision-making: A Case Study from Medicine," *ODJ* 6 (1) (Spring 1988): 22-28 and 4 (2) (Summer 1986): 21-24; portions of Chapter 6 were also previously published as "New Bosses, Old Losses: A Brief Case Study in Organizational Culture," *ODJ* 8 (2) (Summer 1990): 1-5. Permission to reprint is gratefully acknowledged.

Advances in Organizational Psychodynamics

Michael A. Diamond, Series Editor

Dedication, Second Edition

To Seth Allcorn, Ph.D., and Michael A. Diamond, Ph.D.
With gratitude and friendship

Dedication, First Edition

To Richard Smith, M.D.
In friendship

Contents

Foreword to the Second Edition

The writer of a foreword may approach this work from many different perspectives. I write this foreword both to acknowledge the new, expanded, and updated book, and to complement the foreword written by Michael Diamond for the first writing of the book 22 years ago. Much has changed in how Howard Stein sees, understands, knows, and explains listening deeply. It is a challenging perspective not only to understand but also to apply in practice, something he has now more than two decades of additional experience in doing. His grounding of listening deeply in psychoanalytically informed theory remains much the same but better explained and explored. This book is a bold new effort to provide consultants, managers, executives, and students of organizations with a way to grasp group and organizational dynamics using one's inner knowledge of what is going on. By listening deeply to one's own evoked thoughts and feelings, there is a metaphoric amplification of sensing the dynamics of individuals, groups, and organizations. There is in this appreciation a wonderfully complex but also simple approach to grounding consulting and management in the realities of work life.

I feel it is important before proceeding to take a moment to provide some transparency. Howard Stein and I have been friends and colleagues for a great many years, and we have collaborated on writing books and scholarly papers, as is also the case with Michael Diamond, the author of the foreword to the first version of this book. We share a common perspective and approach to understanding organizations and their many and ever-changing dynamics. Our shared psychodynamically informed approach to the study of organizations forms the basis of this book. It is therefore with this very deep appreciation of Howard Stein's work that I provide this foreword.

I begin by saying I wish to echo Michael Diamond's appreciation of being there for others as a thoughtful, reflective listener who draws upon many contemporary psychoanalytic theorists to create insight and understanding. Giving others a chance to be heard is a gift to others. The book is both scholarly and also available to all readers, and the many stories make the theory accessible and usable. The author takes the reader through the complexity of the multidimensional nature of organizational life by combining theory and practice, illuminated by the many stories that operationalize listening deeply.

Those who study, consult to, or manage organizations usually do so from the perspective of a theoretical lens. These lenses may be acquired from reading, study, courses, and degree programs; from life experience and observing role models; or they are sometimes simply self-fabricated in an organic sense to fit one's self and are seldom open to learning and reflection. In practice all of these may apply to understanding organizations, and they will vary over time, as well as be altered to fit the context of the moment. Howard Stein presents the reader with an opportunity to learn about what is an entirely different approach. He grounds listening deeply in the telling of stories infused with insight about the workplace, and how the lenses may be used to peel away the surface of organizational life. He reveals discussable and ignored aspects of the inner life of organizations that are always present, influencing daily life, events, decisions, and responses to change, however adeptly conceived and managed. The author leads the reader through an applied psychodynamically informed organizational landscape, revealing many treasures along the path. He offers us for consideration a humble approach for consulting, organizational research, and management, one that is not grounded in knowing and one not defended by a cloak of specialized language and expertise. The abandonment of knowing, specialized language, and expertise leaves the consultant naked before everyone and in a sense vulnerable; but by so doing, the consultant becomes an instrument of listening deeply, using empathy and respect and the self as the center of knowing via reflectivity.

Consultants must ultimately mediate between the known and unknown, knowable and unknowable, while containing the attendant anxiety for self and others in the service of helping the organization and its members to hear from the consultant an accessible story of their lives at work. Those who listen deeply must appreciate that their lives are largely the basis for selecting questions, ordering observations, collecting data, and influencing our interpretations. Consultants, managers, and others have to bring conscious awareness of these inner dynamics to their work in order to have truly listened deeply. Locating meaning in their subjective experience of self and others is supported by their own authenticity of being there emotionally and accessibly in the moment. To be successful, thinking must be integrated with feeling, to promote reflection instead of compulsive actions aimed at avoiding painful thoughts and feelings. The heart of listening deeply is attentiveness to voices—those of others and one's own inner voices.

The author speaks to a process of discovery, less dependent on theories and methods and more reliant on trusting in himself to come to simply understand in depth. By abandoning control he arrives at a sense of full emergence in the story he is hearing and witnessing. He has empathy. There is a part of him that knows not to rely on filters of theories and social methods, instead placing his faith and trust in himself and relationships with others and groups. This is the basis for this book and his approach to working with organizations. This is the core of listening deeply that has as its main tools: (1) Inquiry into the breadth and historical depth of organizational issues; (2) Empathy combined with the ability imagine oneself as others and groups; (3) Efforts to help organizational members to be heard and understood; (4) Creation of a safe enough and preferably collaborative potential space and holding environment, created by the consultant serving as a temporary container for raw and emotionally toxic emotions; and (5) Sparing use of confrontation and interpretation relative to others and groups. The consultant who promotes listening deeply in organizations must help others and groups to tolerate not knowing and the accompanying anxiety by containing this experience and returning the toxic emotions and workplace experience in an available way that makes accessible the many out-of-awareness and unconscious aspects of work life that ultimately drive much of what happens at work. The professional stranger is empowered to do this critically important work unlike anyone else in the organization (Agar, 1980). The consultant can speak to the underlying dynamics in a way no one else can.

Listening deeply in part arises from analyzing one's own unconscious that has been influenced by the individual and group unconscious. They are interactive in mind and in practice. In this regard every consultation becomes field research using self and other subjectively and intersubjectively as the unit of study. The consultant must avoid premature closure and thinking "you" know when you do not. You have to be comfortable wandering around within the psychic realities of the participants as compared with the official task of studying the group in the present moment; a point well made in the discussion of Balint groups in medical education. In particular you have to be comfortable tolerating what is sometimes collective denial and rationalization where reality becomes distorted in the service of minimizing individual and group anxiety. That these many considerations and challenges speak to listening deeply is wonderfully illustrated in the many informative stories the author provides that evoke a much greater understanding and appreciation of listening deeply. Every story draws in applicable theory and modes of thought that are the organizational principles of this book.

In this book the author begins with theory and ends with stories that tie together the theory with practice, and blend feeling and self-awareness with objectivity and subjectivity, self and other, and group and organizational dynamics.

Through the many stories told in this book, the sweep of organizational experience is revealed in all of its rationality and irrationality, demonstrating how groups function both consciously and unconsciously. Storytelling, it becomes clear, helps to detoxify what has been experienced as emotionally invasive and poisonous. Stories and their telling can be healing. The stories help us, the readers, navigate the theory and understand the potentially therapeutic outcomes of stories and their healing capacity. The stories help us to examine the workplace from many new and different perspectives, often validating, perhaps, the reader's own toxic experiences at work. The stories also underscore how moral and ethical behavior can be encouraged in a workplace if the toxicity is exposed and managed, the harm that has been created is healed, and thoughtful and reflective organizational dynamics are encouraged. Listening deeply contributes to this. The stories provided allow the reader to join with the author in exploring our lives at work. They are, as pointed out, a gift to the listener and the reader, something to enjoy for learning and healing.

Yet another aspect of the book that is unique and an important contribution to consulting and organizational literature is the exploration of the metaphoric nature of work experience and the complexities of leadership within a larger context of loss and grief. Metaphors are helpful in that they condense, organize, and unconsciously represent a group's unconscious fantasy about life in the group while also creating meaning. They sometimes represent the unspeakable aspects of work life, as well as the joyful and pleasurable aspects. The author makes clear how understanding metaphors promotes insight, understanding, and a way of changing the workplace. They must be listened to.

The author also explores in depth the triad of change, loss, and grief that often emerges as a central theme underlying chronic organizational distress. Change, even if well conceived and managed, triggers anxiety. How will this change affect me and us? During the last 30 years, sweeping and abrupt forms of organizational change have transformed the employee/employer contract, marginalizing everyone who works. These destructive types of change, often subsumed under the notion of downsizing and its many derivatives, have become commonplace experiences shared by all workers. Downsizing, we have come to understand, destroys meaning and dignity, and it takes away everything that makes a human being feel worthwhile. People often feel crushed, devastated, angry, fearful, and, in particular, anxious about their continued employment if they survive a downsizing. In the face of this miasma of despair, listening deeply to the stories of people who have been terminated and those who have "survived" (at least for a while) is spiritually as well as psychologically validating. It helps to heal the despair and harm of becoming an expendable, objectified human resource. Miasma is a group response to organization carnage often arising from ill-considered forms of organizational change such as downsizing. It resides in unresolved anger, betrayal, grief, and the loss of hope and meaning for self and the organization, as well as the sense of loyalty and fair play. Listening deeply to change dynamics like this becomes a form of bearing witness and may be in part seen as a gift of the heart for those who have suffered through this top-down imposed carnage that has cut out the heart of many organizations. This outcome of these destructive types of change, sometimes euphemistically referred to as low morale, is ironically seen as undesirable by the same executives who worked so hard to downsize not only their organization but also the performance of their organization. Listening deeply may not stop these management methods from wreaking havoc, but it can become an important contributor to helping those subjected to it to live through it. Some healing is possible especially from listening to the stories of the survivors.

Last, leadership remains not only one of the singularly important aspects of work life, but also one that possesses many complexities, making it hard to understand what leadership is and what is the best way to lead. The author offers us a way out of the dismal swamp just described. He speaks to a form of "good enough leadership" based on safety, listening, and holding that is far removed from often colder and harsher, if not "macho," leaders whom one finds in organizations and politics that have an even greater tendency to arise during periods of high stress, when individual and group regression arises and a strong leader promises safety. The notion of the good enough leader offers an important perspective on leadership that need not be top down, unilateral, and command-and-control oriented—methods that are so often associated with effective leadership in organizations for reasons the author makes clear—are questionable. Good enough leadership is possible.

I conclude by noting that his book provides its reader a rich, sophisticated, and accessible way to learn about organizations, as well as to consult with and manage them. Having worked many years as a midlevel and senior executive in large, complex organizations, I wish to emphasize the relevance of this book to anyone aspiring to a management role, and to managers and executives who aspire to the highest levels of professional management. I know from using the knowledge Howard Stein provides us in this book that it can contribute to better leadership and organizational performance. Enjoy this book. It is one of a kind.

Seth Allcorn
August 2016

Foreword to the First Edition

The reason why we have two ears and only one mouth is that we may listen the more and talk the less.

—Zeno of Citium, c. 300 B.C.

What strikes me in reading this book is how inept we are, myself included, at something as fundamental to the survival of humankind as listening—let alone listening deeply. Stein, a psychoanalytic, organizational anthropologist, views listening as a catalyst for what I call organizational development and repair—making individuals and their organizations whole again by listening deeply. He writes, "To feel heard and understood is perhaps the most precious gift in life. It is a symbolic holding, one that can return the emotionally numbed or deadened to life."

Stein's use of the word *numbed* is, I'm certain, quite intentional and, I believe, critical. In Robert Jay Lifton's *Nazi Doctors*, the author of this terrifying and groundbreaking social research proffers the psychological phenomenon of "doubling" to explain the actions of Nazi physicians who were murderers by day and loving fathers by night. How could they have lived such polarized and opposing existences? How could they have kept these parts of themselves separate? For Lifton, doubling entailed "psychic numbing" of the Nazi group self—a psychological process that depersonalized and dehumanized the physicians' actions, divorcing their actions from themselves. Thus, they could stand on the platform and dispassionately select who might live and who must die and then go home to their adoring families with no apparent remorse or conflict over these murderous actions. The moral core of Stein's book rests in his genuine concern for the potential harm and destructive nature of unconscious group and organizational life. He is not an ordinary organizational consultant.

In this book, Howard Stein explains and illustrates with numerous cases his use of self as a primary instrument for helping members of groups and organizations work more humanely and confidently. His approach to organizational consultation is a psychodynamic one. Stein does not work from the tradition of so-called Freudian orthodoxy, in which the analyst assumes the metaphorical role of archaeologist in search of some objective, historical truth. Rather, Stein seeks and deeply values the narrative truth described by Donald Spence (1984). Stein consults in a pluralistic, contemporary psychoanalytic tradition, one influenced by the pioneering works of Wilfred R. Bion (1959, 1963), Donald Winnicott (1953, 1965c, 1971), and Heinz Kohut (1971, 1972, 1984). Stein employs Bion's notion of the container to describe how groups in organizations use him in his consulting role as a carrier of threatening and anxiety-producing feelings. Stein uses Winnicott's idea of the holding environment to illustrate the essence of listening deeply in the process of group and organizational consultation. And Stein draws on Kohut's therapeutic technique of combining empathy and introspection to establish the necessary degree of trust and affection with clients so that they can discuss and work through negative feelings and paradoxical relationships. In Stein's so-called Balint groups, physicians discuss emotionally difficult relationships they have with their patients, staff, colleagues, and supervisors—an almost unheard-of event in most health science centers.

A consultant with Stein's philosophy must be skilled in the art of reflective practice and self-awareness. As Eric Hoffer (1955, p. 158) puts the matter in *The Passionate State of Mind*, "We can see through others only when we see through ourselves." The application and ongoing utilization of what psychoanalysts call the countertransference in the consultant–client relationship is central to Stein's work with people in a multitude of organizational settings. And unlike many analysts, he makes no apologies for this—in fact, he seems implicitly, if not explicitly, to stress the inevitability as well as the reliability of one's self-experience of the other and the organizational context.

Here the analyst, or in Stein's case the organizational consultant, is in search of what I call organizational identity, the intersubjective meaning of organizational life (Diamond, 1993). Forget the idea of observation without reflective participation; Stein's model of consulting relies on the clinical and fundamentally human skill of listening deeply.

However, Stein does not like commonplace organizational development (OD) terminology, such as *intervention*. He finds it reminiscent of military verbiage and therefore aggressive and confrontational, not unlike the way some consultants actually work. Stein's approach is anything but aggressive, at least as it is presented in this book. One gets the sense of the client being embraced and nourished at the good mother's breast before being lovingly encouraged to travel unfamiliar emotional terrain. Stein provides a safe and comfortable ride for his organizational passengers over rough and often unexplored highways. Through listening deeply, Stein confirms the legitimacy of self (self-in-other) and thereby validates the client's intra- and interpersonal world in the organizational context.

The world of organizations, for Stein, transcends managers' concerns with the bottom line and technical-rational statements of purpose and mission. His organizational world is a deeply moral one. Organizational consultants, he believes, must not ignore the evils wrought by various types of institutions in the twentieth century. After reading this book, organizational consultants and researchers may begin asking themselves the following questions:

What is it like to be a member of their clients' organizations? How do their clients feel about organizational membership?

What in the consultant's own experience can he or she draw upon to better identify and appreciate the client's work world?

What are the intersubjective experiences of people in organizations and the nature of their relationships?

What is the historical background?

What do the stakeholders require of workers, and how does this contribute to their experience?

In what manner are members associated and disassociated from each other, their colleagues, clients, customers, and patients?

Is organizational complexity the result of insulated disciplines and professions fragmented from each other and the organizational system?

Are divisional boundaries unnecessarily rigid and closed off from the host community and task environment of the institution?

Do organizational members trust one another?

If not, are they able to care enough about one another to collaborate and solve their problems and consequently improve the quality of service to the community and the condition of organizational life?

I think the reader will find, as I have, that this book instills a great appreciation for the need to develop and sharpen the ability to listen deeply as an organizational consultant and researcher. I wish to thank Howard Stein for his wisdom and for this book, which makes a valuable contribution to psychoanalytic organizational studies in particular and organizational consultation in general.

Michael A. Diamond, Ph.D.
1994

Preface

To Begin with a Story:
Storytelling and Story Listening as Healing

In the early 1990s, my friend and colleague Seth Allcorn was conducting a year-long study of the experience of downsizing at General Hospital. He had completed his second round of directive but open-ended interviews of executives and employees. He and I were discussing this process on the phone. From his description of *listening* to participants' harrowing stories, it occurred to me that he was not simply eliciting and collecting field data, but was also having a therapeutic effect through the act of caring enough to listen to people's stories. I shared my thought with Seth Allcorn, who thought about it, and realized that he was both obtaining information and actually helping people in the process. For many interviewees, the process was healing.

He then decided to ask an additional, final question in his subsequent interviews: "How did you experience the interviewer and interviewing process?" (Allcorn, Baum, Diamond, & Stein, 1996, p. 15). One woman executive said she had a headache when she came into the interview. "The interviewing was a benign experience. It took an hour of my time. It was kind of nice. I had a legitimate chance to unload. My headache [that she had at the beginning of the interview] is better now" (1996, p. 153).

Attentive, empathic listening, to a person treated as a distinct human being, is never "just" listening. It is a precious gift of the listener to the speaker, just as telling one's story is a gift to the listener. The same holds when one is working with groups as organizational researcher or consultant. I have come to realize that I do my best work listening, and that I try to respond from having listened. This story is part of my personal evolution toward understanding the importance of listening deeply.

Listening Beneath the Surface of Language

This book is about listening. In particular, it is about listening as an instrument of helping people in organizations identify, address, and solve problems that lie beneath the surface. It is also about why so many organizational problems defy resolution. It explores the importance of attentive listening in all facets of organizational consulting. It argues that deep listening is crucial to understanding human behavior in a specific kind of group, workplaces—and far beyond. It is about both language and processes that underlie language. It is about the ordinary that goes unheeded or unnoticed.

This book is about tolerating the experience of not knowing and about not having "the answers" beforehand. Answers become something fashioned in the playfully created space between consultant and client (person or organization), not some abstract expertise already stored in the consultant and waiting to be sprung. Answers are not nouns; they are verbs. They are the always-provisional product of processes, not rabbits a magician pulls from a hat. This book is about what psychoanalysts call "hovering attention" and anthropologists call a "holistic" attitude toward people and their cultures. In not knowing what to listen for, we stand the chance of hearing what we usually edit out as extraneous or incidental but what is, in fact, essential.

Applicability of Listening Deeply

This book shows how much we depend on attentive listening to do our work, enhance our relationships, and unleash human potential. The book demonstrates how far-reaching the consequences of poor listening are, illuminates the causes of poor listening, and develops a theory of deep listening. Although there are numerous works on listening (e.g., Frank, 1998, 2013; Rutter, 2003; Back, 2007), what this book does is to add the dimension of *experiential depth* to what has already been written. Specifically, this is what I will take the term "psychoanalytic" to mean. Psychoanalytic listening goes beyond "just listening" and active listening. Listening deeply opens us to consider the possibility that psychodynamics are not an afterthought or epiphenomenon of economics, but rather that psychological reality shapes organizational processes and creates a "reality" all its own.

I believe that this book is of value whether the reader has a psychoanalytic mode of thinking or not. For me, "psychoanalytic" does not denote some mysterious, arcane language knowable only by the few believers, but rather refers to the psychological depths of human experience, much of which is unconscious, that is, for dynamic reasons, out of awareness to us. My hope is to make this realm more accessible to the reader.

Further, while the focus of this book is deep listening—and its failures and successes—among *organizational* consultants, researchers, and leaders, its method and message are applicable to all the "listening professions," indeed, to everyone. In these days of solitary immersion in the so-called "social media" of smartphones, Facebook, Twitter, and the Internet, there is the urgent need for deep listening whether one is an organizational consultant, organizational researcher, corporate leader, or physician, researcher, attorney, teacher, clergy, police person, firefighter, politician, diplomat, parent, or spouse—in fact, everyone. While the focus of this book is the need for deep listening among organizational consultants, researchers, and leaders, its compass extends far beyond their boundaries.

How I Think I Work

This book is also an attempt to answer the question often posed to me, "What exactly is it that you do?" For more than four and a half decades, I have been teaching physicians and other health care practitioners how to work with patients, their families, their communities, and with each other individually and collectively. I also consult with many types of organizations. Most fundamentally, I help people listen to each other and to themselves. Everything else follows from the ability, willingness, and courage to hear. Although I have written many articles and books that describe physician–patient relationships and American medicine (Stein & Apprey, 1985, 1990), friends and colleagues have urged that I write specifically about *how I work* in day-to-day consultations and conferences. That is, they have asked me to make an explicit methodological road map of my approach, not only of my results. Over the years, I have expanded teaching and consulting from within strictly academic and medical settings to a wide variety of corporate and other organizational cultures.

Much of this book attempts to answer another question: How do people in organizational groups and subgroups "hear" each other (or fail to hear), and what, if anything, can I do to improve their willingness and ability to "listen"? In the stories presented, I identify numerous impediments to listening and describe a consultation approach that is less consultant focused than it is listening focused. My methodological theme is that the consultant who listens attentively to others helps them listen attentively to themselves and to one another. By asking how people hear each other and what this means for how they experience their organization—not only for what they do officially—I am able to accompany them on a voyage to the center of their own organizational identity, history, and sense of meaning.

We are far better at speaking than listening. Often we listen only superficially, waiting for our turn to speak. Often we make up our reply while the other person is still speaking. In the process, we shut them out. How, then, can we truly hear—be capable of being moved, even changed, by what that other person or group has to say? Sometimes the only voice we listen to is our own. This book is about listening to other voices, about caring enough about and valuing the other person or group to listen attentively to them.

Stories, the fruit of listening deeply, are the heart and "guts" of this book (Gabriel, 2000). The dance of *storytelling* and *story listening* (Allcorn & Stein, 2016) will frequently take center stage throughout the chapters. I hope that these stories will "work" with you, the reader, in at least two ways: first, to be of value in themselves in evoking, understanding, and helping to account for workplace life; and second, to remind you of your own organizational stories—and in them, your own life. As your guide through organizational life, I will serve alternately as storyteller and story listener.

In short, *Listening Deeply* explores the pivotal role of listening in organizational research, consulting, and leadership. Business and the wider culture are dominated by visual communication (e.g., PowerPoint presentations, laptop computers, smartphones), while listening is far less valued. Yet, listening attentively to another person or group is never "just listening" or "merely listening." We often *hear* but do not *listen*—we prepare our response while the other person is still speaking. Yet, we do our best work listening—and caring enough to listen and digest what the other person is saying. Deep listening in organizations is about fostering a creative, transitional space (Winnicott, 1953) between people in order to help them feel safe enough to play with ideas, and ultimately, to come up with new solutions to organizational problems. This book explores how deep listening works in organizational communication, and how it improves organizational communication and in turn functioning. At a personal level, the reader will gain a sense of how I listen—or at least *try* to listen—in my own work as organizational consultant, researcher, and sometimes, leader.

The Situation of Listening Deeply

What kind of situation is listening deeply? At its core, listening deeply to another person, and sharing an experience or story with the listener, is a *gift* exchange. When I try to explain what happens, the best I can do is to speak through metaphors. To say that the relationship—even for an organizational researcher who is not a consultant—is "therapeutic" is only the starting point of understanding the gift exchange. What is going on? How does the "therapeutic" process work?

The listener creates a safe space in which to think and feel, to disclose oneself to another. The listener serves as a receptacle to contain all the thoughts, feelings, gestures, and breaths that the storyteller offers. By standing or sitting still and offering rapt attention and sometimes a brief comment, the listener helps to change what the storyteller has said, from being indigestible to being more digestible and even metabolizable. The storyteller senses that the listener is truly there—present—for him or her. The storyteller may even say with surprise, "You really heard me," or "I hadn't thought of it before now" (where the "it" refers to something the storyteller or the story listener has said).

As the story is told in the crucible of the relationship, it often feels to both participants that their boundaries have become fuzzy, ill defined, and that the feeling is good rather than alarming. The story and storytelling are located between them, almost as if it has a separate, distinct reality of its own (what Thomas Ogden, 1999, calls an intersubjective analytic "third"). To the participants, the interpersonal validation feels like an alternate state of consciousness from normal, rational, linear thinking. It feels precious, creative, playful—Real. In this transitional space, there occurs the constant interplay of giving, receiving, accepting, reflecting, processing, and giving back. For both storyteller and listener, the power of deep listening offers the possibility of learning and feeling something new, even as the story itself covers old ground. The story becomes at once past, present, and future. There is space in which a new story might emerge.

All this, I believe, holds true whether one is an organizational consultant or researcher or even leader: The researcher can be also be a healer (as well as a data collector), and the consultant who is implicitly a healer conducts implicit research together with the storyteller. The attentive leader is constantly conducting implicit "research" on his or her organization. Perhaps an image of this situation is the virtuous spiral.

The Psychodynamic Dimension

This book brings the selfhood, both conscious and unconscious, of the listener (researcher, consultant) to the center of the process of listening. The self of the listener, in part experienced by the listener's emotional response to the client or group, is ultimately the fundamental *instrument* of organizational research, consulting, and leadership. Although a psychodynamic orientation (Czander, 1993; Gabriel, 1999; Diamond & Allcorn, 2009; Diamond, 2016; Kets de Vries, 2003) informs much of the book, the language I use is mostly not technical, and strives to be accessible to both nonpsychoanalytic and psychoanalytic readers.

It is my hope that my use of a psychodynamic perspective will be accessible to readers unfamiliar with psychoanalytic concepts and methods. I also wish to be clear from the outset that a discussion of the role of the unconscious in organizational life, and in organizational consulting, research, and leadership, does not replace or diminish the use of other perspectives. Rather, it helps to *complete, supplement, and deepen* more conventional approaches to understanding organizations. It adds another, and I would contend, crucial dimension for explaining, understanding, leading, and consulting in organizations. In fact, listening deeply integrates all these viewpoints.

In this book I explore my own evolution of the method of listening deeply in my work in various organizational settings, how it not only helps in understanding workplace experience, but also in facilitating creative change. Through the medium of many stories and vignettes, which are the experiential core of the book, I apply the method of listening deeply to making sense of organizational groups, metaphors, and leadership, and to examining the triad of organizational change, loss, and grief. It is my hope that this approach will enhance the work and morale of organizational researchers, consultants, leaders—and employees.

Between 1994 and 2016

This new edition of *Listening Deeply* is embedded in and influenced by new contexts. Since *Listening Deeply* was first published in 1994, the United States and the world have seen unrelenting, constant, convulsive, violent, and often traumatic change. With the end of the Cold War between the United States (and, more broadly, the Western alliance of NATO) and the Soviet Union (and its satellites), and the collapse of the Soviet empire, the world has fragmented into countless warring factions and worldwide terrorism.

The late twentieth and early twenty-first centuries have seen enormous technological, economic, political, and organizational change—from globalization of corporations to atomization of work (Diamond & Allcorn, 2009). The presence of multinational corporations, widespread outsourcing of labor from the United States to Third World countries, hostile corporate takeovers, mergers and acquisitions, and the difficult blending of multiple work cultures are all rampant, everyday occurrences, and part of the cultural landscape.

There has been wave after wave of traumatic transformation in corporations and government institutions—known by euphemisms from downsizing and restructuring to offshoring and deskilling (Stein, 1998, 2001). Millions of blue- and white-collar workers have been treated with emotional brutality at work and without warning have been thrown out onto the street without a job. Workplace survivors bear the burden of additional work of those who have been fired. They keep quiet, do their work, maintain a low profile, feel that they have a target on their backs, and fear for their jobs. International terrorism is matched in the American workplace by emotional terror by leaders, managers, and coercive group process.

Then there are the continuous technological revolutions that have brought personal computers, laptops, iPads, hand-held devices such as smartphones, as well as advances in telecommunications. Instant gratification has been matched by instantaneous communication on the Internet, and the expectation of immediate response. For many, the workday lasts for 24 hours of expected availability. What only a few years ago took days and weeks to transmit in the postal system, now takes only seconds.

With the technological revolution, much of electronic communication in workplaces and beyond is reduced to terse, staccato, and cryptic text messaging, tweets, or "sound bytes." The connectivity of electronic social networking breeds more isolation than intimacy (Turkle, 2011, 2015). We are more "related" to technology than to each other. There is little time, place, or willingness for lengthier, nuanced, creative, and subtle conversations. People often meet while looking at their smartphones. What conferences and meetings are not attended by people whose eyes and attention are more on their computer screens and hand-held devices than on the participants or on the content of the meeting? Long-term attention is rare.

Economic Refugees Within

Within the United States, since the 1980s, a vast population of *economic refugees* has been created and sustained by a *symbolic* equivalent of bloody "ethnic cleansing." If there are no literal massacres or mass graves, there are casualties nonetheless. We are manufacturing them at home, and they are largely unseen. A whole landscape ("semantic network") of terms at once evokes and defines this manifestly business ethos. Downsizing. Reduction in force. RIFing. Rightsizing. Redundancy. Restructuring. Reengineering. Reinventing. Outsourcing. Surplusing. Deskilling. Organizational flattening. Vertical and horizontal integration. Retooling. Autonomous self-managing teams. Privatization. Globalization. Deregulation. Shareholder optimization. Productivity. Cost-containment. Survival. Competitiveness. Managed care. Healthcare providers and consumers. Empowerment. Quality assurance. Lean-Six Sigma Black Belt. Open-door policy. And above all: *the religion of the bottom line.*

These are less a string of separate, distinct, words than a core, linked, vocabulary of a world dimly intimated. Culturally we say they are all about "nothing personal, just business" or "economics," as though that explains everything. The words are more correctly understood as fragments of a destructive worldview. They have become moral imperatives in the guise of rational business decision-making. I have discussed these at length elsewhere as euphemisms that mask vast destructiveness and self-destructiveness (Stein, 1998, 2001).

They are markers of the inner experience of work in the American workplace of the 1980s through the present (2016). In their euphemistic aridity, they convey what work *feels* like—feelings about work that become part of work: desolation, the sense of futility, of futurelessness, of toxic miasma (Gabriel, 2005, 2006, 2008, 2012)—at the same time that we hurl ourselves toward the future in the name of "productivity," "competitiveness," and "survival." Bottom-line thinking masks and simplifies the problem of evil that it enacts. Downsizing (and cognate terms), far from being a rational solution, is commonly viewed as the only, and inexorable, solution to the loss or threatened loss of profit. Its automatic thinking—and irresistible action—belies its cultural nature. It is ultimately about organizational rebirth and revitalization through endless sacrifice.

Mass firing or layoff is cultural obsession and compulsion in the guise of economic necessity. So is the creation of masses of temporary workers, gypsy professors ("adjuncts"), and others deprived of any benefit besides a current wage. They are useful until they are disposable. Bottom-line thinking—ranging from downsizing to managed care—is the American way of induced suffering and death in the guise of enlightened, inexorable economics. The corporate spreadsheet—not the firing squad or the gas chamber—is a currently dominant American way of disposing of unwanted people and categories of people: symbolic genocide simply turns people out into the cold. I emphasize that I do not say this for dramatic "effect" through hyperbole. I simply describe the reality that threatens so many.

When, in mid-1998, Alan Greenspan, Chairman of the Board of the Federal Reserve, and admirer of Ayn Rand, proclaimed that the economy of the United States was the "healthiest" it had been in 50 years, including rates of employment, he did not speak of the lower wages and fewer (if any) benefits for which many workers had to settle because they had been fired from better previous jobs. (In 1998 Greenspan could not foresee the devastating 2008 Great Recession that occurred largely because of rampant laissez-faire deregulation. See Allcorn & Stein, 2012; Stein & Allcorn, 2010a, 2010b, 2011.) An attitude of Social Darwinism prevails behind the optimistic doublespeak of the "recovery" now well underway by 2016: If people cannot fend for themselves, it is their own fault. "The Economy"—reified, biologized, and anthropomorphized—is in fine shape again, and that is what matters. As in nationalist ideology, individual lives and bodies are sacrificed (and expendable) in the name of the symbolic immortality of the corporate social unit: from business corporation to nation-state.

Economics is the medium and language of the sacrifice. Americans are simply put out on the streets to fend for themselves or disappear to who-cares-where. The widespread wish that unwanted peoples *disappear* further links the "ethnic cleansings" of recent decades (Rwanda, Bosnia, Kosovo, Darfur, Iraq, Syria) with their equivalent *corporate cleansings* through downsizings, RIFs, and the like. Both these forms create mass *refugee* problems, and are byproducts of the wish to secure boundaries or borders, and thereby organismic-like survival, via *expulsion of unwanted parts*.

Hans Frank, the governor general of Poland under the Nazis, declared, "All that I ask of the Jews is that they disappear." Current leaders of nations and corporations have said the same, in deed if not in word, about their own disposable people. In the process, everyone becomes terrorized. Those who remain behind—the survivors—are by no means free. They wonder whether they will be next. Within the nation-state of the United States, we are witnessing the widespread creation of problems of refugees, (internal) migration, emigration, and the vast social boundary problems that follow in the wake (Where are they to go? Who wants them?).

Largely in part because Americans do not wish to notice this domestic problem, we fail to label it. We all live in Bosnia, or Kosovo, or Iraq, or Syria now. In our world, "there" comes to be "here," "them" comes to be also "us," and "foreign" comes to be "familiar." Long before the September 11, 2001, airplane attacks on the World Trade Center and the Pentagon, our protective bubble had been violated—more from the inside than from terrorists on the outside.

Listening and Participating

It is in this atmosphere of ongoing traumatic change that listening deeply has become more, not less, important to the work of understanding, analyzing, and working to positively change—humanize—workplace organizations. At the same time, it is more difficult to convince people that it is necessary and worthwhile for organizational survival, morale, vitality, productivity, and profit. Listening deeply is more often than not officially spurned in organizations in order to make employees more productive and submissive. Ironically, when someone genuinely expresses an interest in listening to another's story, it is usually welcomed with gratitude and a sense of relief. It is the rare drop of water in a desert wasteland.

This book offers no formulas or recipes. It is not a cookbook in the mechanistic tradition of "how to fix it." Rather through a number of essays and stories, I describe the approach I take in clinical teaching and organizational consulting. It has been a difficult book to write because I am not an outsider to some objective situation I describe and interpret. Therefore, I must wrestle with the nearly insuperable problems of evoking, describing, interpreting, and explaining a world in which I participate. The methodology of this book thus follows from a recognition of how deeply we are part of any subject matter we inquire into, whether corporate, clinical, academic, or tribal.

A Story: The Long Hallway

Consider this very ordinary story in a modern workplace. Around 2014 I was consulting with Atlantic Business Corporation, and visiting with Steve, a senior executive. During our consultation, Steve told me the following story.

It was a Friday afternoon. Harry, a long-time midlevel executive of Atlantic Business Corporation, was walking down a long corridor toward Steve, a senior executive. Steve had long admired Harry as a devoted leader, hard worker, and amiable colleague. As they approached one another in the hall, Steve recognized that Harry was carrying a rather large box with an open top, and piled with things in it. He was streaming several party balloons on long ribbons behind him. They bobbed about in the air as he walked. As the two men came closer, Steve could see that the box was filled with Harry's personal belongings that until now had been placed around his office. Steve had often visited with Harry in both their offices.

They stopped and briefly visited. Harry said that he had received an e-mail from the CEO, Chris, early that morning, notifying him that he was being terminated, effective immediately. Harry was stunned. His colleagues were stunned. After lunch he had filled a copy-paper box with his personal belongings and was walking to the parking lot never to return. His colleagues, many having known him for years, gathered up a quick going-away lunch with food from a nearby store and with those helium-filled balloons that seemed so out of place. Harry said he would receive his final paycheck in the mail. Both Steve and Harry stood silently, awkwardly. Harry had tears in his eyes. Steve did not know what to say: What do you say to a dead man?

Harry was clearly dazed that he, despite his dedication, performance, and longevity, would be fired in the current wave of downsizing. He hadn't expected to be one of "them." Steve extended his condolences and wished him well. However, Steve did not immediately leave and proceed down the hall, but stayed with and listened to Harry talk further.

Chris, the CEO, was known to hold grudges against many people, including those who disagreed with any of his ideas, and to be "out to get" those he disliked, in the guise of large-scale, impersonal downsizing. "Nothing personal, just business" (Stein, 2001) was often a smoke screen for vendetta. Steve stood there and listened to Harry tell his story.

Harry suspected that he also might have had a "target" on *his* back, because of some disagreements he had with Chris some time ago. Steve thought that he might have been put on Chris's "enemies lis," much the same as Harry apparently had been. Steve acknowledged that Harry was in all likelihood right in thinking it was a personal vendetta ending Harry's career at Atlantic. He walked with Harry to the elevator. Harry thanked Steve for listening to his story. When the elevator door opened, they shook hands, the doors closed, and Harry was gone.

This miniature story evokes the quality and ordinariness of listening deeply. Riveted, I listened to Steve's story and storytelling, just as Steve had listened to Harry in the long hallway. This way of being in relation to another human being does not require Special Occasions or something labeled "organizational research" or "consultation." It can happen anytime and anyplace. It only requires readiness and openness for the moment to occur. While the listener may offer "prompts" and share thoughts to help the person tell the story, he or she mostly takes an interest in the other person and in the telling of the story. Sincere caring and empathy go a long way in helping the person telling the story to feel attended to and heard. It cannot be faked. In a phrase, one must "give a damn" (Stephens, 2012).

With respect to the above story, "listening deeply," then, includes the entire experience—(1) the box and balloons; (2) the location in a long hallway between Harry's office and the parking lot; (3) people walking past Harry without acknowledging him; (4) the sense of an enormous institution provided by a long hall within a large building, making Harry seem small relative to the magnitude of the building and the organization; and (5) Steve's gracious act of stopping and listening to Harry's story. There was likewise the vast institutional change itself (downsizing) that swept Harry up, and the undiscussable reality that his termination was very likely the result of downsizing being used as a smoke screen for a very personal brutality.

Further, there is not only Steve's listening to Harry speak, but also *his own self-experience* of the moment—in other words, that it was like talking in a way to a dead man, someone soon to be dearly departed. It was now about *shared* loss and grief. All told, it was a system that dehumanized everyone, creating "organizational fat" to be removed and everyone in the way to be disposed of. Both Steve-the-listener and Harry-the-storyteller embodied far more than words alone. Steve had to emotionally hold onto all the horror he was witnessing.

He did not stand aloof from Harry's world. In standing still and listening, he was conveying his empathy for Harry and his situation. Steve also knew that he was part of Harry's world—beyond the gift of identification, he also knew that he could be next on the chopping block.

It was likewise for me, in listening to Steve tell *his* story. I listened to Steve *through my own self-experience*—which included a close brush with being downsized myself, saved only through legal intervention. I knew that Harry's story had reverberations in Steve's own story, that Steve, too, had more than once "been a dead man" in terminations, and that on several occasions I nearly became a "dead man" myself. In fact, in my own self-experience, my brush with death came over time to feel like I was the "living dead." Steve's storytelling to me, the listener, distills the essence of listening deeply. It encompasses and evokes the book's themes of organizational group process, metaphors, storytelling and story listening, leadership, use of the self of the researcher and consultant, and the triad of change-loss-grief. It is about how the listener is a participant with the storyteller.

Listening as Attitude, a Way of Being

Listening deeply is less a set of techniques and skills than an attitude toward people and an attitude toward knowing, one evoked by Sigmund Freud's psychoanalytic concept of "evenly-suspended [or hovering] attention" (1912, pp. 111–112). The consultant's sense of focus comes later, rather than earlier, in a consultation—even when the client (individual or organization) may well press to focus the consultant's attention on a "problem" from the outset. This approach is a kind of "reverie" (Bion, 1962), a form of attention in which one is comfortable not knowing of what is essential, a suspension of assumptions, of "giving equal notice to everything" (Freud, 1912, p. 112), and a willingness and trust to be guided by the belief that without trying to control destiny, one will be led to where one needs to go.

This form of attention, similar to the Buddhist practice of meditative mindfulness (Pelled, 2007), is the polar opposite of the order for "Attention!" that a military drill sergeant demands (that attention be entirely focused on him and obedience to his orders); a neurotic's obsessive thought on a single thing; and a stern teacher's exhortation to students to "Listen to me and no one else." The opposite of these tense forms of attention is relaxed attention.

The process of evenly hovering attention, moreover, is a *double* listening—a careful attending to the person or group one is trying to help and an equally careful attending to how one is hearing these others, how one is feeling as they speak and gesture, and the dance between the two. I would add, following Thomas Ogden's concept of the analytic "third" (1999), that the "dance" becomes experienced as an entity itself in the space between the participants, making the listening in fact a *triple* listening. The consultant's own feelings, fantasies, and bodily sensations are as crucially diagnostic as what the consultant observes in the client (Reik's "listening with the third ear," 1948; Safran, 2011). In listening deeply, the consultant does not know what he or she is *listening for*. The content or "subject" arises out of the relationship ("dance") between consultant and client (or group).

A Story: Physical Reverberations of Language

Let me tell a brief story that illustrates this process. At a meeting I was facilitating for physician trainees (residents), several participants expressed concern that their medical education was being compromised and that it was not preparing them adequately for practice in the "real world" outside the university a year or two in the future. They felt that they were not learning enough procedures and that the faculty was not as available for supervision or consultation as the residents would like. One physician spoke with a special sense of urgency and personal inadequacy. He was now receiving his medical training on the Great Plains of the United States but was planning to settle and practice in the more competitive and urban West Coast region where he had grown up. Being a family physician, he felt especially vulnerable to criticism and ostracism from specialists in other, more high-status medical disciplines and to discrimination from hospitals.

As he spoke to the group, he used three or four times the vivid image that others would find "a chink in the armor" and puncture him with his own flaws. Each time he used the phrase, I felt an emotional jolt, as if I myself was being pierced through one of those lapses in protection. I had the uncanny feeling that more was going on in his sense of vulnerability and fear of exposure than he was saying. I could accept his wish that professional training equip a person with a certain amount of protection, but as he spoke, I could not help but wonder whether there was something powerfully ethnic, familial, or personal involved, too, whether his turn of phrase was more than a cliché.

After he had used the phrase the fourth time or so, I said that it struck me as a powerful image. I said that I felt awkward in what I was about to say but that I recognized him and his name to be Chinese or Chinese American and that "chink" was an epithet or stereotype Americans had long used to disparage the Chinese people. Each time he used the phrase I felt "stabbed." I wondered whether there was also a vulnerable Chinese man or boy beneath the professional armor of family medicine, whether he dreaded being reduced again to a "chink," a slur against which he could not defend himself. I asked if any of this resonated with him.

His voice softened, and he said as he looked toward me, "You know, I wondered about that, too, as I was talking." He continued by describing a little of his family history in southern California, the experiences of discrimination in the face of an exacting family work ethic, the striving for professional success throughout his family, and his father's experience of pennilessness and bigotry when he came to the United States from China years before. He recounted his father's admonition—heard long before he had chosen family medicine as his profession—to be excellent, exceptional, in order to avoid being considered inferior, "foreign."

We talked about the multiple burdens of being a kind of clinical minority group of family physicians among the high-prestige specialties, about how this minority-hood and sense of exposure in his chosen profession evoked feelings and fears similar to those of his family and ethnic childhood, and about how he was trying to become extraordinarily competent so as to avoid being humiliated, as his father had been as an immigrant. Without ever using the word *metaphor*, we all came to realize that "the chink in the armor" was a metaphor for himself.

It was a moving discussion not only for the two of us but also for the group. Had we limited ourselves to the sense of adequacy or inadequacy that family physicians feel in relation to other medical professionals, we would have addressed only some emotional issues. But my own eerie sense of being struck at the core as he mentioned a chink in the armor, and my association of this metaphoric phrase with ethnic derision and with an even-deeper-cutting contempt and shame, allowed me to bring the issue to our public awareness through *the form* of my own feeling. Stated differently, some of my most important consultant data about him occurred within me. I returned to him some questions about my own feelings. But I first had to find *the chink in my own armor* as an American Jew. Certainly, I listened to *him*. But I also listened to him *via* my own embodied unconscious response.

A Mental Map

In this book I address an imaginary reader, an unseen, invisible companion. By profession my companion may *be* an organizational consultant (corporate, industrial, educational); social or political psychologist; applied anthropologist or sociologist; business or management executive; occupational or family physician; organizational development specialist or theorist; university teacher in business, administration, or management courses; organizational researcher; psychoanalyst; psychohistorian; or even parent. But even to say that my companion is interdisciplinary or multidisciplinary is not enough. In addition, as I write this book, my imaginary companion is everyone with whom I have worked during the past four decades in organizations—not only leaders or managers, academics, facilitators, researchers, and trainers, but also physicians, nurses, secretaries, and janitors.

As I teach, conduct clinical supervision, do field research, facilitate groups, and consult with organizations, I discover my destination by watching where my *feet* take *me*. Even when I have a conscious, willful theory or method for coercing the unknown into the expected, one part of *me seems* to follow faithfully and begrudgingly *comes* to trust that part of *me* that does not need to *be* in control. I increasingly *see* my job as not to stand in the way of the part of *me* that knows better than my current armament of theories and social methods. That growing faith and trust in myself and in my relationship with groups are the basis of this book and of my approach to working with organizations.

Today I can say confidently, "Oh *yes, here* is where I have been heading for forty years," as my reasons and rationale catch up with my heart—to borrow from Blaise Pascal (1670), the French Renaissance philosopher who said, "The heart has its reasons which reason knows nothing of" (*Le cœur à ses raisons que la raison ne connaît point*). I can now condense into a methodological "system" what I have long been doing. But beware of any intellectual system, for it closes at precisely the moment it needs most to be open (Ogden, 1989a, 1993). For science, culture, organizations, and the human spirit to advance, we must retain a childlike wonder at how much the envelope of any idea or feeling might expand to encompass even more experience. Our greatest challenge is not to idolize or worship the envelope—or box.

Where, then, does this book come from? For over four decades, as I have consulted with organizations, as an individual and as a member of teams, I have consistently asked those who invite me—whether a petroleum company, a television-radio media institute, or an academic medical organization—if possible to postpone scheduling my formal presentation until fairly late in the sequence of events. This allows me to become familiar with the group's members and they, informally, with me so that my participation evolves from listener to speaker, from one who is in the role of a respectful participant observer, asking an occasional question or making a brief comment, to one who then conducts a formal seminar or workshop. By the time I speak, we have at least to some degree become real persons to one another. I am not talking impersonally about a topic to a wall of foreign faces and bodies. Instead, I take them and their culture into account in my presentation.

I build into my discussion examples, stories, and illustrations that I have drawn from my hours or days with them. I try to weave their context into some of my content. I try to speak to them only after I have first heard them. I try to contain, to symbolically hold them within myself, before I claim any entitlement or authority to speak. My expertise lies not primarily in some prepared materials I have packed away in my briefcase and brought from a thousand miles away. Content is inseparable from interpersonal context. In organizational consulting, authentic expertise or authority lies *between* myself and those with whom I am working. This is why I try to insist on doing my formal talk, seminar, or lecture toward the middle or even at the end. It has taken me a decade to realize that this is a method, one I extrapolate backward from where my feet have insisted I go.

A Story: The Move to the New Building

Let me offer a brief story to illustrate this process. In late May and early June 1991, I was a visiting scholar in the Department of Family Medicine at the University of North Carolina at Chapel Hill. On the final day of my visit, I presented a formal grand rounds lecture. My subject was the implications of Balint groups for other academic medical groups, such as faculty meetings, business meetings, case conferences, and staff meetings. Named for the physician-psychoanalyst who began them in the 1940s, Michael Balint, Balint groups are havens in which physicians discuss emotionally difficult relationships with patients (and in some groups, staff, colleagues, and supervisors as well), and feel listened to and understood, and can grow.

I had taught and consulted in this same department five years earlier as a visiting professor, so I had some baseline and history of relationships from which to draw. Before I made my presentation to the faculty and residents at the conclusion of my visit, I talked several times with John Frey, M.D., a friend, longtime faculty member of the department, former chair, and former editor of a family medicine journal. He told me, among other things, that his department was now going through major transitions, just as when I had been there in 1986 and the department had gone through a change in chair. Since then, many of his faculty had found themselves recognized throughout the university and nation as leaders in, rather than as newcomers to, the family medicine profession. They felt established and did not have to prove themselves daily and assert their legitimacy. Some, then in middle age, were questioning careerism and competitiveness and were beginning to take a broader, more playful, even spiritual attitude toward life. "What did this value shift bode for family medicine education?" he wondered.

The department, long accommodated in a series of separate house trailers peripheral to the main campus, now had its own, more centrally located building. My visit coincided with the first anniversary of its occupancy. When I made my presentation on ordinary group dynamics of medical organizations, I used some of the faculty's *own* issues to illustrate my concepts and methods. For example, I asked how it felt and how others responded to the fact that many were now successful, established faculty rather than neophytes fighting for a place in the sun. Was it easy or difficult to give up the minority, often protesting, identity-conscious position? Did people enjoy being together in the same building? Did subgroups congregate in their own areas? Did some people prefer the old physical separateness? What did the new, spacious halls feel like in comparison with the crowded quarters of the trailers? I wondered aloud how the new space changed people's relationships and in turn how people used the new space to represent themselves and their groups. I mentioned that where people chose to seat themselves in the tripartite, terraced amphitheater said something about their relationships, values, and power structure—in short, their organizational culture.

In the discussion following my lecture, several participants began thinking aloud about their own department, how it might express some of the group dynamics I had described. For instance, one physician wondered how to discuss emotional issues at ordinary meetings without being branded or dismissed as a whiner.

Despite centralization in a new building, no organizational ingathering is perfect, however. Some members have obligations, loyalties, offices, elsewhere across campus, even across the state. Not everyone is always at home, "together"—itself a powerful fantasy and wish. Dr. Frey, who was then on a fellowship collecting oral histories of rural physicians throughout the state and region, said to me that medical and administrative colleagues on his urban campus often asked him, "Where have you been lately?" and "When are you coming in?" In the large, now much more centralized organization, Dr. Frey wondered how much a sense of culture, a sense of "us," developed and endured. How densely and permanently together must a group be to feel like a reliable "we"? Did a department so widely dispersed geographically still have enough boundaries to constitute a sustainable organizational culture? Most of all, we acknowledged that his department had irrevocably changed, that as something had been gained, something had also been lost. The original void of a colleague and former leader's absence and unpredictable comings and goings was now filled with feelings of abandonment, separation anxiety, guilt, envy, grief, and mystery, all low grade, but present.

In short, I had included their world in the substance of my talk. They were then able to address their own issues—some emotionally toxic and more safely raised by a stranger—during the discussion at the end and in the small gathering after the grand rounds had finished. Moreover, when I ended my formal presentation, I pulled up a chair and sat down near the group, saying that if it would be useful, I would be happy to facilitate discussion of how some of these issues were expressed in the organization rather than simply have a formal question-and-answer session.

This story illustrates how even before I speak to members of a group, I try first to have listened to them. If I expect them to take seriously what I have to say, must I not do likewise for them? The deeper intersubjective imperative is not the speaking but the listening; then and only then can I respond to what I have heard and felt.

To Whom Ought We Listen?

If this book is about learning to listen to others, to help others listen better to themselves and to each other, and to listen to my own self as a tool for hearing others, then no special group may be rightfully singled out as the focus of these thoughts. Although the stories in this book are from institutions called organizations, their lessons and ordinariness extend far beyond workplaces. If our world is to be saved from our own destructiveness, we all must become more comfortable with listening to one another, with tolerating what makes us intensely uncomfortable, with knowing what we do not wish to hear and why we do not want to hear it. In a culture obsessed with formal corporate structures, economic bottom lines, and rationalized strategic plans that purport magically to control the future, we must once again learn to feel. From becoming merely tolerant of hearing, we could *want* to listen more, be *ready* to hear more and respond more fully. This book is about that process, one that, for the sake of our planet's future, must not be limited to professionals, planners, or experts.

This book derives many, though certainly not all, of its stories from health care settings, but the consulting approach discussed herein can be applied to any other work settings. Likewise, if listening deeply is good enough for organizational consulting, it is also good enough for organizational goal setting or strategic planning by leaders, managers, and employees, and even further, for working with couples and families. If listening deeply makes for better medical education, administration, and health care, it also makes for good business, good corporate life, good industry, and good international diplomacy. This book is thus about learning how to become a better listener—to anyone, anywhere. Health care, corporate America, and even American society are but a starting point, an instance in place and time, for what deserves to become universal.

I write these words not as a trainer, formal strategic planner, or licensed OD professional but as an applied anthropologist, who has learned, as a clinical teacher, most of what I know from my students, residents, faculty colleagues, and their patients; and beyond them, from leaders, managers, and employees of many types of workplaces. If this book is the offspring of my own struggle to listen—not wanting, or not being able, to listen is a large part of it—then my true companion in this dialogue and journey is anyone who struggles similarly to understand himself or herself and others. It is about acknowledging and overcoming one's own resistance to listening. Listening deeply ultimately is not about some Western sociological institution called "organizations." Nor is it about a unique species once called the organization man (or woman). Nor is it about waging quasi-military campaigns called organizational *interventions*. Nor is it about advocating and planning brief consultations that promise, but fail to deliver, instant, magical solutions. It is about comprehending the experience of being in the culture of workplaces. It is about a method—not a rigid methodology—that promotes such comprehension.

Workplace organizations in the modern United States—factories, corporations, government agencies, universities, hospitals and clinics, public school systems, print and electronic media—are as rife with intragroup and intergroup conflict and factionalism as was any southwestern pueblo, New Guinea tribe, or sub-Saharan preliterate society described early in the twentieth century by anthropologists. Dramatic, relentless social change in workplace organizations has heightened factionalism and conflict. Large-scale, hostile corporate takeovers and mergers, company closings, massive layoffs, and depersonalized cut-slash-chop attitudes toward employees, all driven by the wish to maximize short-term profit and productivity, have led to a beleaguered, ever-threatened, grief-stricken, self-protective, and hostile workforce. John McDermott (1991) warns that our entire society is coming to be organized around the corporation as its main institution. Any discussion of the organizational consultations I have been involved in over the past four decades also becomes a microcosm of life in this country (Stein, 1985b).

In my formal anthropological training and in much of the folk wisdom of the United States, I was taught that nations, ethnic groups, tribes, and religions are people's primordial, most basic, systems of meaning, feeling, commitment, and affiliation. They express people's core sense of belonging and are their roots. From this it follows that studies of cultural loss and grief, and cross-cultural comparative studies (say, of migration, acculturation, assimilation, and culture change) are most properly done with reference to nations and ethnic groups. So I and we believed 45 years ago. Organizations such as professions, workplaces, occupations, and political parties were presumably of secondary meaning and emotional significance. Yet I have learned that people weave work sites and occupational relationships into their emotional lives, fantasies, meanings, and core identities. Threats to an organization and its boundaries are experienced as assaults upon the integrity of the self.

I am thus led to wonder: Is *immigrants'* loss of century- and millennium-old ways of life in the native country, different experientially and unconsciously from the loss of three- or four-generation employment in a *steel mill* resulting from large-scale layoffs or the closing of an entire plant or industry, such as occurred in the 1980s throughout the once robust steel valley region of western Pennsylvania? Although an ethnic group or multiethnic urban community may have existed only a century through association with a factory town (or a three- and four-generation family farm on the Great Plains), is the disruption of social relationships and inner emotional landscapes any less poignant? Is the inner void any less deep? Since the 1980s, the world of hospitals, clinics, medical colleges, and corporations gives me a resounding "No!" as an answer.

The reader who accompanies me on this organizational odyssey should be able to look and listen more attentively to group issues in his or her own occupational setting, even though the specific types of groups might differ markedly from those I describe. Since we are dealing at once with the human condition, the condition of being a member of American culture in the late twentieth and early twenty-first centuries, and the condition of participating in some workplace organization (from factory to family farm), certain common denominators should be evident in group processes. I hope my imaginary companion on this voyage will readily be able to translate the organizations and processes I describe into those places and idioms with which she or he is familiar.

Although this volume interweaves many threads, its warp and weft, its focus and contribution consist of (1) the presentation of a method for understanding organizations and helping them to heal; (2) a synthesis of concepts, perspectives, and literatures from several academic and clinical fields; and (3) a desire to foster greater healing and integration among people in workplaces through storytelling and story listening. This book is about caring enough to want to listen to others as central to our task as organizational researcher, consultant, and leader. In particular, it is about standing still, being present with the storyteller, and listening to stories that are deeply disturbing. It is about attentiveness. It is both about our resistance to listening to upsetting stories, and the transforming possibilities of our willingness to listen.

Let me say a word about the style and voice in which this book speaks. If this book reads or speaks more like a novel, say, than like a scientific treatise, a procedures manual, or a clinical protocol, I do not apologize. For to write differently would be to violate the very intimacy that listening deeply allows to emerge. It would be to try forcing back into mere description what has leapt from interpretation to evocation. Whatever our profession, we need to ask ourselves what style or styles we require to convey the depth and breadth of human experience as we work with and in organizations.

Many if not most of the stories in this book are emotionally disturbing and reveal the inner darkness in many workplaces. Although some stories have uplifting outcomes, I cannot shrink from the lived bleak experience of countless American workplaces in the late twentieth and early twenty-first centuries. I hope that the reader will join me on this difficult journey into the emotional labyrinth of much of today's organizational life.

Howard F. Stein
May 2016

Acknowledgments

Acknowledgments to the Second Edition (2017)

I am indebted to many people for making this second edition of *Listening Deeply* possible. Seth Allcorn first suggested the idea to me in 2015, and helped buoy my spirit throughout the revision process. Both Michael Diamond and David Rosenbaum, Director of the University of Missouri Press, encouraged me to submit a prospectus. Mary Conley, Associate Acquisitions Editor of the Press, helped me through the many steps of the submission and manuscript revision process. She performed the herculean task of converting the original 1994 published book into a useable Word document. Copyeditor Dana Henricks was far more than a technical editor. She engaged in a running dialogue with me throughout the galley proofs.

I dedicate this book to Seth Allcorn and Michael Diamond, who have been dear friends and colleagues, and, in a way, mentors, for over 25 years. I cannot imagine my life and career without them. Much of the new material in this revised edition owes its origin to weekly hour-long Skype visits that Seth Allcorn and I had in 2015 and 2016.

Shortly after I retired in 2012 after teaching and consulting for nearly 35 years in the Department of Family and Preventive Medicine, University of Oklahoma Health Sciences Center, Oklahoma City, Oklahoma, J. Neil Henderson, a long-time friend and colleague, invited me to serve as group process facilitator for his monthly meetings of the American Indian Diabetes Prevention Center, in the College of Public Health, University of Oklahoma Health Sciences Center, Oklahoma City, Oklahoma, and to serve as informal executive coach to him. I leapt at the invitation, and am immensely grateful for the opportunity to stretch and transfer my years of Balint group facilitation in Family Medicine to the work of his center. My first four years of this work have been a joy of collaboration and creativity.

I wish to thank those many individuals and groups with whom I have consulted for over 45 years. They have all been my teachers, and I their grateful student.

Finally, I must thank Luke, my cat, for keeping me company throughout the revision and expansion of this book. He has been both companion and comfort.

Acknowledgments to the First Edition (1994)

Many people have offered generous encouragement and indispensable criticism in my foray into consulting with organizational cultures. Roy L. DeHart, M.D.; Roger Elliott, P.A.-C.; and Dan Fox, P.A.-C., have enthusiastically supported my annual graduate seminar "Behavioral Sciences in Occupational Medicine," a fieldwork- and experientially oriented approach to the meaning of work in people's lives. Joseph Cangemi, Ph.D., founding editor of *Organization Development Journal*; Joanne Preston, Ph.D., its later editor; and Michael Diamond, Ph.D., have welcomed my approach into their field and assured me that what I do is indeed organizational development—although I had been calling it political psychology, applied psychohistory, or organizational anthropology.

For three and a half decades, the High Plains Society for Applied Anthropology has given me opportunities to present and test my organizational culture ideas and methodological approaches at their annual retreatlike conventions in Ghost Ranch, New Mexico. In 1983 and 1984, Karel F. J. Niebling, a Dutch management specialist, gave me the opportunity to present some of my early ideas at "Uncertainty in Management" seminars to senior executives of Shell International Petroleum Maatschappij, B.V., at the Harvard Conference Center, Mount Pelerin, Switzerland.

Many university-affiliated, private, and corporate medical organizations have taught me a great deal during the course of long-term employment and short-term consultation over the past 45 years. In the Oklahoma City Family Medicine Program and in the community-based Enid, Shawnee, and Lawton programs, University of Oklahoma Health Sciences Center Family Medicine interns, residents, faculty, medical staff, and administrative staff have taught me much about organizational groups over more than 30 years in our ongoing biweekly Balint groups and in a variety of clinic meetings and case conferences. I am especially grateful for invitations to participate at conferences sponsored by the Society for Teachers of Family Medicine. These include two Advanced Forums organized by G. Gayle Stephens, M.D., at Keystone, Colorado, and addresses as plenary speaker in three Forums for the Behavioral Sciences in Family Medicine, sponsored by the Hinsdale Hospital Family Practice Residency in Chicago, Illinois. Visiting professorships at the University of North Carolina, Chapel Hill (family medicine); the University of Virginia, Charlottesville (psychiatry); Saint Joseph's Hospital, Syracuse, New York (family medicine); and the Henry Ford Hospital/

Bon Secours Family Practice Residency Program, Bon Secours, Michigan, provided cross-cultural or multicultural institutional opportunities to compare my Oklahoma experience with the experience of other clinical and academic organizations.

Many colleagues, now dear friends, have been beacons in my effort to understand the organizational culture of medicine and of institutions beyond it: Vamık D. Volkan, M.D.; G. Gayle Stephens, M.D.; John Frey, M.D.; Michael Diamond, Ph.D.; Thomas Maretzki, Ph.D.; Thomas Johnson, Ph.D.; Weston La Barre, Ph.D.; Warren Gadpaille, M.D.; Henry Ebel, Ph.D.; Reverend Julius Thomas, commander, United States Navy; Maurice Apprey, Ph.D.; Johanna Shapiro, Ph.D.; Kathy Zoppi, M.P.H.; George De Vos, Ph.D.; and Robert F. Hill, Ph.D.

To Dean Birkenkamp, executive editor at Westview Press, I owe my gratitude not only for his risk in publishing my earlier *American Medicine as Culture* but also for his encouragement that I write this more widely inclusive, more speculative methods and case book on my work with organizations. Without the convictions of impresario Johann Peter Salomon, Joseph Haydn would not have composed his 12 London symphonies. I am similarly indebted to Dean Birkenkamp for the existence of both these volumes.

Nancy Carlston, acquisitions editor at Westview Press, did far more than acquire the manuscript. She had faith in me and in the yet unborn book hidden in the cumbersome manuscript. In many letters and phone calls, she persevered and kept me honest.

I am grateful to Robert Beasley, M.D., and to Nguyen Anh Nga, M.D., who in 1990 invited me to present some of my ideas at the professorial rounds of the Department of Psychiatry and Behavioral Sciences, University of Oklahoma Health Sciences Center. I titled my talk "'Was It for This the Clay Grew Tall?' (from a poem titled "Futility" by British World War I poet Wilfred Owen [1920] 1963): Organizational Trauma and Griefwork," a topic whose timeliness was uncanny as it coincided with the closing of the in-patient child psychiatry unit in the university children's hospital.

Three reference librarians at the University of Oklahoma Health Sciences Center Library have gone the extra mile for me for this book. They deserve not to be anonymous: Stewart Brower, Jennifer Goodson, and Shari Clifton.

My secretary, Laney Duncan, has painstakingly assisted in the final manuscript editing and word processing. To my longtime editor, Margaret Ann Sheehan, I owe the translation of my handwritten pads and typewriter-punctured pages into the late-twentieth-century world of the word processor.

H. F. S.

LISTENING DEEPLY

Introduction

This book brings the process of listening and the importance of being heard to the center of organizational understanding and consulting, and establishes the listening process as a basis for change in the sense of emotional growth in individual leaders, managers, employees, and in their organizations. This is primarily a work on a method of how to learn—and help those within an organization to learn—the nameless themes that often underlie and then overwhelm an organization's explicit structure and tasks. Further, I regard this approach to consulting with *organizational* cultures applicable to *any interpersonal or group context*. If listening deeply is essential for *consulting* with organizations, then it is equally indispensable for *all relationships*.

In this book I have told many short and long stories from my own over 40 years of experiences with various types of organizations, including medical departments, corporations, school districts, hospitals, and clinics. These stories illustrate how groups become stuck in their histories and how they might get unstuck. To maintain confidentiality, I have used pseudonyms and acronyms in the stories throughout the text.

Learning to Listen

Much, if not most, of life in contemporary United States society is based on doing, achieving, striving, succeeding, competing, winning, intervening, producing—in other words, on outcomes. "Hurry up and get there first" to beat the competition is our modus operandi. Our all-American "can-do" penchant for "fixing things" quickly is more often than not a part of the problem. We are a highly visual culture. We value observing more than listening because the latter often seems too time consuming, too inefficient in terms of the perceived direction and quantity of time available, and too intimate in its demands. From my background as a depth-psychology-oriented anthropologist, I have come to conduct my organizational consulting as a form of ethnographic fieldwork rooted largely in participant observation. In it, I try to listen deeply to cultural members and use what I think and feel I am hearing (as well as seeing) to help the members of the organizational culture understand themselves, feel understood, and change in a way that heals.

Listening deeply is not so much a specialized technique as it is a whole orientation to life and relationships, one that might also be expressed in counseling or therapy as well as organizational consultation. By deep listening, I mean an openness, attentiveness, emotional alertness, and responsiveness to everything the patient, client, family, or corporate group is offering—a willingness to serve as a holding environment (Winnicott, [1954] 1958) that allows everything to be felt, thought, or said. To feel heard and understood is perhaps the most precious gift in life. It is a symbolic holding, one that can return the emotionally numbed or deadened to life.

To listen deeply, we must first allow ourselves to become unfamiliar with everything we think we know. We must wear our knowledge, our certainties, and our methods lightly. We must renounce our culturally sanctioned therapeutic or managerial ambition, our compulsion to change another person, family, institution, or entire nation according to our own values, beliefs, and expectations. Such ambition serves our fragile narcissism more than it truly helps others. We must disabuse ourselves of the illusion that we can fix or mold others. We must give up the need to make the human universe static and both accept and welcome the flux that is at the core of creativity. To listen deeply is to replace our need for intrusive control with respect for another's autonomy and empathy for that person's or group's experience. In such a capacity, an organizational consultant functions less as a strategist and more as a client's or an organization's temporary auxiliary ego. This human instrument of empathy and respect is heir to the mother or other caregiving person as a source of recognition and validation, a person from whom the baby could reliably borrow in earliest infancy.

While listening to the group, the consultant also hears and attends carefully to the music that stirs from within. This activity violates the most revered wisdom in modern science, which holds that the observer is always the worst, to-be-mistrusted, instrument. But the observer is potentially the finest instrument because objectivity is gained not in spite of our subjectivity but through the intersubjective dialogue of conscious with unconscious, soul to soul (Devereux, 1967; Duncan & Diamond, 2011). Thomas Ogden (1989a) writes that "the analyst has no means of understanding the patient except through his or her own emotionally colored perceptions of and responses to the patient. Of these perceptions and responses, only a small proportion are conscious, and it is therefore imperative that the analyst learn to detect, read, and make use of his own shifting unconscious state as it unfolds in the analytic discourse" (p. 16).

This book looks at how to listen deeply in order to elicit the group or organizational story(-ies) underlying the manifest or official story. This book is also about *storytelling*: how we are part of one another's stories, how we tell stories, how we listen to stories, and how storytelling and story listening both affect each other (Gabriel, 2000; Allcorn & Stein, 2016). We can become unwittingly destructive as we routinely weave others into our own individual or group folktales. Or we can become profoundly healing as we are able to hear the painful underlying stories we are struggling to tell or to withhold from ourselves and from others. Genuine story listening is deep listening.

Storytelling and Story Listening

Even though in one sense the stories are "in" the storyteller, they are not offered, or perhaps even consciously known, prior to the relationship with the listener. The listener values the storyteller and the storyteller feels valued by the listener. Contained in a good enough relationship (the quality of being "good enough" will be explored in depth later in this volume), the storyteller feels safe enough to entrust his or her story to the listener. The storyteller remembers a story in the presence of the listener and bestows upon the listener the gift of the story. The good enough listener not only hears, but also contains, both the storyteller and the story by having the desire and emotional capacity to *hold onto* and *bear witness* to the storyteller and the story.

The listener gives the gift of presence, of wanting to hear, and of containment. He or she also validates the worthiness of both the storyteller and the story. By simply listening, the listener implicitly affirms the teller and the teller's experience. By listening, the listener offers the gift of affirmation to the storyteller, for example, as if to "say" to the storyteller: "I believe you that this really did happen, believe it or not." Thus, while stories evoke a *spoken* response, the *act of listening* is in itself important.

The creative process of telling stories to other people, and of making sense of the stories with another person, is profoundly validating. The process helps to detoxify what has been experienced as emotionally invasive and poisonous. It helps both the storyteller and us to better understand what has been experienced. This hoped-for outcome can be transformative, mutative, changing a persecutory internalized experience (bad object) into something less threatening and dominating. The process can be healing, in the sense of fostering greater personal integration and differentiation, creating a sense of feeling more whole—and less fragmented, disorganized, and confused.

There is also a *historical* dimension to the in-the-moment storyteller–listener relationship. The storyteller brings to the relationship the wish to relate the story and yearns for a safe place in which to tell it. Leaders, managers, and employees often have the experience of feeling unsafe in their emotionally persecutory workplace. The storyteller both wants to be heard and is afraid of being heard (disclosed, exposed, punished, even fired). Storytelling in a safe enough relationship is thus liberating. For storytelling in organizations, the story listener's hope is to create a potential space to empower the previously disempowered storyteller to tell the story, and to transmute what was dark, secret, and taboo into the daylight world of conscious experience, verbal symbolization, feeling, and reflection (Ogden, 1999).

Storytelling gives us access to the breadth and depth of workplace experience, what Diamond (1993) calls the "unconscious life of organizations," a world ruled as much by the irrational, dark side of human nature as by rationality and enlightened self-interest (Allcorn & Stein, 2015). Storytelling also helps people and groups to heal when harmful organizational and leadership dysfunctions arise. Stories bear witness to painful events, create a shared moment with a listener, and can become an integral part of organizational consulting and coaching. (The previous five paragraphs are adapted from Allcorn & Stein, 2016.) As the following story attests, countless workplace stories and their telling could echo the common refrain: "You couldn't make this [story] up."

A Story: "You Couldn't Make This Up"

Just about everyone I know who has worked in an organization has stories that they begin or end with saying, "You couldn't make this up," or "You Wouldn't *Believe* This." We Americans have an economics-based view that organizations, and the people who work in them, are rational, realistic, objective, and they make decisions exclusively based on productivity, profitability, and efficiency. Yet the stories we tell each other every day suggest the opposite—a lot of things that happen in workplaces defy reason. For instance, countless organizations lose hundreds of thousands, even millions, of dollars, because the CEO's pride, or self-image, or the need to be right, or the need to exercise power, supersedes economically sound decision-making.

It is in the *stories* people tell and listen to, rather than the official "party line" of how an organization is supposed to function, that the lived reality of the workplace is revealed. Visions and mission statements, strategic plans, and goals and objectives are often only part of the picture, if not the deceptive official surface picture of the organization. If you ask leaders, managers, and employees, "What's it like to work here?" you will be given stories that go counter to what we expect and prefer to believe about organizational life. And of course, workplace stories do not exist as disembodied entities. Rather, they are told and retold, and are *empathically listened to.*

More often than not, "ego" rather than economics prevails. In one organization some years ago, a manager was orienting new employees, and as part of his presentation said something close to: "We expect a full eight-hours' work from you. If you think that you're essential to this organization, that we can't get along without you, you're wrong. There are hundreds of people just waiting out there to take your job. Imagine sticking your finger in a bowl of water and then taking your finger out. Look at the water. The water will never remember that your finger was ever there. That's how much you'll be missed."

That was hardly a welcoming speech. The manager not only *told* his official story, but the new employees *listened* to it as he inflicted it upon them. It was a threat to the new employees who had not even begun their job. It was even sadistic, vicious. Psychologically, it was a death threat. There are many organizational executives and managers who unnecessarily inflict psychological trauma on their employees, even terrorize them for the sake of feeling powerful and in control.

This is not to say that all organizational leaders and managers are like this, but rather to bring out into the light of day the fact that management by bullying and irrational decision-making are far more common than we would like to acknowledge. You, the reader, can test this for yourself and be the judge. Think about the workplace stories you have heard and that you have told. The beginning of addressing this common workplace problem is first *acknowledging* that it exists. Recognizing that "You couldn't make these stories up" is the first step in accepting the reality of life in countless workplaces. We have to begin to believe what "You won't believe"—what we don't wish to believe. We have to listen deeply.

In workplaces everywhere and every day, people tell those who empathically listen stories that are unimaginable, except that they really happened. It is the listener who makes the speaker feel safe enough to tell his or her story that allows the unthinkably bizarre to be imaginable.

Creating Potential Cultural Space

Where, then, do the stories exist? This book describes the potential space between myself and the groups with which I have worked (Winnicott, 1967, 1971), for this is where the new stories are created. It is an account of working relationships out of which data emerged about organizational culture and about change that is healing. The main tools of listening deeply are (1) inquiry into the breadth and historical depth of any organizational issue presented; (2) empathy, together with the ability to identify with or imagine oneself as the other person or group; (3) efforts to help organizational members feel understood (both by the consultant and by one another); (4) creation of a safe potential space, a holding environment (Winnicott, (1954] 1958) or container in which emotion-laden group issues may be explored (Bion, 1959); and (5) sparing use of confrontation and interpretation by the consultant or group facilitator.

The approach of listening deeply draws from, and attempts to integrate, many perspectives: anthropology, psychoanalysis (including classical psychoanalysis, ego psychology, self-psychology, and object-relations theory), existential psychology, political psychology, management psychology, counseling psychology, small-group theory, family systems theory, psychohistory, social psychology, sociology, and organizational development. For instance, in consultation psychiatry, according to Thomas M. Johnson (1987, pp. 288–289), an anthropologist can serve as a "culture broker" among patient, family, and physician and other medical staff, as well as between the culture of psychiatry and those of other health care professions. Not unlike the "shuttle diplomacy" of Cyrus Vance, Henry Kissinger, John Kerry, or Hillary Clinton in international relations, this consultant role consists of developing "an increase in understanding and flexibility of interaction between various subsystems in the hospital milieu."

Within the field of anthropology, listening deeply can be situated at the intersection of applied anthropology, psychoanalytic anthropology, hermeneutic or narrative anthropology, and symbolic anthropology. Together they constitute the anthropology of experience. The intellectual roots of listening deeply are broad; its methodological foundation is simple. Organizational consultation, intervention, facilitation, and training must be—whatever else they are—a species of *ethnographic fieldwork* (Duncan & Diamond, 2011). A consultant must study the group culture in which he or she intervenes as a participant observer.

Furthermore, the consultant must also study the intervention or application process itself, not only the group with whom she or he is consulting; and the relationship with group members, not only their relationship with one another. Moreover, the consultant must situate herself or himself as part of the consultation itself. Certainly, the organizational anthropologist learns about the client, individual, or organization through naturalistic and participant observation, through open-ended and focused interviews, and through an examination of the "material" culture, which includes documentary sources, such as organizational charts on the psychogeography of space use in the workplace (Stein, 1987a; Stein & Niederland, 1989). More important, the consultant learns how to help through the "intersubjective resonance of unconscious processes" between self and client (Ogden, 1989a, p. 17), soul to soul. The key instrument of understanding, feeling, comprehension, and action is the self of the observer, facilitator, or consultant.

A Musical Analogy

Let me make an analogy with performance and interpretive styles in music. In music, numerous schools of thought on orchestral conducting exist, as represented, for example, by Bruno Walter, Arturo Toscanini, Wilhelm Furtwängler, and Otto Klemperer. Opinions vary passionately over which conductor is *the best*, the most correct, the most profound. With the advent of phonograph recordings and compact discs, those "bests" become not only readily available commercially, but also ossified. The argument is no longer confined to concert hall memories but extends now to definitive interpretations recorded and preserved forever. No matter how moving an interpretation—and a great interpretation reveals new details and synthesis with each new playing—it is still but one.

As several different performances of, say, a symphony or an opera by the same conductor become available, we recognize that even a single artist interprets differently at different times. Which, then, is *the* definitive Klemperer or Furtwängler Beethoven "Eroica" symphony? Worse, as later conductors emulate the masters, these copyists and disciples are inferior to the originals they imitate while fancying themselves true to their source. Worse yet, music critics and the public often categorize new interpreters as so "like" the master that the individuality of the "disciple" is not noticed. Guido Cantelli is not profound because he is like Toscanini, who had declared Cantelli his successor! Similarly, George Szell, Fritz Reiner, and William Steinberg are distinguished interpreters not because they are supposedly "like" Toscanini.

Whether in music, in theory building, or in day-to-day organizational consulting, we must not adhere to a tradition and listen only through it, for it will teach us to hear our theory and nothing else. It will teach us not to listen to the people with whom we work. To hear or perform a familiar Beethoven or Schubert symphony as if we have never before opened the score but are fully ripened by everything we have heard and lived—this is what I mean by listening deeply when consulting with organizational groups.

What, then, is the lesson of Beethoven and Schubert interpretation for becoming a better organizational listener as consultants? Listening deeply can be thought of as the paradox of listening carefully, with our entire being, for wholeness without deceiving ourselves that we have achieved completeness. Just as listening deeply requires that we yield to a subject, rather than try to control it and its outcome, the process likewise liberates both consultant and client from having to repeat the same story. It gives all participants an opportunity for continual renewal. It allows organizational stories to contain surprises and participants to be surprised, to rediscover histories they had never consciously known, to feel what they had not before felt. Self-knowing, whether by an individual or an organizational group, is a matter of access to knowing anew, and the key to that is what the consultants can first bear to know anew about themselves.

The Evolution of Method

The approach I use for consulting developed out of a style of teaching, supervising, and facilitating I have developed with intern and resident physicians in family medicine, occupational medicine, and psychiatry, and with physician assistant (P.A.) undergraduate and graduate students. In each class, seminar, or large lecture, I invite and encourage the group to be an inherent part of the subject. For me, teaching and learning are to some degree always fieldwork in which at least some aspects of the participants' lives are elicited and made a part of the course content and process (Stein, 1987c, 1988; Stein & Apprey, 1985, 1990). Contrary to the tenet of professionalism that in order to be objective, we must control for and discount, if not eliminate, inclusion of our lives, I explore with the group precisely how our lives do count in selecting our questions, ordering our observations, collecting our data, and influencing our interpretations and policy recommendations. Everything we do is both influenced by our biography and expressive of it. Part of my goal is to bring that biography—together with the shared biography of the group, our group culture—to greater and more accessible consciousness.

One of the institutionally sanctioned avenues for doing this in medicine, especially family medicine, has been in what are often called Balint groups. Michael Balint (1957), a Hungarian-born psychiatrist, had founded and led seminar groups (later dubbed Balint groups) of British general practitioners in discussions of difficult physician-patient-family-staff-colleague relationships. Their subject or topic of study was themselves, their emotional responses during patient care. As coordinator and facilitator of Balint groups in the Oklahoma City, Enid, Shawnee, and Lawton, Oklahoma, family medicine residency programs (all largely rural, community-based residency programs), I collected process notes between 1984 and 2012 from working with nearly 2,000 Balint group meetings with family medicine interns, second- and third-year residents, faculty physicians, and alumni physicians in private community practice. I have learned much about the subjective experience of organizations through participation in these Balint groups.

Through medical or clinical teaching and Balint groups, I came very ordinarily to incorporate my and other group members' observations and interpretations of our own group process over the days, weeks, months, and years as a key to understanding all culture. Thus, to understand culture—ethnic and national groups, adolescents and the elderly, Oklahomans and Texans, occupational groups—we do not merely look "out there" beyond ourselves but also "in here" within ourselves and in our own learning, occupational, or church groups. We study our values, expectations, roles, and feelings as crucial instruments or tools for studying others. The reverse is also true.

Irrespective of the official organizational subject matter—business, medicine, corporate mergers—I have come to realize that participants and their experience of the group (its culture) are always a part of the topic. Recognition of this as well by participants over the years has convinced me to pay close attention to the fact that *the subject of the group is always the group itself* as well as its formal agenda and explicit work tasks. This book brings to fruition that repeated discovery in multiple types of organizational settings.

Negative Capability, an Attitude of Not-Knowing

In leading Balint groups, and later in consulting with other organizational groups, I explore what happens—what *can* happen—when less *exclusive* attention is paid to enforcing what is supposed to happen and attention is given to understanding and addressing what does happen. Over the years, I have moved from thinking I know what should be happening in Balint groups to thinking that I *also* do not know what should be happening in Balint groups. I found it essential to address and attempt to understand the discrepancy between the aims and processes for which Balint groups are designed, and what actually happens in them in intern, residency, faculty, and community settings.

For me, the essence of all inquiry and effort to help others is the cultivation of living and working at the boundary, the edge, between knowing and not knowing, of being inside and outside the group (Duncan & Diamond, 2011; Stein, 1982a), of knowing while at the same time knowing that I do not or might not know. Poet John Keats, in an 1817 letter to his brothers, George and Thomas, distilled this disposition. He called it "Negative Capability . . . when a man [person] is capable of being in uncertainties, Mysteries, doubts, without any irritable reaching after fact and reason" (1974, p. 705). It is less a strictly cognitive strategy than it is a way of being in the world with one's entire being—including one's unwieldy emotions (Stein, 2007; French, 2001; French & Simpson, 1999; French & Simpson, 2014). Robert French and Peter Simpson (1999) even titled one of their papers on organizational research and consulting "Our best work happens when we don't know what we're doing."

To live in this mode of "negative capability" is to hold onto and embrace both knowing and not knowing. Relative to Balint groups, it is to suspend knowing what is supposed to happen in Balint groups so that one can learn in and with them. This approach draws upon the ethnographic method of learning via immersion in the life of a group. One can only learn so much from theory—sometimes too much, so as to create a defensive, closed system of scholarly or clinical ideology. Balint groups are not immune to this seduction.

Balint groups were designed to nurture physician self-exploration of their relationships with patients and in turn to improve these relationships and patient care. I neither defend Balint orthodoxy nor advocate local variation. Instead, I ask and attempt to answer the question: What happens in the life and work of a group if the leader/facilitator pays as much attention to the needs and psychic realities of the participants as to the official task, agenda, or purpose of the group?

For me, acknowledging and addressing these group needs and realities are not a deviation from the official task or purpose of the group, but are essential to the group's eventual emotional capacity to take on the official work for which the group is designed. Put differently, acknowledging and addressing these needs of the group become part of the work of the group: They serve as its emotional foundation. This process creates a group atmosphere in which the capacity to think and feel in relation to the task becomes possible. I find that *I must study the group in order to be of help to the group*; that is, I must listen deeply and attend to the group with all my senses. Negative capability is at the core of listening deeply in consulting—and in life.

The Role of Consultant

I define my consulting role as one in which (1) I am either a short-term, time-limited, rather than day-to-day regular, participant in the organizational group, *or* a longitudinal internal group participant observer and processor; (2) I am at least to some degree an outsider, if not a stranger (although I might be a regular guest); (3) I am attempting to learn about and emotionally encompass a cultural system in order to help describe and interpret it to its members so that they can be more knowledgeable of the breadth and depth of their own culture; and (4) I am ascribed or assigned little or no formal authority or official power but acquire my status informally through my ability to network, mediate, or speak with people in the organization.

My experiences as an organizational consultant and a group facilitator have placed me in far more active roles than the traditional fieldworker doing participant observation. To be asked to intervene as an agent of change—even if this change is also resisted—differs from recording or chronicling a group's way of life for another audience (readers such as anthropologists, political psychologists, or organizational researchers).

Lorna Amarasingham Rhodes's (1986) term *institutional analyst* better characterizes my methodology than does interventionist, trainer, or manager. However, since the relationship between observer or consultant and the group is the key to the cultural content that will be revealed, there is far less difference between fieldworker and consultant roles than I had first imagined. Even if I say, "I listen," rather than "I do," listening is itself a powerful, if under-recognized, form of doing. Listening is a form of healing.

Consultant and trainer roles have taught me to distinguish between the content and context dimensions of any consultation, intervention, or collection of field data. Traditional content consultants offer organizations such items as group exercises, presentations, suggestions, policy recommendations, interpretations, confrontations, questions, and reflections back to the group. When I began working with groups, although I tried to be a good listener, I did not realize how central this role would be. I assigned far more importance to the official, ostensible tasks I would do or be asked to perform.

It turned out that the contextual role of providing a holding environment, a safe container, an empathic setting in which the communication of affects (emotions, conscious and unconscious; see Diamond, 1993) can occur, was not only as important as any specific idea I or another facilitator might come up with, but was also developmentally and group-historically more fundamental. The relationship context was everywhere the foundation upon which any idea or task would be built. I came to visualize the relationship between content and context in a spatial manner, as if specific contents, issues, insights, tasks, ideas, and, yes, mistakes, were always contained, physically housed within the symbolic membrane of the group members' relationships with one another. My own authenticity in being there emotionally with them, and in using my perceptions and feelings as clues to what they were feeling and seeing but not acknowledging, became the foundation for everything else. Theory might inform experience, but group experience itself became my foremost teacher.

Some Guiding Principles

There are several principles that the consultant can use to guide himself or herself in performing the actual work of consulting (see Table 1). *First*, the consultant must recognize that group structure and function are both unconsciously and consciously organized (Gabriel, 1999; Stapley, 2006; Diamond, 1993, 2016; Kets de Vries, 2003; Kernberg, 1998). Political, economic, and structural "reasons" are only part of an organization's story. Group life is complex, not neatly packaged. The surface picture presented to the consultant often is a symptom and symbol in which people invest because it protects them against pain. Both vertically and horizontally in organizations, people defend against knowing, emotionally as well as cognitively, precisely what they need to know in order to mature, become more integrated.

Client organizations and individuals often do not want to know what they, at some unrecognized level, already know too well. The consultant's role becomes that of mediating between the known and the unknown, the knowable and the unknowable. This brings me to the central role of projective identification in unconsciously "organizing" many workplaces.

Beneath the Surface

For a *second* guiding principle, although the consultant must elicit and acknowledge the initial viewpoints and presenting "problems," he or she must not take them at face value as the entire reality. They are starting points. Susan Scott-Stevens (1988) warns that

> the [organizational) consultant must be wary about taking at face value the client's descriptions of the issues at hand. The anthropologist/consultant should already be cognizant of the fact that few people are aware of the details involved in the working of their own culture or subculture. This phenomenon is as true of smaller subcultures, such as groups of people in corporations, as it is of larger societies. (p. 11)

In the safety and playfulness of the consultant–client relationship, the often-painful mutual discovery of unconscious agendas (Freud, [1937] 1964; French & Simpson, 2014; Czander, 1993) is discrepant with the widespread anthropological tenet that "the native is always right" or that "only the native can define and treat or solve his or her problem" or that "text is all" (postmodernistically; see Spiro, 1986, 1988). Katherine P. Ewing (1991), for instance, reminds us that

> what goes on overtly in social interactions may be at variance with covert processes that participants themselves (much less observing anthropologists) are not always aware of. Taking an absolutely interpretivist stance, in which the culturally particular formulations of informants are assumed to be the only data about interactions that are available to the observer, would make the elucidation of covert processes (and their overt consequences) epistemologically impossible. (p.156)

In consulting, the consultant pieces together as much of the whole story as possible, something that cannot be reduced to the initial presentation of the problem, issue, or task. Through listening empathically, using temporary identification, interpreting, gently confronting, asking questions, and spending time with personnel on their own turf throughout the organization, I have discovered repeatedly the untold story behind the manifest story. This approach does not trivialize what

TABLE 1. Principles of Listening

What to do	What not to do
Listen carefully to many people, different subunits of the organization.	Do not trivialize or dismiss the identified problem or "presenting complaint" or those who make it.
Track metaphors, silences, verbs, expressions of emotion; do a "fantasy analysis" of group process (deMause 1982).	Do not take the presenting problem or issue to be the entire picture.
Build trust.	Do not try to solve the problem prematurely or promise to solve the "wrong" problem.
Give yourself time; ask for more time.	
Get to know "the whole" organization.	Do not listen only to one component, person, or unit of the organization.
Use your own emotional responses as cues to organizational experiences.	While you are trying to be efficient, expeditious, or helpful, do not overidentify with the urgency the organization is inducing or projecting onto you to solve the problem.
Assume that the presenting complaints, issues, problems, are not the whole story.	
Ask what has been done before to "solve" or address these problems; ask what other types of problems the organization has had.	Do not say that the problem is only or really different, deeper, or unconscious; advise that new facets of the problem initially presented emerge over time.
Help the organizational group find out what the characteristic problems of the organization are.	
Learn who constitutes the informal authority structure as well as the formal authority structure, and work with both.	Do not say that the group is crazy or resisting change; do not accuse the group of being stuck or not accepting reality.
Help the organizational group to understand the complexity, breadth, and depth of its own culture, that in every culture things are more than what they first seem; help the group to tolerate not knowing for a while through identification with your toleration for uncertainty and anxiety.	
Help the organization to accept that to experience intense emotions around occupational settings and issues is as ordinary as it is in families, ethnic groups, and religions.	

a consultant hears at any given moment. It accords everyone dignity, but not finality. It also acknowledges that there is more to be pieced together and that the consultant is there to serve as a liaison between persons or units and to help integrate storylines. The consultant might at least consider presenting problems to be metaphors of larger contextual issues in addition to real, concrete issues.

For instance, in recent years I have been asked to examine, address, and "fix" a number of problems that turned out to be vessels carrying the burden of organizations' history: difficulty scheduling meetings between groups, employee evaluations, factionalism between organizational groups, decreased productivity, poor team morale, conflict between the vertical chain of command and horizontal responsibility for carrying out tasks, staff turnover, and role demand. In each of these, I would have missed (and sometimes did miss) the opportunity to help the organization address the deeper cultural and unconscious issues had I failed to pursue the possibility that the part first presented to me was metaphoric of a still-elusive whole.

Emotional Responsiveness: Depth of Relationship

The *third* principle is that the consultant not only listens and watches for this story to emerge in others but also, through introspection, identification, and empathy, constantly monitors his or her own emotional responses as crucial data about the organization. Some of the most important cues are our own feelings and fantasies, even strong visceral reactions (such as heart pounding, cramping, headache) (see Boyer, 1993). I often offer a description or interpretation to a group about their own emotional tone that I sense, or I describe my own.

Whether a task is called fieldwork, organizational consultation, or clinical healing, the relationship is the foundation of the edifice that is eventually built. The crucial ingredient is our emotional responsiveness to one another. What this responsiveness should be cannot entirely be known beforehand, say, by reading everything ever written and published about tribe A or corporation B. People are more alive than the paper on which accounts and taxonomies of them are narrated and enumerated. Anthropologist Oliver La Farge ([1945] 1967), for instance, tells a poignant story of how in 1927 he came to learn sacred lore from the shaman Antel, The Shower of the Road, among the Highland Maya of Guatemala.

The renowned shaman received La Farge and a Ladino interpreter. Both Antel and La Farge grew more confident in each other. Soon, however, La Farge (p. 355) realized that "the Ladino was a hopelessly incompetent interpreter" of the Jacaltecan language. The interpreter would summarize five minutes of explanation with, "He says, 'Yes'" (p. 355). Moreover, Antel did not speak Spanish and was trying to convey serious matters of theology and cosmology correctly. La Farge feared their communication was being destroyed. La Farge persisted, hearing his long questions rendered in a few words and Antel's long reply returned merely as "No."

La Farge explains,

The trouble was that the [Ladino] man didn't understand the full of what Antel had said. I think I understood as much as he did.

Digging into my brain for all the Jacalteca I could summon, I asked the next question for myself. Antel hesitated. Then a lovely look of relief came over his face in the candlelight, and he answered me in halting Spanish. The interpreter was astonished; so was I. It was a beautiful tribute, the laying aside of a shield, an advantage he had guarded for years. We worked together from there on, helping each other, piecing the two languages together in co-operation in order to deal with sacred things. Of all my work among Indians, this remains the highest moment. (p. 356)

Surely part of the issue was linguistic, a lack of comprehension from the outset of who spoke what. Yet as the example shows, language can be a tool and badge of honor, a means of avoiding shame, a kind of self-protection. When the compassionate interviewer, La Farge, took the first risk of revealing his vulnerability by trying haltingly to speak in Jacaltecan, Antel took the risk of replying in Spanish, thereby revealing how much of both cultures he indeed knew. This is what I mean by placing context, relationship, always ahead of any cultural content.

What psychoanalyst Harold F. Searles (1975) writes of clinical work with autistic patients can be extended to consultants' efforts with individuals and organizational groups:

For the analyst to help the autistic patient become able to participate in a therapeutic symbiosis (that is, a symbiosis similar in nature to a healthy infant-mother symbiosis), the analyst must first have become able to immerse himself in the patient's autistic world. This then fosters the patient's identifying with the analyst who can so immerse himself in the other's world: the patient, partly through such identification, becomes increasingly able to immerse himself in the analyst's more usual "own" world, and the rapid flux and interchangeability of a therapeutically symbiotic kind of relatedness flows from this. (p.104)

Ethnographic Fieldwork and Immersion

Listening deeply draws heavily upon psychoanalytic and anthropologic fieldwork approaches (Hunt, 1989; Duncan & Diamond 2011; Volkan & Hawkins, 1971;

Stein, 1982a) in which consultants immerse themselves in another's world in order to comprehend it. This world consists not only of verbal meanings but also of the feelings, gestures, postures, facial expressions, unconscious affects, and fantasies that underlie and accompany these meanings. As a consultant, I then try to return this comprehension to organization members in an effort to understand them and to allow them to feel understood. I not only observe and interview "them," but I reflect upon my own emotional responses to them as crucial data about the relationship, and ultimately about the people with whom I am consulting.

In organizational consultation, I temporarily serve the dual function of a real person and an "auxiliary ego" (or Theodor Reik's "third ear," 1948; Safran, 2011) for the client or group. I try to acknowledge the participants' real self that has become buried by defenses against anxiety (for instance, annihilation, death, abandonment, separation, castration) (Masterson, 1985). I pay special attention to the affective or emotional dimension of communication, not only to the spoken words. Being insofar as possible in an I-thou relation with the group (Buber, [1923] 1958), that is, a relationship in which the other person or group is valued as separate from the consultant, I acknowledge and serve as a refueling station for the real self to take the chance to emerge.

Sense of History and the Creation of Space

The *fourth* principle is that the consultant must obtain a good history of the presenting problem, the organization's problem-solving style, and how leaders address problems. This is not a once-and-for-all storytelling event. The client or organization's sense of history will also emerge over the time of the consultation. A longitudinal approach to the present is essential. The consultant must be an exemplary historian in helping clients to reconstruct their own history.

He or she should refrain from solving the wrong problem or trying to solve the presenting problem prematurely or alone. The consultant first finds out what problems have been presented before, by whom, their statuses in the organization, what has been done and not done. The next step is to determine different people's sense of what the problem is, how it developed, and why it has persisted, and find out what the channels of information distribution are, the media used (computers, meetings, memos, even bathroom conversations), and how earlier ideas have been received. In short, what prevented them from working?

The approach of listening deeply in organizational consulting relies heavily upon clients' and groups' free associations, that is, their choice and sequence of words, phrases, and sentences together with their feelings, whether expressed by an individual or built up over time by a group. I learn to trust the group process to reveal key themes, patterns, meanings, feeling tones, and metaphors. When

I work with groups, I seek opportunities to hear them on their own terms and even on their own turf (hospital ward, nurses station, or corporate headquarters), rather than in my office, before I feel I have earned the right to contribute my own reflections.

Ernest Jones (1953), in his biography of Sigmund Freud, writes of how Freud himself came to listen more and to ask less of his patients. While working with Josef Breuer, "Freud was still given to urging, pressing, and questioning, which he felt to be hard but necessary work. On one historic occasion, however, the patient, Frl. Elisabeth, reproved him for interrupting her flow of thought by his questions. He took the hint, and thus made another step towards free associations" (pp. 243–244). To use free association in organizational work is to lead by first following. It is to take emotional and cognitive cues from clients, to take in, absorb, and process what the group is doing. It is to respect group members, foster in them mastery of conflict, participate with them in problem-solving.

Learning from Mistakes

The *fifth* and final principle is that the consultant acknowledges her or his own mistakes. Our Western Judeo-Christian history, together with its secular inheritors, has emphasized the importance of being right, of winning, of striving for perfection in thought, if not also in deed. We pay people handsomely to have the right, cost-effective, and short-term answers. In the past century, Frederick Winslow Taylor's (1911) principles of scientific management and Peter Drucker's (1954) later management by objective are two prevailing symbols of our cultural preoccupation with eliminating possibilities of error, of totally foreseeing and planning outcomes. Most recently, *strategic planning, total quality management (TQM)*, and *Lean/Six Sigma* processes strive for efficiency and predictability. We devalue serendipity and surprise. Mistakes are costly, we say, in time and money.

Yet can we learn without errors? Can we foresee everything and therefore never have to learn in the first place? Fear of mistakes is fear of our own limitations, vulnerability, mortality, ambivalence about values, aggressiveness, and creativity. Acknowledgment of mistakes in the group can open a kind of nonextensional space to greater emotional breadth and depth and to greater creativity in planning task accomplishment. Much creative "cultural space" (Winnicott, 1967) can be liberated from rigid group routine when group members and consultants acknowledge that their precious ideas were dead wrong.

I turn now to two stories where my recognition and acknowledgment of my mistakes I had made created the opportunity for new ideas—new potential space—to emerge.

A Story: Discovering and Creating Space

At the end of August 1990, I was a visiting faculty member for a week at the Poynter Institute for Media Studies, in St. Petersburg, Florida, for a seminar called "Ethics in Broadcast News." The group, consisting of newspersons, reporters, station managers, and photographers from television and radio stations around the United States, totaled approximately 25 participants. At the conclusion of a role-play and interview exercise, I stood toward the front of the room. This location was identifiable as the place where previous speakers (faculty) had spent virtually all their own presentation times, as the location where the video screen was placed (retractable electronically toward the ceiling), and as the direction toward which end everyone was facing.

Through the exercise, many people had begun to realize that, despite their ideal of objectivity in reporting or photography, they often felt uncomfortable in changing roles. As group members and I interacted, I wrote some of their key concepts, phrases, and images on the many green chalkboards in the front. At about this time, I noticed that my handwriting on the chalkboards had become smaller and smaller and that my notes were getting increasingly crowded in the space. I felt somewhat panicky since I wished to keep up with the participants and to have their comments immediately available for them to view and integrate with the discussion.

Suddenly it dawned on me as I looked across the entire room that at the *opposite* end of the room, above the shelf where the slide projector and other audiovisual aids sat, stood an entirely clean, unused, green chalkboard. I interrupted the group discussion of the role-play content and shared my realization about all this unused board space. Hesitantly, cautiously, but increasingly playfully, I walked into this hitherto unoccupied space, sharing aloud both my consternation and the unspoken rules in which we had all colluded. Without uttering a single word, we had emotionally divided up space right there in the seminar room. Here, I realized aloud, lay the very creation of "newsroom" culture or any culture.

What—I wondered aloud as I now stood confidently at the "back" of the room and began to write on the board—did it feel like for the people in the back to be there at the front, while those once at the front now sat in the back? They earlier might not have heard or seen or been heard or seen as easily. I proceeded with the exercise, describing my feelings and asking theirs about the new space we had together created.

I openly apologized for my former bias in my perception of the room and of the group members themselves. The mistake was one I had not realized I was even making. I, too, had accepted the implicit group cultural rule about faculty staying in the safe, "commanding," front of the class rather than venturing toward the back. On the face of it, not to use a chalkboard and not to walk to the back or side of a classroom appear minor issues. Yet this seemingly small matter was a metaphor for unstated cultural assumptions, rules, fantasies, and relationships—all of which had limited the learning experience in the room. We collectively realized how much additional relational (newly cultural) space we had available all the time but had not claimed or used on previous days of the seminar.

A second story also illustrates how a client or group of people feels free to be creative when the consultant or leader publicly admits that he or she had made a wrong assumption. Mistakes do not have to be disastrous and embarrassing. They can be liberating, so long as the person or people who acknowledge them are not humiliated or punished.

A Story: Not Needing to Be Right

Let me offer a second example of the lesson of acknowledging mistakes. On March 28, 1990, I was a speaker at the centenary celebration of the Calgary General Hospital in Calgary, Alberta, Canada. The occasion was, in fact, a double anniversary. Called "one hospital on two sites," the original hospital, the Bow Valley Centre, was celebrating its hundredth year. The Peter Lougheed Centre—the Calgary General Hospital site at which the conference was being held—was exactly one and one-half years old. I titled my presentation "The Interplay between Understanding Health Care and Family Culture."

In the months prior to the presentation, I had tried to do what I regarded as my homework. I had spoken at length with one conference organizer about the hospital's history and about the populations it served. I had read the celebratory brochures about the hospital's proud history and humble, log-cabin-like origins a century earlier. During my formal lecture I speculated about what it must be like to work there during the centenary, that it must be a joyous time of increased organizational group pride and sense of purpose. I asked whether there was anything special about this moment in the hospital's history that affected how hospital workers perceived, experienced, and responded to the diversity of family types that they treated.

As I finished my formal presentation, I stepped out from behind the podium on the five- to six-foot-high stage that was located in front of the room. I walked down to the level of the group. During the following lively half hour or so of discussion, the participants at first timidly, then candidly, expressed how many of them felt: (1) there was little to celebrate; (2) they had been removed from an old, comfortable, familiar hospital work setting with friends to a new building that few people wanted; and (3) the new hospital had been foisted on them by the administration and the remote federal government. Let me add a further note of context: Not only was the entire conference being videotaped, but it was also being played live on television monitors throughout both hospital facilities, including the offices of the hospital administrators who had organized the centennial celebration. Far from being in a mood to celebrate, the participants felt deep loss, grief, and anger.

I acknowledged to the group that I had been utterly wrong. I attempted to change my role: to serve now less as an *outside expert* lecturer and more as a *group facilitator* for expressing issues, articulating feelings, and strategizing. Perhaps as a fantasy figure, I served projectively as a "good" or "nurturing" parental or authority figure and safe "container" who let participants speak the unspeakable, who did not punish them for acknowledging these thoughts, who allowed himself to be the target and container for what had been toxic (symbolically poisonous) thoughts and feelings. Participants entered into a spirit of play. The group and I together created a safe space in which emotionally explosive issues could be raised and discussed.

Encompassing Systems

A consultant who can truly mediate between people or groups avoids taking sides. He or she is foremost one who can encompass internally—hold, integrate—both or all viewpoints or factions of organizational conflict and who can therefore imagine alternatives (see Stein, 1985c, 1987b). One who can listen deeply to both (or all) sides to a problem or conflict creates the atmosphere for clients to identify with his or her style and creatively imagine alternatives *themselves*.

To encompass a system emotionally is to stretch the sense of affiliation and common humanity so as to exclude no one in the system. It is an act Martin Buber (1965) calls inclusion. Heinz Kohut (1971, 1984), and Arnold Modell (1984), among other self psychologists and object-relations analysts, call it empathy. Sigmund Freud ([1921] 1955b) and other classical psychoanalysts term it identification, and Jean Piaget terms it decentering (Piaget & Inhelder, 1969). Maurice Friedman (1985) emphasizes that in this process of inclusion, "the therapist runs the risk of being changed by the client, but never loses his or her own separateness or identity in the process" (p. 199).

Emotional inclusiveness of others is made possible as we cease imposing idealizing and demonizing projections onto the world, and recognize them instead as parts of ourselves and then reincorporate them. To encompass conflicting, even fragmented systems, we must be able to withstand the temptation that pulls us to take sides as a means of reducing anxiety. One form this inner siren takes is to split groups—say, subdivisions in a corporation, factory, or hospital—into an all-good "us" with whom we identify and whom we like, and an all-bad "them" from whom we distance and whom we dislike. It is easy to be an advocate for the former but difficult to see any of their flaws. Likewise, it is difficult even to listen to the latter, let alone acknowledge they possess any virtues.

In the early hours and days of organizational consultations, I invariably feel as if I am going crazy, descending into chaos with so much emotionally "hot" material forcibly entering my thoughts and sentiments. But only as I can tolerate taking it in, rather than fending it off, can I help my clients look at, hear, feel, and be handed back all that they are as I experience them. My first task is to emotionally and intellectually encompass everything I encounter (Stein, 1987b), to expand the boundary of the imaginable. I am ready to "say" something, to return something to them, only when I have begun to feel what it is like to be a member of that group, to harbor its group fantasy (deMause, 1982; Stein, 1985b; Stierlin, 1973). Here my subjectivity is a crucial ally of any objectivity, one that helps clarify the group's own largely out-of-awareness subjectivity.

Reason and emotion are not necessarily foes. Nor is "group" inevitably a foe of intellectual development or of love. Love is not, at least ought not to be, a subject alien to organizational consultation but deserves to be brought to its core. Writing of ethnographic fieldwork, George Devereux (1967) says, "There is information based on the experience of Love, which is valid precisely because it is not distorted by an obsessive pursuit of (pseudo-) objectivity and is based not on participant observation, but on a shared experience" (p.119). Furthermore, "The anthropologist can seldom find real love in the field. He can, if he be worthy of it, find friends [in the field] and thereby learn all anyone can know about the Epiphany, in that particular culture, of the universal Eros who is at the root of all life" (p. 120). This poetic view of the depths of fieldwork deserves to be central to organizational work. Devereux follows in the footsteps of Sacha Nacht (1962, p. 160), who argues that a psychoanalyst must love his or her patients and that love is in fact the main curative factor in healing, by saying that in fieldwork as well "one must love one's subjects."

Let me turn now to three stories that illustrate much of what I have discussed above. The first story is about time and listening, giving a client or group sufficient time for out-of-awareness material to emerge. The ending of the story has a far different emotional tone than the beginning, but was possible only because I intuitively sensed that there was more to the story than the presenting account.

A Story: How Crazy Was Internship?

A crucial element in listening, and in helping individuals and groups solve problems, is to give time for materials to emerge rather than jump to conclusions and give premature closure on a subject. The following case illustrates the importance of time and timing. At a February 1991 two-day retreat by interns, residents, and faculty of my family medicine department, much of the opening group session (about 25 people, including spouses and children) was devoted to talking about experiences of the internship year. Participants testified that, despite the hardships of internship, it was doable, survivable: "So far the worst thing has been the night shift on obstetrics, keeping the kids quiet while daddy [the intern] is home from the hospital sleeping. . . . Second year residents get more sleep. We made it! Internship is survivable. I even have forgotten most of it! Each year gets better and better. . . . I don't remember my husband's internship year. It's faded."

As I listened in this large group, I formed the impression that either the trauma-ridden intern year had improved retrospectively with memory and with better subsequent experiences, that internship was really not so bad as many had claimed at the time, or that the "fading" of internship in memory was some kind of self-protective armor against the pain of the experience (see Stein, 1990a, 1990b, for a more comprehensive discussion of medical training).

Eight hours later that same day, the retreat was divided into three smaller discussion groups, each composed of interns, residents, faculty, and spouses. Husbands and wives were assigned to different groups. I facilitated one group of eight people. Our task was to discuss one or more stimulus questions. I emphasized that this was not a questionnaire but a way of prompting them to think, feel, and talk about what was important to them.

From the start, several participants offered detailed, passionate testimonials about traumatic experiences from their own or their spouses' internships. One spouse, himself a biomedical professional, spoke of a time when his wife, then a family physician resident, was on 36-hour call at the hospital and did not come home until 16 hours after she had left the hospital. She had been exhausted from hospital work, had had trouble seeing the road, and had pulled over in a parking lot, thinking she would sleep for a half hour. She woke up 16 hours later, confused about what day or place it was.

Another physician's spouse gave a vignette from her days in graduate school, which took place while her husband was in residency. He had always insisted on driving the car, even when he was tired. He would never admit he was tired, but while driving, he would miss exits on a familiar freeway or veer off the road onto the shoulder. She would become furious because he would not acknowledge he was so exhausted from being on call, nor would he ask her for help. Several others, physicians and nonphysicians, offered "war story" examples as if they were emotionally reliving, rather than distantly reporting, experiences from their intern year.

As they spoke, I remembered many of the disavowals made earlier that day. I was disturbed by the disparity between the feeling tone of this group and of the larger group while talking about the same subject. I used the disturbance within me as crucial data about the recollection of internship. I commented on how different these present testimonials were from my initial impression. As facilitator and interpreter, I was using what Peter Giovacchini (1969) calls linking interpretations between words and feelings I remembered through free-floating attention to the initial group and those in the current small group.

I shared with participants my uneasiness about accepting at face value the earlier fading view of history. I said I was inclined to see their vignettes shared within the safety of this smaller group as evidence for how emotionally overwhelming internship had actually been. I wondered whether emotionally distancing themselves from it via repression, denial, and isolation had been a way to protect themselves from feeling and remembering how traumatic it in fact had been.

I use this example to illustrate the importance of giving groups time to allow more, and deeper-leveled, material to emerge. One of a consultant's or facilitator's crucial functions is constantly to try on earlier material with current material; to look for disparity, congruence, conflict; and to present those patterns as questions or hypotheses to the group.

The following story is about a telephone consultation with a physician client with whom I had worked years before. It turns out that the explicit reason for the call differed considerably from the implicit reason for the call—that latter of which came to the surface as a result of attentive listening to her.

A Story: "I Knew I Called You for Something"

For decades, approximately twice a month, I receive a long-distance phone call from a physician, psychotherapist, family therapist, medical administrator, or corporate consultant or executive who asks my advice on some personal or group problem he or she is facing. More often than not, we discover as we talk that the solution is contained in my client's own story—if only I have the patience and compassion to listen to and evoke the story. My role is then to help my client tell and feel the full (or at least fuller) story.

Furthermore, no consultant can know beforehand how occupational and other areas of life, current and past, connect. Rather this is something that emerges out of the material supplied by the client or organization, together with the thoughts and feelings of the consultant. A consultant can help a client solve a problem only if enough of the breadth and depth of the problem is known first. Otherwise, the consultant will, in good faith, "solve" the wrong or at least address only the superficial problem. The following vignette illustrates how the problem and solution gradually emerged during a phone conversation I had with a physician.

In the late 1990s I received an unexpected phone call from a physician I had last seen two years earlier, having counseled with her for more than a year. She had been a family medicine resident and single parent and had been unable to afford even a reliable car. She had left a residency situation in which all the trainees and faculty—most of them men—with children were presumed to have a significant other available to take care of home, children, car, and all nontraining "support" activities. She said she was calling "just to check in and see how you are and to let you know what I'm doing. It's been so long since we talked." I listened. Most of the consultations I have been involved with have begun indirectly like this.

She had worked full-time as an emergency room (ER) physician in a rural community, making good, stable money, which enabled her to care for her family and control her schedule. She said that her contract would expire in five months. She was trying to decide what next to do in her life. Although ER work paid the bills handsomely, helped her pay off her large family debts, and gave her quality time with her children, she did not want to practice this type of medicine for the rest of her life. In particular, she did not like the procedure orientation of ER work and the fact that she hardly got to know her patients as people. After a single, intensive ER visit, she rarely saw patients again.

She said that she had applied to a small town in a northern midwestern state that was looking for a full-time family doctor but that she was not sure she would like such a long and snowy winter or that she would want to do the type of practice in which she took care of every type of medical problem in people's lives. She felt that the town had made her a generous offer but that she was not sure her children would like to live so far north or that she would want to live such an isolated life, 60 miles from the nearest city. She then told me of a second possibility, a psychiatry residency at a state hospital, to which she had also applied and which had expressed great interest in her.

Remembering our earlier conversations, I told her I was not surprised to learn of her interest in psychiatry. I said I remembered many of our earlier counseling sessions in which she had talked about how much she had enjoyed visiting with patients in their hospital rooms while she was doing an internal medicine residency. I thought aloud of the many areas of her life she was probably trying to reconcile and integrate: training, career, income generation to provide a living for herself and her children, dating with the hope of finding a marriage partner, social and environmental (ecological) concerns, love of the outdoors, and artistic and literary talents. I gave her my perception that increasingly even small towns are seeking board-certified physicians. I worried that, although the town might welcome her now, she might eventually be shut out of a good, long-term practice if in the future the town attracted board-certified physicians and she was licensed only from her rotating internship. In short, I relied heavily on my imagination and memory in response to what she was saying. She said she was having a hard time deciding which to choose, although she was inclined toward psychiatry.

I then recalled patterns from our earlier counseling sessions when she had faced some difficult career or family decision or felt she had reached an impasse. Instead of urging her to weigh all the alternatives logically or to make an accountant's tally sheet, which she had already been doing to little avail, I now encouraged her to listen to her heart and then compare its voice with realistic options in the professional world. "Try sketching, writing your poetry, or reading your recent entries in your diary, or as you play your flute in some secluded place in the woods, ask yourself what you are trying to say to yourself, what these different facets of you are trying to tell you."

With a sigh of relief and a smile in her voice, she replied, "I knew that I called you for *something*. That's why I must have called you, and I didn't even know it. I was calling because I was stuck on how to make my decision concerning my career and family. I knew you could help me get unstuck. You keep reminding me of how important a part my art is in my life, that it's like a barometer if I'd only trust it."

I said I enjoyed hearing from her and had wondered "Why now?" when she had first called. I had trusted the unfolding of our conversation to answer the question without my ever having to pose it. During our visit, I used my current emotions and ideas, and my own mental associations from prior conversations, as bridges or links between issues or feelings then and now and gave them to her to try on for size. As she told her story with few interruptions from me (what psychoanalysts call free association), I occasionally interjected a remembrance, question, or comment on a feeling tone in what she was saying. This in turn became part of the flow of the phone consultation.

This phone visit reminded me that the process people use to make life decisions is of a different order than an exclusively rational assessment of specific choices or outcomes themselves. We had not started thinking about an occupational consultation but about her life. I was able to be of some help to her by backing off at the outset and listening for—and facilitating her telling—more of the story so that we could both gather a sense of where she was heading, which she did not know at the outset. By the visit's end, I not only had helped her identify numerous content issues in her decision but had also reminded her about styles or modes in her own world that she could use to help herself get unstuck in her decisions. For her, painting, canoeing, writing poetry, making diary entries, and drawing in charcoal were forms of creative self-healing—just as for others going turkey or quail hunting, fishing, or backpacking was their therapeutic medium.

I did not enter the telephone consultation with a preordained notion as to what the right outcome ought to be. With trepidation, I trusted that this was something no "expert" had the right to decide or dictate, that the solution was one we would construct together. In a sense, I trusted my physician colleague to lead the consultation to where she needed it to go. My role was to help her tell the story she did not even know she had within her. Answers would not arise *in* me (ostensibly the "expert"), but *between* us, the fruit of the dialogue of storytelling and story listening. This is the essence of this book.

1. Key Concepts

Introduction

In this chapter, I identify five key concepts that serve as road maps and guide-posts for the chapters that follow. These key concepts emerged inductively over the years from consultations. I did not know or apply them beforehand. Organizational work taught me what tools and language I needed. I first discuss the importance of understanding *group dynamics* in work sites. I describe how the *self of the observer-consultant* provides crucial data about groups. I then discuss the roles of *metaphors, leadership,* and *the triad of change-loss-grief* in regulating the life of organizations. I begin to raise and answer such questions as: What is a group? Why should we pay attention to group process in work sites and not only to tasks? What does it feel like to be a member of a group? What is an organization? What is its culture and that culture's consequences for decision-making, produc-tivity, profit, and morale? How does a consultant know what to pay attention to during the course of a consultation?

Before I offer the key concepts, I want to situate this book in relation to a sampling of other recent works that have fruitfully applied psychoanalytic theory and methods to organizational research and consulting. No study stands alone, but rests on the shoulders of its predecessors and contemporaries. Together, they emphasize the importance of our attending to the psychological reality of leaders, managers, and employees, for that reality molds and drives much of what hap-pens in the workplace.

A Selected Overview of Recent
Psychoanalytic Organizational Literature

In recent decades there has been a convergence of perspectives, thinking, and findings on the part of psychodynamically oriented organizational researchers and consultants about the profound irrationality that characterizes and governs much of organizational life. Across many books and years, their goal is to make the inaccessible (unconscious) more accessible, and to translate this into consulting approaches.

In a book on organizational identity, Michael Diamond (1993) questions the widespread myth of the techno-rational workplace. Instead, relationships are rooted in emotion and projected emotion, and fantasies largely govern the relationship between leaders and subordinates, among employees, and between managers and workers. In a similar vein, William Czander (1993) applies psychoanalytic theory to understanding unconscious as well as conscious dimensions of management–employee relationships and conflicts, and offers suggestions for organizational consultants.

In *Managing People During Stressful Times*, Seth Allcorn and Michael Diamond (1997) systematically explore how psychological defenses and defensiveness that arise in the face of change, stress, threat, loss, and anxiety actually have the opposite effect from what management intends and make the workplace increasingly dysfunctional.

In a study of ideology, conflict, and leadership in organizational life, Otto Kernberg (1998) describes the role of libidinal and aggressive impulses, regression, authoritarianism in small and large groups, and the psychodynamics of leader–worker relationships in the workplace. In his encyclopedic *Organizations in Depth*, Yiannis Gabriel (1999) offers a systematic account that psychoanalysis can make to understanding workplace organizations. Likewise, in *Storytelling in Organizations: Facts, Fictions, and Fantasies*, Yiannis Gabriel offers a comprehensive account of the role that stories and storytelling play in organizational life. Gabriel shows how employees' stories can reveal the emotional life of organizations that lies beneath the official, rational surface picture and leadership-authorized stories.

In *Leaders, Fools and Impostors*, Manfred F. R. Kets de Vries (2003) addresses the darker side of human nature in organizations. He questions the dogma of rationality as driving leaders' and followers' behavior. Instead, employees, for example, often become subservient echoes to narcissistic leaders, who insist they are always right and accept no criticism.

Michael Diamond and Seth Allcorn (2009), in *Private Selves in Public Organizations*, build on Diamond's theory that questioned the beliefs about techno-rational principles and practices in the workplace. They observe the fragmentation of the workplace into silos of exclusivistic identity, the role that transference and countertransference play in workplace relationships, and the importance of rampant local and global change, loss, and mourning in regulating organizational life.

Lionel Stapley (2006) examines the role unconscious forces play "beneath the surface" of organizational systems, and how out-of-awareness forces influence work. In a similar vein, in *Beneath the Crust of Culture* (Stein, 2005), I explore many areas of American life and uncover the influence of unconscious factors in numerous cultural institutions and history.

In *The Conscious Leader* (2014), Shelley Reciniello reveals unconscious forces beneath the surface of organizational leaders' and leader–employee relationships. In her award-winning book, Reciniello shows how out-of-awareness forces sabotage organizational planning and productivity, as well as how leaders and managers can become more reflective and self-aware and, in turn, more creative.

Finally, in a study of work in organizational groups based on the theories of Wilfred Bion, Robert French and Peter Simpson (2014), I explore how group purpose, focus, and attention to tasks are often distracted by unconscious fantasies, wishes, and agendas.

Key Concept 1: Understanding Groups

Psychoanalytic scholars and consultants have contributed much to our understanding of organizations. Perhaps their most important—and difficult to accept—discovery is that workplace groups are governed largely by psychological processes outside the awareness of their own members, and that these processes affect major policy development as well as minor, everyday, decision-making. Furthermore, in diverse areas, such as the study of leadership (Levinson et al., 1962; Kernberg, 1998; Kets de Vries, 2003; Stapley, 2006; Reciniello, 2014), self and organizational identity (Diamond, 1984, 1988, 1993; Diamond & Allcorn, 1985, 1986; Allcorn & Diamond, 1997; Diamond & Allcorn, 2009), evil in organizations (Alford, 1990), bureaucratic structure (Baum, 1987; Gabriel, 1999; Diamond & Allcorn, 2009), and the metaphor of management (Zaleznick, 1989), psychoanalytic investigations and consultants repeatedly find that organizational members imagine and act as if their group is a distinct entity that somehow possesses a life of its own.

In describing ethnic, national, or organizational cultures, outside interpreters and insiders alike can easily slip into reifications and speak as if a group is a self-standing entity, a living organism rather than an association of individual people. Although in one sense reification distorts reality, in another sense it performs vital mental functions for group members. Warren Shapiro (1989), for example, shows how reification of people's social group serves the purpose of denying death. People everywhere perceive and characterize their group or society as an immortal, ontological, if not supernaturally created entity.

While studying how peoples in Europe and the United States reify society, Lloyd deMause and Henry Ebel developed the concept of group fantasy (deMause, 1982; deMause & Ebel, 1977). It refers to the fact that people perceive, define, identify, and experience themselves as members of a group that constitutes some kind of "us." They do so actively and to a large extent uncon-sciously. The process of constructing and "sharing" a sense of we-ness does not exist apart from constantly imagining an otherness. It is, in short, a never-ending hammering out and shaping of group contents. A group fantasy consists of what it feels like to be a member of a group at a particular time. Through the oscilla-tion of projection and introjection (and identification), one reincorporates into the self an image of the group as the outer social skin of the self, the protective outpost or border for security operations. The group self-image becomes an ide-alized object, the representation of which is then taken back into the self.

Yet groups do not really exist apart from the people—and their motivations—who constitute and "belong to" them (e.g., La Barre, 1972; Bion, 1959; Czander, 1993; Diamond & Allcorn, 2009). There exists no such thing as a "group mind" or group entity beyond the individual feelings and perceptions of the people who constitute the group. It is people who believe in and negotiate a sense of we-ness and who create and experience the very group they describe as possessing a separate existence beyond themselves. For purposes of defense against anxiety, motives and character may be ascribed to, projected upon, or externalized upon the group. All organizations and cultures are created, constructed, and sustained by those who in turn experience themselves as belonging to these groups and who are loyal to "them" (Berger & Luckmann, 1966; Diamond, 1993, 2016).

Implicitly building on Melanie Klein's (1946) concept of projective identifi-cation as regulating both internal and interpersonal environments, Yrjö Alanen (1990) refers at the individual level to

> those defensive functions through which the individual tries to protect him-self against anxiety caused by internal or external threats by using or exploit-ing other persons and/or fantasies about them. A successful warding-off of anxiety will then depend upon whether the other person behaves in the way he is expected to do, or whether at least such a fantasy can be maintained. At the world community level this conception is very relevant to a better understanding of the deeper causes of the so-called enemy stereotypes, pro-jectively tinged apprehensions of the "other part," giving at the same time an acceptable and guilt-relieved motive for one's own aggressive feelings and actions directed at it. This also includes the psychological paradox that a feared and—rightly—condemned aggressive intervention of the other part may also be experienced as an unconsciously welcome event, just because it gives additional evidence in support of the "correctness" of our prejudiced stereotype of that other part.

In families, we not infrequently also see actions exercised by one member to provoke the other member to behave in ways corresponding to the safeguarded conceptions of the first member. These kinds of provocations play their part in international politics as well, and may have contributed to the outbreaks of many wars. (p. 8)

In groups, mental operations of members differ from those of dyads or of the individual. There is greater proneness to regression; to the eruption of primary process, irrational thinking; and to action governed by it (cf. Alford, 1988, p. 579; Kets de Vries, 2003; Stapley, 2006). The larger the group is, the deeper is the regressive potential; the greater are the depersonalization, dehumanization, and abstraction of adversaries and the diminution of reality testing; and the more unfettered is the dominion of fantasy (Volkan, 1997). Organizational culture, like ethnic and religious cultures, rests upon deeply personal, conflictual, and emotion-laden foundations, most of which drive people unconsciously. Consider, for instance, the crucial role of projective identification as organizational "glue."

The Work of Projective Identification
Finding a Suitable Dumping Ground

One of the most common ways that workplaces are unconsciously as well as consciously *organized* is by splitting off from oneself, then transferring and psychologically injecting unacceptable parts of oneself or one's group *into* another person or group. As a consequence, one of the most pervasive and emotionally damaging ways of not knowing a major part of oneself is to put it outside of oneself and into another person or group. One can, in turn, feel good and unconflicted about oneself. Of the many inner maneuvers we use to rid ourselves of unacceptable thoughts and feelings—for example, projection, externalization, and projective identification—*projective identification* is one of the most indelible, silent, and emotionally destructive tactics. (Its pernicious work is a theme throughout this book.) It imprisons and torpedoes organizations and their tasks.

By extension, one of the most difficult, yet central tasks of a consultant is to recognize and help people in organizations recognize and relinquish the need for projective identifications, and to take back and psychologically "own" painful and disavowed self-images, wishes, fantasies, and beliefs that are psychologically "stuffed" into other people, who are in turn provoked to enact precisely what has been dumped into them.

For example, let us say a person or group prizes self-control and rationality, and despises anger and aggression. They cannot allow themselves to feel aggression toward others, even to the point of disavowing they even have it, and so they self-righteously deny that they harbor any angry thoughts and feelings. The way they deal with the fact that they nonetheless unconsciously have them, is to rip or split them off from themselves and find another person or group into which to deposit and dump these unacceptable thoughts and feelings. They are thus bound in a relationship in which this dumping and containment of the dumping become a bond. One studiously notices one's own aggression in the other person or group.

This is not the end of it. The person or group that has done the dumping then acts toward the other person or group as if the intolerable thoughts and feelings were now *the property of them*. So now the *others* are experienced as angry and aggressive, which justifies acting aggressively toward them in order to protect oneselves. Further, those engaged in projection *provoke* this disowned behavior in the other person or group, often to the extent that it becomes an internalized part of the other and their experience of themselves. That is, *their*-rage-in-me becomes experienced as *my* rage. This "confirms" their projected perception about me. This dynamic happens all the time in workplaces, between leaders, managers, and employees, and within each group.

Projective identification is thus a defense mechanism and a relationship regulator that often plays a crucial role in group functioning. A term introduced by Melanie Klein (1946, 1955), it refers to the complex mental process by which an unacceptable emotion and fantasy-driven idea is first projective identification split-off from one's conscious awareness, ejected onto another person, and finally perceived and responded to as though the other person was the source and embodiment of this affect (see Apprey & Stein, 1993). As Maurice Apprey (1986, pp. 115–116) discusses this complex concept, one of its main functions is to attempt to avert painful separation and its associated feelings through the unrelenting control of another person.

Projective identification serves simultaneously as a defense, an unconscious fantasy, a mode of communication, and a vehicle for a wish. Donald Meltzer (1967), discussing motives underlying projective identification, lists among the most powerful "intolerance of separation; omnipotent control; envy; jealousy; deficiency of trust; excessive persecutory anxiety" (p. 14). Projective identification can cement and stabilize intrapsychic, interpersonal, familial, organizational, and intercultural relationships (Jaques, 1955; Zinner & Shapiro, 1972; Kets de Vries, 1984; Stein, 1986; Diamond & Allcorn, 2009; Czander, 1993; Kernberg, 1998). Along with other protective strategies that keep inner strife at a safe distance, projective identification is an often insurmountable obstacle to listening deeply. When shielded by this mechanism's armor, we are likely to be self-righteous, to reject and exclude others, even to wage war, under its protective gaze.

Psychodynamic Group Organization

Wilfred R. Bion (1959) describes groups as organized around three types of unconscious basic assumptions: (1) dependency upon a leader or upon the group as an entity (the sense that the leader[s] will sustain the group by nurturing and protecting it or that the group itself is a mother-child unit); (2) fight/flight aggression (heightened vigilance, a sense of imminent danger, readiness to attack or to withdraw, heightened aggressive impulses); and (3) creation of a group savior through "pairing" (the group hopes for rebirth via a redeemer who is a product of the fantasized pairing of two group members or of outside parent figures). Bion addresses the relationship between intellectual activity and group fantasies:

> The individual, conforming with the behavior imposed by participation in the basic-assumption group, feels as if his intellectual capacity were being reduced. The belief that this really is so is reinforced because the individual tends to ignore all intellectual activity that does not fit in with the basic assumption. In fact I do not in the least believe that there is a reduction of intellectual ability in the group, nor yet that "great decisions in the realm of thought and momentous discoveries and solutions of problems are possible to an individual working in solitude" (McDougal,l 1920); although the belief that this is so is commonly expressed in the group discussion, and all sorts of plans are elaborated for circumventing the supposedly pernicious influences of the emotions of the group. Indeed I give interpretations because I believe that intellectual activity of a high order is possible in a group together with an awareness (and not an evasion) of the emotions of the basic-assumptions groups. If group therapy is found to have a value, I believe it will be in the conscious experiencing of the group activity of this kind. (pp. 159–160)

In *Group Psychology and the Analysis of the Ego*, Freud ([1921] 1955b) argues that groups are formed and perpetuated by bonds of identification based on father–son conflict and its resolution. Bion (1959) proposes that this facet of group psychology rests developmentally upon even earlier mother–infant relationships and infantile defenses against massive anxiety. Alan Dundes (1980, 1984) notes similarly that the plausibility of a depth psychology interpretation lies in the very cultural material—the folklore, slips of the tongue (parapraxes), metaphors, myths, and taboos—of people themselves.

The method of listening deeply discussed here has been especially influenced by the clinical and theoretical work of such object-relations psychoanalysts and psychiatrists as Harold F. Searles, M.D. (1975); Vamık D. Volkan, M.D. (1981); L.

Bryce Boyer, M.D. (1983, 1989); Arnold H. Modell, M.D. (1984, 2006); James S. Grotstein, M.D. (1981); Thomas H. Ogden, M.D. (1989a, 1993, 1999); Otto F. Kernberg, M.D. (1976, 1998); and Wilfred R. Bion, M.D. (1963). What resonates most strongly with my work in organizational groups is how *earliest* developmental issues of boundaries, continuity, sensation, rhythm, integrity, cohesion of the body, and life and death are the foundations upon which organizational group identities are built and destroyed.

In *The Meeting: Gatherings in Organizations and Communities*, Helen Schwartzman (1989) distinguishes between formal decision-making and the ebb and flow of meetings in which decisions take place. Our culture has widely shared categories, such as decisions, decision-making, outcomes, outcome measures, mission statements, strategic plans, policy manuals, goals, and objectives, according to which the official or formal work of groups is assessed. Schwartzman looks behind bureaucratic language, explicit genres, and official group self-representations to explore the eventfulness of meetings themselves for those who participate in them. Decisions become only one of the many elements of the meeting and not necessarily the most significant one for those participating. The meaning that meetings hold for their participants often diverges widely from the formal agenda and espoused meaning. Moreover, decision-making occurs outside the boundaries of what we officially and formally define and recognize as decision-making (Allcorn & Diamond, 1997; Kernberg, 1998; French & Simpson, 2014).

Despite the common belief that decision-making in organizations is governed by realism and rationality, unconsciously motivated hidden agendas affect group thinking, interaction, and action (French & Simpson, 2014; Diamond & Allcorn, 2009). There are often informal, if not formal, prohibitions against acknowledging certain ideas or feelings in groups—power, membership, leadership, insidership, outsidership. Participants enforce a group fantasy of ignorance that sustains the illusion that the group is really only about decision-making. Group members can unwittingly play out issues of insiderness/outsiderness and conflicts over power via some formal topic (budget, curriculum, production quotas, quarterly reports) that embodies what cannot be spoken. Similarly, participants can rally around a tightly bounded agenda to divert attention from, and even avoid, an emotionally toxic subject, such as what it feels like to be a member of the group or meeting at that moment. Often the most powerful forces in organizational life are undiscussable.

Unless these unconscious agendas are given their due and addressed in group meetings, they will contaminate, if not sabotage, official roles and tasks; distort reality; and perpetuate conflict even if for a while they artificially boost morale. To the degree that unconscious agendas fail to be brought to conscious awareness for greater access and control in work groups, organizations will fail to mature and evolve. They will instead continue to repeat old patterns, often called mistakes. Conversely, as groups acquire better insight into these powerful underlying factors, they will increase their ability to be liberated from the pull of the past and to explore genuinely new alternatives.

A number of authors who are noted throughout this book have discussed unconscious influences in what we today call the industrial psychology or management psychology of work groups (Stein & Fox, 1985). Early psychoanalytic literature about workplaces was often identified as clinical, which made it seem exceptional, unusual, and exotic rather than mundane. In more recent decades, a considerable literature has burgeoned from investigation of and consultation with workplaces as themselves types of groups. These are forms of applied psychoanalysis.

Although this book is not social psychology or sociology per se, neither is it their adversary. The psychoanalytically informed approach taken in this book complements and helps complete the analyses of groups, organizations, and work offered by social psychologists and sociologists (for example, Erikson & Wallas, 1990; Lindsmith & Strauss, 1968; Argyris, 1990). Decision-making processes, consensus, conformity, the construction and use of group norms; the nature of leadership, task and process roles; group cohesiveness; power and status; and the relationship between individual and group decision-making are all topics long addressed in these fields—fields now integral to schools of business and management training. What a psychodynamically oriented approach strives to do is add yet another *dimension* to an understanding of these processes, that of the unconscious and its relation to the conscious.

Let me briefly illustrate this by drawing from a classic experiment performed by Solomon Asch (1952) on how individuals in groups often conform themselves to their social environments as a means of conflict resolution. Richard S. Lazarus (1961), summarizing Asch's work, writes:

Asch (1952) has performed a fascinating experiment on the effects of social pressure on perceptual judgments. The subject in his experiment was required to match a visually presented series of lines with comparison lines of different lengths. In the same room with him were other persons who the subject thought were also being tested but who, in reality, were allied with the experimenter and said what they had been rehearsed to say when they were asked publicly to make their judgments. A large portion of the time they gave incorrect answers so that the actual subject often found himself a minority of one. Even though the correct answers were quite obvious, tremendous social pressure was exerted on the subject to modify his judgment in favor of the group.

As Asch (1952, pp. 4–5) wrote, "There was a marked movement toward the majority. One third of all the estimates in the critical groups were errors identical with or in the direction of the distorted estimates of the majority. The significance of this finding becomes clear in the light of the virtual absence of errors in the control group, the members of which recorded their estimates in writing." . . .

In response to this situation, the subjects conformed to the pressure of the group about 30 percent of the time. In fact, some subjects, when questioned later, seemed to be entirely unaware that they had responded to this pressure, believing that they actually perceived the lines in the same way as the majority. (Lazarus, 1961, p. 18)

Asch's experiment parallels Irving Janis's (1982) later studies of "group think," except that in Asch's, conformity occurred with a leaderless group rather than in a group rallying around a leader. A person obliterates his or her distinctiveness in the service of fitting in. Reality distortion and abrogation of personal judgment are two consequences and casualties of this subtly coerced conformism. Organizational groups of all kinds lose in reality testing and creativity what they gain in consensus. Groups can be wrong but insist that they are right. People will change what they "know" and perceive in order to belong. Concepts such as separation anxiety, identification with the aggressor, and dependency wishes help us to explain why people in organizations often behave as Asch discovered in his experiment six decades ago. Furthermore, these concepts direct the consultant to largely out-of-awareness dynamics that influence perception and judgment in decision-making.

The pioneering small-group research of Janis illustrates the promise of depth psychology in understanding group life. Janis studied decision-making in the circle around President John F. Kennedy to understand how the calamitous Bay of Pigs invasion of Cuba was conceived. Janis (1982) also studied corporate policy-making processes and coined the Orwellian term *groupthink*. Janis (1971) describes groupthink as

a mode of thinking that persons engage in when *concurrence-seeking* becomes so dominant in a cohesive group that it tends to override realistic appraisal of alternative courses of action. . . . The term refers to a deterioration in mental efficiency, reality testing and moral judgments as a result of group pressures. . . . Groupthink involves nondeliberate suppression of critical thoughts as a result of internalization of the group's norms. (pp. 43–44)

In groupthink, the participants' goal of group cohesiveness through unanimity of thought and action overrides individual perception and judgment. Members subordinate themselves to the group in making decisions about taking a course of action. Participants stifle one another's and their own autonomy. In the group-think mode, members overestimate the power and morality of the group, they close their minds to views different from their own, and they pressure one another toward uniformity ('t Hart, 1991, p. 259). In an overview of Janis's contribution to the study of groups, Paul 't Hart (p. 247) concludes that "the results [of groupthink] are devastating: a distorted view of reality, excessive optimism producing hasty and reckless policies, and a neglect of ethical issues. The combination of these deficiencies makes these groups particularly vulnerable to initiate or sustain projects that turn out to be policy fiascoes."

Janis (1971, p. 75) inquires into human motivation to explain why group-think occurs: "We can best understand the various symptoms of groupthink as a mutual effort among the group members to maintain self-esteem and emotional equanimity by providing social support to each other, especially at times when they share responsibility for making vital decisions." Janis often alludes to the anxiety-allaying function of groupthink's presence. In doing so, he helps us comprehend more clearly what self-esteem, emotional equanimity, and morale are about. At one point, for instance, without using the term *defense mechanisms*, he enumerates the defensive uses of various symptoms of groupthink:

> Shared illusions of invulnerability, for example, can reduce anxiety about taking risks [denial, regression]. Rationalizations help members believe that the risks are really not so bad after all [intellectualization, isolation of emotions from cognitive process]. The assumption of inherent morality helps the members to avoid feelings of shame or guilt [projection, splitting, externalization]. Negative stereotypes function as stress-reducing devices to enhance a sense of moral righteousness as well as pride in a lofty mission [projection, idealization]. (p. 76)

Consider how groupthink operated in such seemingly rational (heavily rationalized) an activity as the development of military technology during the prolonged Cold War between the United States and the USSR. Knud S. Larsen (1986) argues that behind the culturally compelling language of discourse on behalf of military technology lies "ideological competition" between superpowers. "Ritualized ideology" places the armaments race in "the realm of moral absolutism" (p. 397). "Ritualistic ideology serves as the perceptual screen which continually confirms threat perception" (p. 396) and regulates standards of conformity.

"Perceptual screen" is an especially felicitous phrase in that it can be linked to the psychodynamic concept of screen memory (a filtered perception of the past that masks more disturbing feelings and fantasies). We studiously watch the screen, not realizing we are imposing a distortion. We do not even know there is a projector.

Long ago, in the 1980s, President Ronald Reagan referred to the USSR as "the focus of evil," which transparently alludes at least in part to the Soviet Union as the focus of our own evil. Much later, in the aftermath of the September 11, 2001, terrorist attacks on the United States, the psychological focus of evil of President George W. Bush and Vice President Dick Cheney became Saddam Hussein of Iraq and his supposed "weapons of mass destruction," which were later demonstrated to not have existed. Today, a similar focus of evil are terrorist groups such as Al Qaeda and ISIS, and nations such as Iran and North Korea.

In armaments negotiations and in the current war against terror, as in all group processes, multiple layers of perceptual screens interact. For instance, economic and political defense of massive military technology is shaped by ritualized ideology, which is likewise shaped by participants' unconscious, unacknowledged fantasies and defenses. Group enemies can be places, locations in space or time, where we reexperience outside of ourselves, yet do not recognize or accept as our own, childhood hurts, identifications, and wishes for revenge. Likewise, we can safely displace our aggression onto adversary organizations and nations.

Clearly, the us/them splitting of groupthink is hardly limited to the Cold War that (ostensibly) ended in 1990. With the ending of the Cold War in 1990 and the fragmentation of the Soviet empire, the world erupted in group fragmentation and into numerous us/them splits. Further, in the aftermath of the September 11, 2001, terrorist attacks on the New York World Trade Center and the Washington, DC, Pentagon, United States President George W. Bush addressed a joint session of the United States Congress on September 20, 2001. He admonished his listeners: "Either you're with us, or you are with the terrorists." This was a variant of the much-used notion throughout history that "You're either with us, or against us." It quickly turned into an ideological split between the good people, the victims, the victims' nation, and the bad people, "Muslim Terrorists," "Radical Islam," and for many Americans, all Muslims. The rigid boundary delineation helped set the stage for war with Iraq with its alleged, but nonexistent, "weapons of mass destruction."

For many Americans, the "War on Terror" was in fact a war on Islam. Many of the 2016 Republican candidates for U.S. president capitalized on an emotion-laden split between Americans and Muslims. One thinks, for instance, of presidential candidate Donald Trump, who wished to prohibit Muslims from entering the United States. In times of great anxiety over identity, people fear for the weakness of their boundaries, and their vulnerability. One's ethnic, national, or religious group is (regressively and via projection) imagined to be a literal, living organism, a human body under attack and in great peril of invasion. The "invading" groups in turn are objectified by one's own group into metaphorical infection, cancer, insects, or rats (Koenigsberg, 1975).

In such times, group boundaries, from ideological to geographic, become rigid in the service of keeping the good inside, and keeping—and often expelling— the bad outside, if not killing them. In the America of 2016, for much of white America, Muslims, Hispanics, blacks, non-heterosexuals, and so on, have become a despised and excluded "them." Presidential candidate Donald Trump called for the deportation of 11 million Hispanic people in the United States, the construction of a giant wall between the United States and Mexico, and for the closing of American borders to Muslims who seek to enter the United States. Free-floating anxiety and unbound aggression are focused on groups experienced to be threats.

All organizational as well as national groups have an official subject matter (such as strategic planning, prioritizing, preparation of goals and objectives, research, design, production and deployment of military technology), the boundary of which serves as a heavily guarded group taboo. Far from being exclusive work- or task-related, it is an identity marker of where "we" end and "you" begin. Outside is not permitted to enter the inside; sometimes those from outside are expelled, even killed.

As a result, the shared image projected onto the perceptual screen of one's group and its enemies is a negotiated, fantasy-based consensus that constitutes the only acceptable "reality." In groups of all types, whatever else we "defend" (territories, economic interests), we muster vast arsenals to protect the sanctity of our perceptual screens, and the identities behind them, as though our very lives depended on them. These groupthink screens are the mental skin of our group identities. Genuine reality testing is both forbidden and impossible.

The shared unconscious purpose of groupthink is to prevent the emergence into consciousness of enormous anxiety. Group members use one another and "the group" in fantasy as bulwarks against experiencing that anxiety. Much as we may complain about the sterility of endless corporate meetings, this numbness also keeps at bay vast, often frightening portions of ourselves while we act them out and express them metaphorically. By understanding the purpose of thought, of getting together at all in organizational group cultures, a consultant can better know how and when to intervene in those organizations. The consultant can know that an underlying purpose of groupthink activities is to *prevent* thinking and feeling.

Decision makers must examine their own individual and group subjectivity in order to diminish the distortion that emotional investments and conflicts impose on tasks and on one another (see Devereux, 1967; La Barre, 1978; Diamond & Allcorn, 2009). We may extrapolate this perspective to all group decision-making and urge that those hidden agendas that are collectively brought to work groups be routinely acknowledged and addressed. This effort would help organizations mature, not merely enact defensive chimera of change. Organizational groups often select and focus on concrete, isolated, tangible, "fixable" problems in order to displace attention from the fact that group members are always part of the larger problem they study and in which they seek intervention. People's ability to hold near, to reinternalize and examine, what they have defensively displaced and projected away from themselves, is an often unstated condition for real development.

We will do virtually anything to avoid persecutory delusions, psychotic anxiety or, worse still, the intolerable sense of being utterly alone, empty, unenclosed, annihilated, falling to pieces, dead (Ogden, 1989a, 1989b, 1993). We defend the membrane of our group fantasies with a ferocity greater than that we muster to assure our "mere" biological survival. For organizations as well as for ethnonational cultures, their main psychological purpose is not what we consciously compartmentalize as economic, political, rational, realistic goal orientation. Rather, it is to locate ourselves *inside* something safe and secure that will give us life, take away our hurt, and avert death (Becker, 1985, 1997). That is what groupthink and group fantasies serve; that is, ultimately, what groups are for.

In his memoirs, Henry Ebel (1990) writes:

That human beings insist on getting together in all kinds of *groups* . . . is a stable pathological pattern that can be traced back to the earliest stages of individual biological development. The "group" is a uterine hallucination that we rationalize with an infinite fertility. We join nations, cliques, committees, associations, churches, armies and clubs—not to mention political parties, factions and cabals—because life without them would confront us with an inconceivable anxiety traceable to prenatal, birth and early infant experience. (p. 42)

He (p. 42) then adds courageously, "But one can talk about group fantasies until one is blue in the face without ridding oneself of the need to be accepted *inside* one of these collective hallucinations. Or inside several of them simultaneously."

In the profession of medicine, Michael Balint (1957, p. 76) describes the phenomenon of the "collusion of anonymity," which is a common form that organizational group fantasy takes: "When the patient offers a puzzling problem to his medical attendant, who, in turn, is backed by a galaxy of specialists, certain events are almost unavoidable. Foremost among them is the 'collusion of anonymity.'

Vital decisions are taken without anybody feeling fully responsible for them." (p. 76). Western health practitioners often protect themselves from their anxiety and un- certainty by ceding individual responsibility to an externalized fantasy of the group itself as final authority. As a result, if everyone is "responsible," then no one really is. The unconscious purpose of this collusion of anonymity is to post- pone as long as possible confrontation with their own frailties—life and death, loss, separation, sexual desire, and decay—by creating a depersonalizing distance between themselves and the patient. By merger with the fantasied group self, practitioners seek and find refuge from themselves, individuality, and personal responsibility.

Devereux (1955) has formulated a group or cultural psychology of crisis. He explains how we try to treat and diminish our anxiety through groups. By taking refuge in groups, we place the source of distress beyond ourselves. Crisis illus- trates this.

A crisis comes into being through the following process: In a situation of stress, which elicits *fear*, time-tested and traditional mechanisms of orien- tation and of action no longer produce the expected results. This leads to a schizophrenia-like disorientation and to catastrophic behavior. *Fear*, which is an objective appraisal of the magnitude of a real danger, is replaced by *anxiety*, which is a sense of the inadequacy of one's resources in the face of stress. Since anxiety is harder to endure than fear, society rapidly becomes more preoccupied with alleviating its state of anxiety than its fear, and prac- tically ceases to do anything about the danger which elicited fear in the first place. Figuratively speaking, a society in crisis clamors for "cultural bromides" rather than for tools and weapons. This means that an autistically evolved intrapsychic "*threat*" replaces the objective "*danger*," and comes to occupy the center of the psychological field. Society then attempts to bring into being in reality—to "materialize"—precisely the kind of objective *dan- ger* which corresponds to the initially intrapsychic *threat* . . . . From then on society fights the phantoms—the Frankenstein's monsters— . . . in compli- ance with its needs to project its intrapsychic *threat* into the outer world it brought into being, and therefore ceases to fight the initial, objectively real, *danger*.

In brief, crisis behavior is characterized by the presence of self-defeating mechanisms leading to a downward spiraling, ever expanding, vicious circle where the very attempts to cope with the problem on hand only exacerbate the stress and create new difficulties. (p. 147)

A group consultant helps the organization diminish the distance between where anxiety is displaced and its inner source. In openly saying what often cannot be acknowledged and must not be said in the organizational culture ("The problem is us"), the consultant offers himself or herself as a person (observing ego, container, holding environment) with whom organizational members might identify as capable of holding onto their anxiety and not being destroyed by it. In turn, having metabolized this new positive object (person) representation, they proceed independently with their group work. Such acknowledgment, as well as its power, is not limited to the mother-infant bond. It extends throughout the life cycle.

Acknowledgment by the environment is "necessary for development of the self in infancy" (Masterson, 1985, p. 56). Furthermore, following Erik H. Erikson (1968), James F. Masterson stresses that "a healthy sense of self-identity and ego identity are always dependent not only on acknowledgment during the developmental years but on a continuing dialogue of acknowledgment with the environment during the rest of life" (p. 57). John D. Sutherland (1990), following Bion (1959), writes similarly of people who have developed a distinctive adult identity beyond the earlier separation-individuation stage it rests upon: "This new development . . . has its own needs for group relatedness, namely, in groups in which his identity is affirmed and enriched by the extent of the ego's reality involvement in them" (p.135).

Groups are not invariably regressive or oppressively groupish. People can also develop and mature in group settings. Not only can intellect and task performance flourish in groups under the right circumstances, but also the emotions themselves can mature. Bion (1959) describes fight/flight groups as expressing "the sense of incapacity for understanding and [for] the love without which understanding cannot exist" (p. 146). Few clinicians and consultants today have such courage to identify love as the foundation upon which any therapeutic change builds.

Key Concept 2: Use of the Self

Every consultation is a field research project; its main instrument is the self of the consultant (Diamond & Allcorn, 2003; Duncan & Diamond, 2011; Volkan & Hawkins, 1971). Diamond (1988) summarizes what I (Stein, 1982a, 1990b) have been describing as a psychodynamically informed fieldwork approach to organizational cultures: "By placing himself in the other's experience through identification (empathy) and by acknowledging how he is responding to others (countertransference), the organizational analyst and administrative practitioner are more responsive to (interpret) how organizational members feel and think in present circumstances" (p. 172).

I have long advocated the image of a circle or, better yet, virtuous spiral to describe the relationship between practical work with people and theory building. We can learn about human culture and its roots in the process of working with people on some common task or project. The perennial battle between the "pure science" or "pure research" faction and the "applied science" or "practical work" faction is counterproductive and downright silly. Theory and practice, explanatory natural and social science, and interpretive hermeneutics, objectivity, and subjectivity, need not be foes (Spiro, 1986; Paul, 1987; Grolnick, 1987). They can be allies in a common enterprise.

This circular or spiral image of theory and practice does not go far enough, however. What happens to doing and model building when change agents are profoundly moved by the process of facilitating others? What happens to what we do, our supposed effect upon others, when instead of being a pseudo-scientific, Aristotelian "unmoved mover" (the Greek philosopher's image of God), we are perhaps the most moved "movers" (Abraham Joshua Heschel's image of God; following Rothschild, 1959, p. 24). Where in that intersubjective process is the organizational culture, which we are studying and in which we are intervening, *located*? That culture is not strictly or objectively "out there"; it is a co-creation of something new between and within us. It is intersubjective, between.

Our modes of inquiry, our methodologies, can be shared resistance to discovering and feeling disturbing realities about life (Devereux, 1967), or they can be vehicles to help us along the journey. How do we know what we know? What are we looking for? A ghost question follows, like a negative for a photograph: What are we trying to avoid seeing (hearing, touching, feeling)?

Abraham J. Heschel (1965) writes that "we formulate and debate the issues while oblivious to, and alienated from, the experiences or the insights which account for our raising the issues. . . . We not only describe the 'nature' of man, we fashion it. We become what we think of ourselves" (pp. 2, 7). Heschel connects method (doing) and theory (imagining, thinking). We refract individuals', families', and organizations' worlds through our own personal and cultural prisms. Scientific methodologies can become as much prisons as can any religious or political ideology. It is not that an objective world or human nature does not exist, but that it is difficult for us to know when and how we are distorting reality through our needs, wishes, and feelings. In all research, in every consultation, what and who we are defines what we count and discount as data.

How might we gain access to these crucial inner data that color all we hear, see, and do as consultants and as human beings everywhere? One answer is supplied by the "experiment" begun by Michael Balint among small groups of physicians in England. In the 1950s, this British, Hungarian-born psychoanalyst and his wife Enid Balint invited general practitioners to present spontaneous cases about their thoughts, feelings, and conflicts during patient care. These groups, later termed Balint groups, were based on the recognition that physicians' feelings and attitudes toward patients affected not only the clinical relationship itself but also diagnosis, treatment, and outcome (Alexander, 1981; Waxler, 1981). Governed by confidentiality, these groups offered participants a safe, trusting, supportive, nonjudgmental haven in which professionally related fears, hopes, ambitions, losses, expectations, and failures could be examined, and in which self-disclosure could be risked.

Historically, the *original* purpose of Balint groups was to help the presenting physician understand what had made a specific difficult doctor–patient relationship so troubling, frustrating, or depressing. By understanding those personal issues that clouded the relationship, the physician might improve it. Through attentive listening, transitory identification with the presenter, the sharing of emotionally similar cases, and reassurance that he or she was not altogether alone in these feelings, the group helped the presenter work through difficulties in patient care. For Balint, the group provided a Winnicottian "good enough" holding environment in which participants felt safe to express their vulnerabilities so that they might then repair old wounds (Winnicott, [1954] 1958). The leader practiced respectful, profoundly attentive listening, with little confrontation and interpretation, although these were not absent. Rather, the leader tried to create a safe space in which creativity and healing could emerge.

Balint's group approach derived in part from his (1968) theory that all human beings have a "basic fault" in which they feel something inside to be missing from their wholeness. Balint's individual therapy and group approaches attempted to create an atmosphere of trust in which all participants could begin to repair that fault. John D. Sutherland (1980) writes of Balint that

> in the treatment of individuals who manifest the basic fault regressed to a marked degree, Balint concluded that the standard analytic method of giving only verbal interpretations was unable to alter the stalemate produced in the regression. The patient's state was not one that could be "analyzed away" so to speak. What the patient needed from the analyst was the opportunity to make good a deficiency. The analyst had therefore to be the kind of object or environment with which the patient could discover his own way in the world of objects. With all basic fault states, the analyst had to convey through his relationship with the patient that he understood his needs and that in doing so he recognized the patient's own inner life and valued his own unique individuality.

In an article on Balint, Leonard J. Friedman (1971) writes similarly that

> Balint exemplified in his teaching that learning about human experience is a collaborative enterprise: a mutually creative endeavor of doctor and patient in therapy and analysis, of psychiatrist and general practitioner in the study of psychological medicine. . . . The essential aspect of psychoanalytic experience which Balint conveyed was the experimental mode of respectful participant observation. He used his psychoanalytic experience to foster in physicians the development of their skills in the professional use of human understanding, aware that a degree of personal growth was necessary in the process. (p. 95)

Balint's (and later, Harold F. Searles's) psychotherapeutic approach has as its parallel Buber's ([1923] 1958, 1965) concept of genuine "dialogue" in I-thou relationships and Paul Tillich's (1955) theological existentialist position of "the courage to be." More recently, writers such as Kohut (1984), Modell (1984, 2006), and Volkan (1988, 1997) have discussed the role that empathy plays in understanding other persons and groups.

The late George Devereux (1967), a psychoanalyst and anthropologist, insisted that all people understand others—and distort others—via themselves:

> In interpreting their reverberations within himself, the analyst professes to interpret *also* the unconscious of the patient.

> This is, clearly, a hypothesis and, moreover, one which involves the subsidiary assumption that the unconscious of the analyst is much the same as that of his patient, chiefly because one's unconscious is a relatively undifferentiated function or portion of the psyche and can therefore resemble that of another individual more than can one's highly differentiated conscious. Any analyst who believes that he perceived *directly* his patient's unconscious, rather than his own, is deluding himself. (p. 304)

An analyst or group consultant presents to the patient or to the organization an interpretation of the unconscious process by first absorbing and analyzing his or her own unconscious response to them (p. 305).

For example, Otto F. Kernberg (1965), Ira Stamm (1987), and Donald B. Colson et al. (1986) have described the psychotic-like anxieties often evoked among *staff* in psychiatric hospital settings. Such painful, often violent, emotions are often a key to what is taking place in *patients'* inner worlds. To use the image of the thermometer: The staff's own "temperature" is an accurate reading of the patients' "fevers." Analysis of one's own unconscious response is the basis for the interpretation of others' unconscious, individual or group. As Devereux (1967) writes:

> The unconscious is no more *directly* observable than is the heat of the bowl of water in the experiment analyzed by J. von Neumann. What is directly observable, and therefore constitutes a datum, is the reverberation—the disturbance—which the patient's utterance sets up in the unconscious of the analyst. It is the inspection of these internal disturbances which yields data "at the observer" and, naively speaking, even "within" the observer. (p. 303)

Emotional features of group life are not extraneous or epiphenomenal to structure and action, but instead take us to the heart of human experience in groups (Bion, 1959). Likewise, emotions and fantasies evoked in the therapist, consultant, or facilitator during the course of work in organizations are a crucial—if not the most important—source of data about the group. The self of the investigator or counselor is invariably the prism through which the reality of organizational work is refracted. The consultant learns about the organizational culture via herself or himself. To enable others to "change," the consultant must be ready and willing to be "changed" by them, to be emotionally permeable to them. This self can either distort or correct, be antitherapeutic or therapeutic, depending upon the researcher's or consultant's access to his or her unconscious issues and defensive organization, including the symbolic significance the organization and the identified problem hold for the consultant.

What Modell (1984) writes of Winnicott's ([1954] 1958) concept of the holding environment and its role in two-person psychotherapy applies as well to my work with groups: "I have understood the idea of the 'holding environment' to contain the principle that conflicts, especially those of separation/individuation, are carried forward symbolically into the analytic process" (p. 4). The holding environment of therapy and consulting alike is symbolic heir to the mother's (and other reliable caregivers') earliest actual physical holding, her reassuring presence, countenance, and reliability, which served as a "container" for the infant's physically experienced hopes and dreads (Bion, 1959).

"The analyst communicates to the patient an image of the person that the patient can become" (Modell, 1984, p. 245). So does the organizational consultant with the client. A consultant performs the fundamental function of metaphorical holding via "the communication of genuine affects" (p. 89). Winnicott ([1963]

1965) writes, "The analyst is *holding* the patient, and this often takes the form of conveying in words at the appropriate moment something that shows that the analyst knows and understands the deepest anxiety that is being experienced, or that is waiting to be experienced" (p. 240).

Modell (1984) distinguishes between two types of symbolic facets of the holding environment: "the setting itself, the area of relatedness, between the patient and the analyst" (p. 4) which is the locus of therapeutic action, and the "truth-giving function" of verbal interpretation to patients who are well differentiated from the therapist. Ogden (1989a, 1993) emphasizes that even highly individuated people never outgrow the need to provide membrane- or envelope-like affective surfaces for themselves and for their relationships. We emotionally touch and house each other. Words are symbolic skins; the exchange of words is symbolically the touching of skins. What we do is always contained within, and builds upon, such visceral touching and housing. No matter how abstract symbolic relationships become, including clinical and consulting ones, the experiential bedrock on which they are founded remains a sensory holding environment. In it, people can learn to hold onto and internalize their best and their worst because another person in their presence has contained it first within himself or herself.

To visualize this process, I draw upon a vignette of Ogden's (1989a) in which he describes having turned on a heater in his cold office and his patient's response:

I said, "It's cold in here," and got up to turn on the heater. She said, "It is," and seemed to calm down soon after that. She said that for reasons that she did not understand she had been extremely "touched" by my saying that it was cold and by turning the heater on: "It was such an ordinary thing to say and do." I believe that my putting the heater on acknowledged a shared experience of the growing coldness in the air and contributed to the creation of a sensory surface between us. I was using my own feelings and sensations in a largely unconscious "ordinary way" (perhaps like "an ordinary devoted mother" [Winnicott (1949) 1964]) which felt to the patient as if I had physically touched her and held her together. The sensory surface mutually created in that way was the opposite of the experience of "coming apart at the seams"; it facilitated a mending of her psychological-sensory surface which felt as if it had been shredded in the course of the patient's interaction with her mother. (p. 34)

Ogden (p. 34) continues, saying that "this sensory 'holding' [Winnicott (1960) 1965a] dimension of the analytic relationships and setting operated in conjunction with the binding power of symbolic interpretation." Although I had "done" this, functioned in this way, in organizational work for years, formulations by analysts and psychiatrists who have worked with narcissistic, borderline, and schizophrenic patients ring true for the dynamics of what I am engaged in as a consultant. Their formulations evoke the intersubjective nature of the ethnographic style I use in helping organizations. Collaborative field research in this holding environment constitutes the intervention itself (Hirschhorn, 1988; Duncan & Diamond, 2011). Likewise, this symbolic holding lies at the heart of the storyteller/story listener relationship in organizational research and consulting (Allcorn & Stein, 2016). The story emerges, is formulated, and is told and shared within the crucible of this relationship. It does not exist apart from the intersubjective—soul to soul—dance in which it is created.

As an organizational anthropologist, I find myself offering what I imagine as a symbolic membrane around those with whom I work by listening deeply for long periods of time. I try to make room for their worlds within mine before I offer anything in the form of descriptions, questions, or interpretations. Within the safety of this envelope-like holding environment, I try to provide a sense of being heard, seen, and understood. I often feel that group members reciprocate this holding to one another, then to me, as they try harder to hear what each is saying. Enclosed safely in a membrane of words and feelings, they offer a membrane in return. Feeling understood, they can tolerate their anxiety and understand themselves better and then to extend the gift of empathy to others in the group. When this affective knowledge is working best, I can sit back almost as if I am (in my fantasy) an outside observer enclosed within the group, which now functions on its own. I can then infer that "client" persons and groups have identified with my auxiliary ego, containing, and holding functions. They now listen more attentively to each other unmediated by me.

Key Concept 3: Metaphors

In consulting with and conducting research on organizations, why should we concern ourselves with metaphors? Metaphors are commonly associated with literature and poetry. Let us step back for a moment and ask: What, then, is a metaphor? It has long been regarded as a "figure of speech" that compares and links one idea to another. Metaphor is seeing and thinking of one thing or idea in terms of another thing or idea. Unlike simile, metaphor does not say that something is *like* another. A man may say to the one he loves: "You are a rose" (rather than "You are *like* a rose."). With metaphor there is less distance between the symbol and the symbolized, or the symbol and its meaning, or the signifier (symbol) and the signified (the ultimate significance or object of the symbol).

But metaphors are more than linguistic and cognitive devices. They are also deeply *affective* or *emotional*. Often, metaphors feel physical (Lakoff & Johnson, 1999). We often feel deeply about the metaphors we use. Further, in the connection and transfer of one thought to another, the deeper significance and affect may be unconscious, and in turn, embodied. For instance, as Kirshner writes:

> "Metaphor, Modell proposed (pp. 25–27), following the work of Lakoff and Johnson (1999), is a process of cognition and can function as an interpreter of unconscious memory. In this way, what he called "the metaphoric imagination" provides a means of making sense of experience, linking the meaning-making need of the self to neurological and corporeal processes (p. 27). (Kirshner, 2010, p. 335)

Further, Michael Diamond (2014) adds that through metaphor,

> one understands the present in view of the past, and the past in view of the present. Memory is *recontextualised* and is linked to unconscious metaphoric process (Modell, 2006, pp. 35–38). This viewpoint broadens the notion of metaphor towards a supra-linguistic and psychoanalytic perspective. Metaphor is not only a phenomenon of language but of mental activity; its units are not only words but psychodynamics (Borbely, 1998). (Diamond, 2014, p. 108)

Thus, while metaphor involves language, it is not only about language, but gives words to what is otherwise inexpressible in language. Metaphor is about *what language is about*, the referent of language. Metaphor is key to transference, where a metaphor in the present represents, and exists *in terms of*, the unconscious past.

Consider the language of countless organizational leaders who have championed and executed downsizings since the 1980s. They often refer to employees to be terminated as "dead wood," "dead meat," "excess fat," "useless fat," even "muscle that needs to be trimmed down to the bone" in order to make the organization "a lean, mean fighting machine" to compete in today's market. Six Sigma programs have as their goal "*lean* management." To users of such metaphors, employees are not valued, sentient human beings, but disposable objects to be thrown away. The result is often what has been metaphorically called "anorexic organizations." Among other things, symbolic war for the salvation of organizations is waged on and through *living bodies*.

To cite another metaphor: In a corporation the CEO might be called "The General" for his demeanor of giving orders that he expects to be unquestioningly obeyed, for his calling his employees "troops," and for his insistence on business competition as "war." Employees might feel that when he is around, "We have to salute him and jump to attention." The metaphor is what midlevel executives, managers, and employees think, feel, and fantasize about their leader.

In unconscious *transference* from the past to the present, the CEO might represent aggressive, angry, or abusive father figures (and fantasies about them). The CEO *becomes* in fantasy the metaphor, and is responded to as if he *embodies* the metaphor. That is, the metaphor is now experienced as inside him, part of him, so that what is projected into him corresponds to the aura that he projects outward from himself. Further, the metaphor is felt inside managers and employees: They can feel their muscles stiffen when he comes around the workplace, or when they are summoned to one of his meetings (Modell, 2009).

Consider the following brief workplace scenario: Academic faculty and corporate management meetings early in the workday often begin something like this: People get their morning coffee, orange juice, and donuts from a long folding table outside the conference room, then mill around and talk informally. They continue to visit around the conference table before someone calls the meeting to order. For instance, at one such meeting, I heard the following interchange among 15 members of a medical corporation:

> A Soviet cosmonaut is stranded in space. . . . Russian astronauts, up six months . . . stranded. . . . There's a lot of garbage lost in space, a lot of garbage floating around. A return date didn't occur for the cosmonauts because the Soviet political structure changed. They were Soviet. What were they to come down as? Who would have the authority to call them down? Who will arrive and depart on our faculty next? [group laughter] Can you imagine a list, like at airports: "arrivals" and "departures"? [The group broke into side-splitting, hysterical laughter, many in tears.] Imagine the agent saying, "You are on standby for this flight"! [group laughter again]

After a brief silence, one midlevel manager queried, "What are the vibes when the CEO is in? He is hardly ever in. He says he has an open-door policy, but does he really?" Another manager said:, "It's a catch-22: 'When I'm in, I'm out; when I'm out, I'm in.' That is what it feels like he is saying." That is to say, the CEO insisted he was available even when he was not. The CEO's door was mostly closed when he was in, and though he insisted he was often in the office, the CEO was often out of town. A second manager asked the manager who had just spoken, "Are you feeling stranded?" He replied, "I'm feeling stonewalled on this position I'm supposed to be chairing a search committee for." Fantasies of separation, abandonment, even symbolic death were contained in group *metaphors*.

A consultant often can quickly assess the emotional tone of an organizational group through the metaphors its members "float" and seize upon even before the formal agenda begins by the leader. The emotional substratum, the foundation of a meeting, can be sensed in premeeting visiting. Metaphors are not of merely academic, intellectual, or literary interest (Lakoff & Johnson, 1980). Knowledge of them can help the consultant become oriented and later draw group members' attention to emotional agendas half-revealed and half-hidden by symbols. *Metaphors embody the organizations they represent.* They convey what it feels like to be "part of" and contained in an organization (Diamond, 2014). Even before the manager introduced the first formal agenda item of the meeting, the informal, humorous visiting had already set the tone in metaphors of drifting, abandonment, ambiguity of authority, fear of falling to death, all safely displaced onto Russian/Soviet cosmonauts, abandoned children of a former enemy father- and motherland—topics of seemingly casual conversation.

Cultural metaphors, including organizational metaphors, are one of several (congruent or competing) symbols in widespread use that condense, organize, and consciously represent a group's fantasy about what it is like to live or work in that group. To some degree, metaphors organize organizations and are part of organizational infrastructure and identity. Beneath the official belief system of rational management, productivity, and financial bottom lines (themselves metaphors), still other unstated metaphors compel how people think, act, and feel.

Metaphors crystallize personal or group meaning systems. They are the idioms through which a group expresses its deepest concerns and feelings. Cultural metaphors, expressions of unconscious fantasies, influence how we feel about our bodies and ourselves, what we believe our bodies and lives to be and to mean, and the kinds of relationships and actions that take place in such a world (Koenigsberg, 1975).

Group metaphors are the royal road to an organization's core fantasies, affects (conscious and unconscious feelings), relationships, conflicts, and values. The *experience* of working in an organization is intrinsic to the organization's structure. This structure is not limited to formal organizational hierarchy charts, procedure manuals, and official policy statements. Metaphors influence all facets of that institution's life.

Organizational culture, together with its formal structure, rests upon organizational identity in the same way as consciousness rests upon, and is a compromise formation to, underlying unconscious processes. Metaphors simultaneously articulate and disguise a group's deepest feelings and thoughts. Diamond (1988, p. 169; see also 1993) writes that "organizational identity is the totality of repetitive patterns of individual behavior and interpersonal relationships that taken together comprise the unacknowledged meaning of organizational life" (1988, p. 169).

Consider the workplace in which employees "hunger for recognition" from a narcissistic CEO who "drills down his will" into the company and is psychologically abusive. Consider the very word "*manage*(-ment)." In American society there is hardly anything that we do not try to manage, which becomes a metaphor for control (managed [health] care, waste management, project management, weight management, process management, urban management, etc.), and further, unconscious meanings of control, such as rage and aggression.

Discussing work groups, Jean-Paul Larçon and Roland Reitter (1984) write, "The group gradually works out a common mental definition, a common image of the structure of the group in which every member can find a place to his satisfaction" (p. 346). Whereas organizational images consciously depict what and who "we" are, organizational metaphors, although expressed symbolically, are more closely tied to shared unconscious processes. During rapid social change or group trauma, any shared image of wholeness is fractured. This often leads to a search for new meanings and metaphors to articulate and attempt to mend the threatening situation and avert catastrophic feelings. Protective skin has been punctured; people must deal with feelings of vulnerability and violation, if not the bleeding out of their very essence.

Larçon and Reitter (1984) write about the roles that myths, rites (rituals), and taboos play in corporate organizations:

> Like all human groups, the organization has a collective life style—a culture—which it manifests in symbolic form: myths, rituals and taboos. These symbols . . . provide clues to the collective imagery, their usual function being to allow for the tensions which may arise in the group from the organization's basic choices, and to assert the unity of the group over and above these differences and tensions. . . .
>
> The business firm, like any other human group, engenders myths, that is, stories about its history. The origins of the firm naturally constitute an ideal subject for myths, for it is there that the firm's values generally have their origin. . . . In very broad terms the purpose of the myth is to create—or to support—an ideal image of the firm. This image will cover problematic or obscure aspects and show them in a favorable light. . . .
>
> Rites are practices which reflect the myth and which have no significance in themselves other than providing an occasion for a consensus on the important problem which the rite masks. . . .

Taboos can pinpoint the organization's sensitive spots; only those things which strike at the heart of the organization—its basic values, its secret conflict, its contradictions, its traumas—are taboo. Since the taboo is what should be denied, hidden, exorcized, wiped out, it is a fundamental part of the equilibrium of a company. (pp. 350–351)

Organizational stories and the occasions on which they are told do not necessarily mask problems, although official stories often do. All stories (all histories) are not myths. All dramatizations are not rituals. All proscriptions (interdictions) for behavior are not taboos. It is when groups say and do one thing in order consciously and/or unconsciously *not* to talk about, feel, or do something else that we enter the realm of secrets, mythologizing, ritualizing, and taboo manufacture.

We can determine whether something is myth, ritual, or taboo if its purpose is to displace organization members' attention from a painful, depressing, anxiety-evoking, or guilt/shame-arousing subject to another subject that alleviates these bad, dysphoric feelings by defending against them. Organizational myths, rituals, and taboos all intensify what Janis (1982) calls groupthink and what deMause (1982) calls group fantasy. That is, organizational myths, rituals, and taboos can serve as metaphors that crystallize the meaning and "feel" of an organization for its members. They create and enforce an altogether new "reality principle," one based on wish, fantasy, and defense against anxiety. Perhaps it could be called an un-reality principle.

Organizations and all cultures possess metaphors during ordinary, calm times. They also develop metaphors of catastrophe, disaster, and trauma during times experienced as menacing and tumultuous. Among these are natural and social disasters: For instance, tornadoes, floods, earthquakes, wars, death camps, toxic wastes, industrial layoffs, corporate mergers and takeovers, and plant closings. I define as traumatic those events and experiences in which participants feel overwhelmed, their defenses and routines are broken, and conflicts, fantasies, and feelings usually kept at bay return to consciousness (Lifton, 1979; Luel & Marcus, 1984; Niederland, 1961). Trauma (or crisis) refers less strictly to the objective character of the event than to the psychological response to and significance of it (Devereux, 1955; La Barre, 1972). Groups psychologize and mythologize around a "chosen trauma," which Volkan (1991) defines as "an event that causes one large group to feel helpless and victimized by another group" (p. 13). La Barre (1971, 1972) has argued that the stress to which people adapt can rarely be reduced to the physical "stressor" alone (such as natural disasters) but lies in its emotional, overdetermined significance.

We can feel emotional tremors as much with respect to workplace firings and employee turnover in a corporation as to the separation anxiety unleashed by a world-shattering earthquake. How members of an organization experience and imaginatively depict a crisis is a constituent part of that crisis and influences its outcome. Because metaphors symbolize organizational identity, language used during critical events such as trauma offers insight into organizational structure unavailable during less disruptive, more routine periods.

Recognition of group metaphors is a powerful way of understanding what knits organizations together. From clinical and consultative work with various groups, I have learned to pay attention to the language and images of group process as a key to emotional and fantasy-laden issues, of "basic assumptions" (Bion, 1959), that underlie, if not often override, official, rational, "work" agendas. The group is often really about fulfilling an unstated metaphorical agenda *and* addressing the explicit, official group task. Close attention to metaphorical language in a group allows a consultant or facilitator to formulate and speculate aloud about possible underlying issues, themes, agendas, conflicts, and feelings. Through the disclosure of affects that are out of conscious awareness to group members, metaphoric analysis of group process can help demystify organizations to their members and in turn improve human relations, group morale, and task performance. Group metaphors exist as the "tip of the iceberg," as safe, manifest content of shared fantasies of organizational and larger cultural identity systems (deMause, 1982; Diamond, 1988, 1993; Larçon & Reitter, 1984). The consultant's task is to learn the meanings behind the official meanings, what is felt as well as what is said and what is kept secret; then to help translate this understanding into an idiom acceptable to the client, individual, or organization.

Consider the ubiquitous, lowly *cardboard box,* not only as an instrumental artifact and as a container in which to put or store objects, but as an organizational metaphor and symbol. In the era of downsizing, reengineering, restructuring, and outsourcing that dates to the early 1980s, the cardboard box has come to represent separation, loss, rejection, abandonment, even symbolic death. Boxes have been provided to countless numbers of employees who, out of the blue, are ordered to put their personal belongings in them, and carry them out of the building to their car, when employees are peremptorily fired and told never to return. The employee herself or himself is like a flimsy cardboard box that is used while it is considered useful and then thrown away when it is no longer needed. These boxes contain and embody horrible feelings, fantasies, and bodily states as well as objects. Boxes have become group as well as personal metaphors.

Key Concept 4: Leadership

All leadership and change in leadership are fraught with emotion and dense with metaphor. Whether by secret ballot, house coup, assassination, or revolution, political order and succession in any organization or large culture are psychologically complicated processes. In many preliterate societies, a people measured much of its sense of well-being by the leader's health, sexual potency, and vigor. When they sensed his powers waning even slightly, he was forcibly removed and replaced by someone who could assure the success of the people, their crops, their herds, or military campaigns.

Since my days as a graduate student in anthropology in the late 1960s and early 1970s, I have been fascinated by the divine kingship of the Shilluk along the upper Nile (Evans-Pritchard, [1948] 1964), where I first encountered this process. Although its local flavoring is unique, it speaks to the shared human wellspring of all attitudes toward authority, our ambivalence about it, and our dependence upon it.

How a whole people feels about itself is embodied (via projective identification) in the leader. Emotion-laden fantasies about leaders absorb people's deepest anxieties, their best and worst images of themselves, their ideals and their inner demons, their conflicts over independence and dependence, their feelings about dimly remembered childhood caregiving figures, and their feelings of sexual potency and impotence. All work sites imbue leaders with their own members' wishes and expectations, hopes and disappointments, victories and defeats. Leaders and followers, superordinates and subordinates, endow one another with parts of themselves and live as though these parts are independent of them.

Discussing what binds people to a group, C. Fred Alford (1988) first quotes Sigmund Freud ([1921] 1955a), who defines a group as "a number of individuals who have put one and the same object [person] in the place of their ego ideal and have consequently identified themselves with one another in their ego" (p. 116). Alford (1988) continues with a succinct discussion of the leader and the group itself as representations of narcissism's derivatives:

> It is apparent that what binds the group is not love (at least not love for one another, object love), but narcissism. Individuals identify with one another; they feel bound to one another in some way, because they share a common ego ideal, represented by the leader. It is because of the shared common ego ideal that the group is bound together by narcissistic ties, understood as a self-love that extends to others because—and only because—they are like ourselves. It is also apparent that it is not an illicit abstraction, a reification,

to speak of a group ego and group ego ideal. Both exist, in the form of attitudes and emotions directed by individuals toward the leader (who embodies the group ego ideal), and other group members (who together embody the group ego). (p. 579)

Volkan (1980) says of the leader, "The identification with idealized external object creates an illusion that supports its [the self's] cohesiveness and stability" (pp. 138–139). I rephrase the sentence to read, with respect to work groups, that identification with idealized, mutually shared externalized *symbolic* objects, such as companies, departments, hospitals, and blast furnaces, creates an illusion that supports group members' cohesiveness and stability. Mental representations of groups, corporations, and cultures often serve as fantasized external outposts of the self and the person's defensive organization. These are inner, imaginative equivalents of medieval castle walls and moats that people build to give themselves boundary and distinctiveness, pride and uniqueness, separation and enclosure. These are both sanctuary and border for what and who are contained within and what and who are excluded—even expelled or killed.

Harry Levinson (1984), discussing the work of Elliott Jaques (1955), notes how in organizations, people regress (that is, emotionally return to developmentally early psychological states) to ward off developmentally early anxiety by rigidly compartmentalizing coworkers, managers, or leaders into categories of all good and all bad:

Dividing people into good and bad, commonly observed in clinical practice, is one way of handling paranoid anxiety. The "bad" impulses of people in an organization may thereupon be projected onto a "bad" figure or figures. Jaques calls attention to the way in which the first officer of a ship is commonly regarded by the crew as the source of all trouble, permitting the men to idealize the captain and identify themselves with him. There is often a similar polarity in the army between the executive officer and the commanding officer or "old man." Industrial psychologists will recognize key figures in other divisions of a company who are seen as the bad ones who cause all the problems. (p. 269)

Howell S. Baum (1986) portrays the emotional structure of bureaucracies as the

hierarchical organizations in which authority is centralized and responsibility is diffused. . . . The authority who assigns, variously controls, and evaluates a subordinate usually is relatively distant, relatively anonymous, and more or less autonomous. This situation of being controlled by someone powerful but poorly visible—a situation not unique to bureaucracy— encourages subordinates to fill in reassuring details by transferring past assumptions about authority to contemporary authority. Some of these transferred assumptions, deriving from infantile and childhood experiences, make bureaucratic authority seem larger, more powerful, and more puni- tive. . . . Workers may respond to organizational authority associated with earlier images of the superego and ego-ideal. (pp. 159–160)

Moreover, as Volkan (1980) describes narcissistic leadership:

Clinging to the illusion of being powerful among others, some narcissistic people ambitiously seek the leadership of groups, organizations, or even na- tions. In their relentless search for power they use other people, discarding them without compunction whenever it seems advantageous. The success of such a person bent on leadership is obviously contingent on many variables, some of which may depend more on the psychology of the group itself than on his own. For example, a group may have undergone humiliation and defeat and be impelled on this account to seek a glorified leader who will lift them up. (p. 136)

Volkan then identifies "the 'fit' between an individual's grandiose ambition and his potential followers' need" (p. 138), specifically the leader's need for power and control (together with his or her charismatic aura of power) and the group's sense of powerlessness and vulnerability (pp. 139–141). Corporate leaders *are* the shamans of capitalistic society.

In a psychobiography of Atatürk, founder of modern Turkey, Volkan and Nor- man Itzkowitz (1984) distinguish among types of leadership style. Writing of narcissism and leadership, they propose that

narcissistic leaders can be divided into two general categories. One is the destructive leader who attempts to protect the cohesion of his grandiose self, chiefly by devaluing others in order to feel superior. The destructive narcissistic leader poses a considerable danger. History shows that an exces- sive need to devalue a group often leads to the destruction of that group. For the destructive leader the devalued persons or groups become targets for the externalization of his split and devalued self and object images, and those people and groups have to be suppressed.

The other type of narcissistic leader is reparative, and Atatürk is representa- tive of this category. The reparative leader wants adoration from his "valued" followers and may attempt to uplift them in order to build his support on as impressively high a level as possible. The followers are idealized so that their mental representations can be fused into the grandiose self of the leader, making the cohesiveness of his inner world more stable.

In some respects the distinction between the reparative and destructive grandiose leaders is artificial, since one may turn into the other under certain circumstances. (p. 358)

Reparative leaders tend to allow, if not welcome, the work of grief as a *necessary* part of change, whereas destructive leaders tend to forbid it, to press on with their own projects or exploit and "freeze" mourning by turning it into vengeance. It is a mistake, however, to think that when reparative leaders are removed by election, coup, or assassination, the group feels sad, but when destructive leaders are replaced, the group feels only relief. People feel a sense of loss toward leaders who terrorized them as well as those who were beloved and respected; consider Josef Stalin and John F. Kennedy. Some form of grieving accompanies all change in leadership, even for despots who have been hated and ousted.

Grief is often so difficult that people will do anything—have physical symptoms, kill, wage war—to avoid its pain. Unresolved group losses often complicate transitions to new leadership, ideas, or personnel. Losses contaminate choices and role relationships in the present; they shackle the future to an unresolved past. Aggression is often mobilized and channeled toward enemies when traumatic loss cannot be fully mourned by the organizational group.

For example, a new leader often aborts a grief process by launching new initiatives without allowing his or her employees and managers to say good-bye to their old world and work through their experience of loss. This new leader commands his or her employees to "forget the past," and insists that, while the future promises to be great, the past had nothing good about it. Here the purpose of aggressive policy is to ward off painful feelings of separation, abandonment, guilt, and helplessness. This brings me to the fifth and final key concept.

Key Concept 5: Organizational Change, Loss, and Grief

A powerful subtheme of many organizational stories is grief (and the prohibition of grief) for lost relationships, pasts, leaders, selves, values, and missions or for an anticipated threat of corporate loss. The "unit" of this triad of change-loss-grief can be as much workplace organizations as nations, ethnic groups, and religions. I come by this emphasis honestly, if reluctantly, through the experience of change and loss in work environments throughout my professional life.

During my six years in the Department of Psychiatry at Meharry Medical College in Nashville, Tennessee (1972–1978), I saw one internationally prominent chairperson leave after only a few years. Soon a second nationally renowned chairperson came and went within a few years. I witnessed firsthand—although I did not have a name for the process then—institutional ambivalence toward outstanding clinical practice, scholarship, and leadership and the unacknowledgeable loss created by such ambivalence.

Now living in Oklahoma since early 1978, I was until my retirement in 2012 the last remaining faculty member of the *ancien régime* among the Oklahoma City, Enid, and Shawnee, Oklahoma, family medicine residency programs, which include(d) approximately 50 physician and nonphysician faculty. Over time, some 60 faculty members have come and gone. For many years I was the only remnant and often unwelcome reminder of a repudiated past.

These years have taught me considerable adaptability in the face of continual, unpredictable change. They unleashed what felt and still feels like interminable mourning for the loss of increasing numbers of those with whom I had worked more as close friends than as academics or colleagues. I often felt as if I were in a family with a chronic illness that could not be acknowledged or discussed. This is a world haunted by disappearance and symbolic death, by official secrecy over death and its shames and guilts, by endless shadow, together constituting what Yiannis Gabriel calls "miasma" (2005, 2006, 2008, 2012). This experience has alerted me to similar processes in other organizations. It has also taught me immeasurably about American culture.

For the most part, organizations that request my consultation or project management do not define their problem as the triad change-loss-grief. They invite me to assist them on some other, usually specific issue, task, problem, or project. Through the process of listening, asking questions, and spending time with personnel throughout the organization on their turf, I discover the presence of loss and unspent grief as well as other underlying, uncompleted stories.

Organizational cultures, like societies everywhere, often lunge into the future with unresolved losses and attachments. From individuals and families all the way to international relations, the work of mourning what has been lost and letting go of what cannot be kept is not only one of the most difficult and unending of human tasks but also one of the most powerful impediments to greater maturity (Diamond, 1984, 1988; Fornari, 1975; Pollock, 1977; Volkan 1981, 1988). Many writers have explored organizational and international conflict, change, and loss from the framework of psychoanalytic object-relations theory (Fornari, 1975; Kets de Vries, 1984; Levine, Jacobs, & Rubin, 1988; Mack, 1986; Montville, 1989; Volkan, 1979; Allcorn & Diamond, 1997; Diamond & Allcorn,

2009). A recurrent theme among these writers is the role of mourning as a means of liberation from the past and in turn a diminished need to *repeat* the traumatic past and cling to its loved and hated inner representations.

Anyone who looks at the social history of the United States since the late 1970s and early 1980s through the present (2016) must be struck by the atmosphere of belligerent competitivism, commercialism, corporate groupism, minimalism, and rampant survivalism. This is a renewal of a callous "live and let die" Social Darwinism (Stein, 1982b, 1982c, 1982d, 1985b). As we approached and crossed the millennium, catastrophism pervaded ideologies of the inner as well as the outer environment. We read almost daily of hostile takeovers of one corporation by another, of numerous mergers, of the insatiably large devouring the vulnerably small, of short-term planning based on immediate profit (e.g., the sacred quarterly report). Bank failures and closings, farm and home foreclosures, the virtual disappearance of the once-flourishing steel valleys of the upper Midwest and the Northeast, rampant termination of long-term employees, and the replacement of solo and group medical practices with corporate outpatient and hospital conglomerates—these are but several instances of society-wide rapid transitions and losses of identity (Stein, 1985b).

The greedy, gluttonous "junk bond" empires of culture heroes such as Donald Trump, Michael Milken, Ivan Boesky, Carl Icahn, and other ambivalently admired high-risk financial speculators of the 1980s (equivalents of the nineteenth-century robber baron industrialists) collapsed into the 1990s. Cutbacks, austerity, increased temporary employment ("temps")(Morrow, 1993), and social dislocations have followed excess, expansionism, and collapse. In the 1990s and 2000s, ruthless CEOs from Albert Dunlap ("Chainsaw Al" of Sunbeam) to Jack Welch ("Neutron Jack" of General Electric) to Irwin Jacobs ("Irv the Liquidator" of Qualcomm) to Kenneth Lay (of Enron) and Dennis Kozlowski (of Tyco) thought nothing of firing and psychologically abusing millions of employees in waves of downsizings and restructurings that were supposed to make their corporations instantly more profitable but put them in instead in greater danger. An exclusive focus on short-term gain almost invariably led to long-term financial disaster. All this set the stage for the economic collapse of 2008. Appearance was and remains everything. "Yuppie" is now a dirty word.

Most of the organizations described throughout this book situate within the era beginning with Ronald Reagan, through the Clinton and two Bush presidencies, and the Barack Obama presidency in the United States It has been a time when retreat from values of compassion, social commitment, the psychological contract of mutual loyalty between employer and employee, and social responsibility is the norm. The American dream (ideal) of opportunity retreated into self-aggrandizing opportunism. Fragmentation and rage abound in every area of life. This is the deeper ocean of group fantasy in which many of the organizations to be described in this book continue to reel in unending onslaught of chronic, traumatic change and loss, followed by an inability to mourn and a frenzied quest for greater productivity and profit.

Tawdry social values such as economic bottom lines, ruthless self-advancement, corporate greed, and immediate profit trashed deeper values and turned people into mere producers, consumers, and disposable commodities themselves. Top-level management often had little knowledge of, or interest in, the actual industries or companies they bought and sold with both poor guidance by conscience and an absence of federal controls. Executives brought in from the outside often knew nothing of the products or the processes of the organization they led. They knew and know only spreadsheets and computers and how to manipulate abstract numbers. Part of what remains to be mourned, then, is what we as Americans have allowed ourselves to become in the shadow of the 1980s through the present (2016).

The "Teflon president" (a term often used to characterize Ronald Reagan) represented a culture that had renounced its own mettle, its own ideals. The ethos of greed and flamboyant individualism continues in 2016 in the form of the right-wing Tea Party and those aspiring national leaders who represent it. There is no place in this ethos for mourning loss. By contrast, sincere grief, and grief's repentance, is a path of reclamation and restitution, of genuine rebirth, whether in corporations or in nations.

The era from President Reagan through the present (2016) can be characterized as one of mostly uninterrupted *deregulation* (Allcorn & Stein, 2012; Stein & Allcorn, 2010a, 2010b, 2011) of corporations, banks, businesses, and virtually all other organizations. The result of *laissez-faire* economics has seen the reign of magical thinking that unlimited growth and profit will occur. For many companies, however, deregulation has been disastrous, as many grandiose executives are tempted by ever-greater risk taking and expansion. Deregulation led largely to the precipitous Great Recession (the word Depression was magically avoided) in 2008. Even after the economic collapse the call for greater regulation went largely unheeded, and many economists warn that the United States is on the road to yet another economic catastrophe.

What are such notions as guilt, shame, responsibility, empathy, and compassion when a nation elects to public office those who embody the widespread privatistic, greedy, callous indifference and neglect that became governmental laissez-faire and deregulation in public policy? We suffer, then, at the hands of those whom we appoint to exact deep "cuts" and "sacrifices." If America has become a latchkey society of mutual abandonment, workplaces are but one site where we live out our abuse and neglect of one another. We are all at risk for homelessness. Street people are metaphors of our collective inner scorched-earth landscape, a contemporary embodiment of T. S. Eliot's *Hollow Men* and *Waste Land*. Our social problems are in part our self-contempt wandering among us. The *organizational* traumas, loss, and unspent grief described in this book then are artificially bounded only by a kind of heuristic punctuation. The grim ethos pervades all our social "units" and institutions.

We press on, business as usual, indifferent to suffering, as if nothing has happened. We are the ghosts we are haunted by, the ego ideals we disavowed because we could not live up to them. We flee from the pain of guilt, shame, and anxiety that their reminders would awaken in us (Alford, 1988; Stein, 1998, 2001). We have so long poisoned our own well with the tyranny of forgetfulness, our mandatory cultural "normalcy," that we mistake this poison for sustenance. Although we might claim to have temporarily repudiated it and made some amends in the form of the Clinton and Obama presidencies, in the guise of company and university planning, public policy, and electoral politics, this group fantasy is largely what still governs us in 2016. Vicious racism toward blacks, widespread hatred toward immigrant Muslims and Hispanics, attempts to legally exclude LGBT members from jobs and restaurants, the creation of laws that make it difficult for members of minorities to register to vote, and so on, attempt to dehumanize and exclude millions of people from basic dignity and rights.

During the 1960s and 1970s, large-scale American urban redevelopment and relocation disrupted networks of meaning, information, succor, and mutual assistance and inspired terror in many ethnic populations for which home and neighborhood had been experienced as coextensive with the world (Stein, 1980). Similar societal disintegration and rampant self-destructiveness have occurred among Native North Americans experiencing rapid acculturation, but over a longer time period (Fry, 1970; Shkilnyk, 1985). Common Native American responses include emotional numbness, passivity, disorientation to time and space, substance abuse, and random aggression, which together constitute what Wolfgang G. Jilek (1974) calls anomic depression (see also Jilek-Aall, 1986). The relentless drive for "progress" and "development" continues to destroy many communities.

From two decades of fieldwork in the Monongahela steel valley (late 1960s through 1990s), principally among Slavic-American steelworker families (Stein, 1980; Stein & Hill 1979), I have witnessed once bustling mill towns become virtual ghost towns in which the demoralized, the retired, and those unable to move are trapped. During twice-yearly visits to the Pittsburgh-McKeesport region through the early 1990s, I saw and read (in local newspapers) the same scenarios repeated. For example, in the mid-1980s, officials of USX (formerly United States Steel) urged greater economic realism on the part of devastated communities, admonishing them to relinquish their understandable but pathetic symbolic attachments to the steel mills (for example, the "Dorothy Six" blast furnace at the former Duquesne Works; as maternal symbols, most blast furnaces were given female names, and steel making was often likened to procreation).

Meanwhile many newspaper editors urged greater regionalism and less localism and pressed for a more cosmopolitan spirit of development. For example, they asked readers to think more of the entire greater Pittsburgh area than of microdevelopments in individual towns along the "Three Rivers." But many townsfolk were members of multigeneration families for whom mill-church-tavern-market was the world, not merely a job. For such people, symbols are never merely symbols. Some communities have diversified and flourished, but many still languish, left behind from "progress." Since the 1980s, the constellation of globalism, deregulation, deskilling, and offshoring has fractured the identities of millions of people.

Attitudes such as cosmopolitanism, parochialism, localism, tenacious resistance to change, and tenacious adherence to change are all emotionally charged, symbolic operations that are as much about identity as they are about economics. Not only in steel valleys but also in all corporate policy development and planned change, we would do well to understand both those who have everything to lose and those who have nothing to lose (see Grieco, 1988, on organizational culture and conflict). For the former, the boundary of the self lies beyond the skin in a way of life. For a way of life to "die" is for a person's sense of self to perish, for historical continuity to be forever severed. For the latter, the boundary of the self lies in discontinuity, rather than in continuity, in a new future severed entirely from the past. Urban revitalization involves stretching a new social skin (boundary), one consisting of a wider, even global, geographic compass (Stein, 1987a; Diamond & Allcorn, 2009) and a new way to have a proud economic identity ("clean" informatics, telecommunications, or banking, rather than "dirty" coal and steel, white collar rather than blue collar). Countless people are simply left behind.

Ironically both extremes—those who cling to their past and those who fling it away—are ways of dealing with grief to avoid its sting and inner growth. Those who cling tenaciously to the past, who hope even to resurrect the old way of life, avoid grieving by insisting that the old way is not really or not necessarily gone. They do so either by sheer denial, by angry protests against corporate executives, or by a numbed, chronically depressed attempt to live life as usual amid the decay. Those who attempt to cast the past from their view, to efface it from memory and landscape, often show a kind of manic denial, a restless need to do and change the outside to avoid feeling inside the loss and pain. Yet what is needed most by all participants to the calamity does not occur: A public acknowledgment of the profound extent and depth of change and public grieving on the part of all "interest groups" so that the past can be collectively worked through and only then relinquished.

As a result, organizational retrenchment, regression, and factional splitting (for example, between radicals or progressives and conservatives) occur. Far from healing, wounds become more injured and gaping, even as business ostensibly flourishes in some sectors. When an individual or a group cannot bid farewell to an era, when that era is either clung to or hurled away, organizational renewal is aborted (see Owen, 1986, 1987). All sides become stuck perceiving another side as a "betrayer."

What Kohut (1972) describes as chronic narcissistic rage (relentless hatred and often violence toward people who embody what we despise in ourselves) assures that constant battle prevents deep bereavement. Neither flight into the past nor flight from the past permits an organization, a community, or a culture to grieve what has been irrevocably lost, even to acknowledge a loss has occurred. Moreover, attenuation of ties to the past becomes all the more unbearable when some external force is perceived as assaulting, if not severing, those ties. In a number of studies (Stein, 1984, 1985a, 1987a), I have discussed individuals' and groups' representations of themselves and their identities in terms of place and space. *Who* we are entwines with *where* we are. Under the rubric of psychogeography, I have described how developmental issues over separation and individuation are depicted in terms of the fusion of personal boundaries with spatial boundaries of culture, workplace, and social organization.

American culture, with its pioneer-inspired flight from the past into the self-made future, is vulnerable in a particular way to being haunted by what has been hurriedly left behind. Propelled by widely shared values such as future orientation, insistence on optimism, individualism, success or achievement, and mastery over nature (Kluckhohn & Strodtbeck, 1961), Americans and our organizations live according to such attitudes and maxims as "Burn your bridges," "Never look back," "Cut your losses and run," and "Think about the living; forget the dead." We have difficulty standing in one place emotionally (or occupationally, as a result of our emphasis on continued mobility) long enough to mourn the irreparability of all that has befallen us.

Yet a present that cannot pause to grieve and bid farewell to its past will in some way breed a future enslaved to that past. For a consultant to help a corporate group *remember* and *feel* is also to help it *perform* better. Although it is against the American grain to say so, only through the reclamation of the painful past do we become liberated to create a future that does not repeat that past because it is not yet finished. Freedom comes as much from unshackling the inner life as from throwing off the yokes of oppressors. The intergenerational transmission of trauma (e.g., between current workers and new recruits) occurs in workplaces as much as in traumatized families.

Short of genocide, organizational groups, like ethnic and religious groups, that experience rapid change do not literally die. Yet their members often keenly feel that the groups are dying or that they are endangered. Groups are often experienced intrapsychically and represented symbolically by their members as living organisms that contain and define the membrane of the self (Koenigsberg, 1975). Threat to group meaning is felt as threat to life itself, if not worse. The prospect that a person's group might disappear evokes a horrified shudder among those who fuse their very selves and destinies with it and who represent that very self by it. For many, the prospect of group disappearance is a fate worse than death.

In the face of loss—whether individual or group, actual persons or abstractions of the self, such as land, institutions, leaders, values, or ambitions—people often mobilize aggression to lessen the pain and anguish, to deny an irreversible loss has occurred, to try reclaiming or reviving the dead object, and to exact vengeance upon the real or imagined source of the separation or loss (Volkan, 1997). The inability to mourn rests upon the inability to let go of the past because what it represents is too sorely needed for a sense of dignity, cohesiveness, security, and absence of guilt and anxiety.

Here aggression serves what Klein (1946) calls the paranoid-schizoid position. It affirms and acts on persecutory fears and the need for greater self-defense, if not offense. We see adversaries as all-bad villains responsible for our present misery. Correspondingly, we perceive our own selves, group, institution, or culture as all good and victimized. What Klein (1946) calls the working through of the "depressive position," leads, through mourning, to the experience of disavowed guilt and anxiety, to greater ego integration, and to the capacity for empathy and reparation. We see others now more as whole persons than as evil things. We seek to repair those persons or groups whom we have injured.

From birth to death, we spend our lives losing. Each gain is also a loss. Each advance requires some giving up (Stein, 1985a; Diamond & Allcorn, 2009; Gabriel, 1999). Developmentally, we do not become aware of our distinct selves without the price of awareness of our separateness from earliest caregivers and from nature. Human history is an odyssey of change and the struggle toward and away from awareness of separateness. Social change, even rapid change, is not a peculiar affliction imposed exclusively by the industrialized, secularized, modernized, capitalist West. Nativistic and revitalizational ghost dances (La Barre, 1972; Saffo, 2005)—from the ancient Hebrews with their golden calf in the desert journey to freedom, to the 1991 upsurge of nationalisms in a Europe bereft of the protective ideological fist and scourge of communism, to the recent explosion of terrorist groups in the Middle East—arouse groups when the finality of real and symbolic death is too shatteringly painful. Workplace organizations are equally rife with their revitalizing ghost dances intended to "turn around" and "give new life" to ostensibly declining, if not failing, organizations.

Volkan (1988) defines mourning as "an involuntary human reaction to changes that occur when the loss of possessions or objects of affection or objects of hate either threatens or actually takes place. When this reaction is worked through, something is gained: The mourner feels a new surge of energy that may be expressed in his undertaking new projects or new personal attachments. Mourning, although marking a loss, also eventually brings a kind of new power" (p. 155). What cannot or must not be grieved finds some internal or external way to be revived and enacted in new, updated situations. George H. Pollock (1977) writes that "to be able to mourn is to be able to change. To be unable to mourn, to deny changes, carries great risks to the individual and to the organization" (p. 29). People must first feel safe enough to allow themselves the vulnerability of mourning.

For example, writing of international diplomacy, Joseph V. Montville (1989) observes that

> if the abstract losses one can identify in so many ethnic and sectarian political conflicts—for example, losses of territory, or self-respect—can be seen as Freud, Pollock and Volkan, among others, have seen them, that is, as genuine, profoundly meaningful losses of a sense of permanent, predictable security, then the discovery of ways to complete political mourning is critical to the art of political conflict resolution. A people cannot "let go" of a lost abstraction of the ability to feel safe. And they should not have to "let go" of the hope for a secure future. It would seem almost impossible to reestablish ego equilibrium if one's survival seems threatened.
>
> . . . If security is assured, then mourning of past losses can be completed. The negative, oppressive historic past can be "let go" to be replaced by a new adaptation based on a reasonably confident future. (pp. 304–305)

In a family, factory, corporation, or nation, how can so essential a sense of safety, of sanctuary, be nourished? Montville (p. 309) gives many examples of the transforming quality of acts of contrition by former adversaries, specifically "the concept of accepting responsibility for one's flaws and asking forgiveness of those who have been hurt by one's hostile acts" and by those of the historical group with which one identifies oneself. It is no different (and no less difficult) with corporations or hospitals as it is with nations.

In an essay on change, mourning, and reorganization in Moscow in the wake of former Soviet president Mikhail Gorbachev's reformist policies, Volkan (1990) writes:

> When we lose someone due to death we mourn; we also mourn when we lose our land, our self-esteem, or our social order, even if it was an order that we objected to or rebelled against. An adult in psychoanalysis will not get well unless he mourns giving up his neurotic attachments which served him so long in the past.
>
> When a loss occurs (and any drastic change is a loss) we unconsciously review the images and the meanings of what is gone. Depending on the nature of what is lost and how it is lost it may take a year or two to get through the "disorganized" state, to struggle between the unconscious reviewing of the meaning, recapturing the lost object, or letting it go. After going through expected stages mourning comes to a practical end and the new internal and external reality, which includes the acceptance of the loss or change, is accepted.
>
> While my above reference is to an individual, groups also mourn when a drastic change or loss occurs and it is shared. For example, the loss of ancestral land due to war, or natural disaster, or abrupt political change, imposes the necessity of a shared mourning process, through which everyone involved can adapt internally and externally. (p. 4)

Individuals and organizational groups suffering loss review their history as a part of grief work. Consider corporate mergers and hostile takeovers. When organizations are "merged" or "acquired," people become disoriented and ask, "Who are we now?"; "Where are our boundaries?" When people feel they have lost "footing" on their very "ground," they consciously and unconsciously, often obsessively, tell stories about their history as a way to work through the intense separation anxiety rekindled by loss.

Organizations and larger cultures are symbolic "objects" to which we attach ourselves (Koenigsberg, 1975, 1989; Stein, 1987a; Stein & Niederland, 1989; Diamond, 2014), with which we feel connected, and onto which we project images of security, symbioses, and separation from our earliest mothering figures. When we lose organizations or coworkers, we feel as if we are losing a part of ourselves as well as losing real, external persons and things. We narrate our painful histories via private and shared metaphors and storytelling, and only gradually, if ever, peer into their deeper significance.

Social organizations as well as natural, geological "bodies" of land and water, come to be experienced in terms of our own body senses and our deepest dreads (from engulfment and death to separation, abandonment, and castration). Corporations often experience psychological earthquakes when downsizing, restructuring, and reengineering occur. Developmentally, the first and most fateful "ground" to which we are attached is not the earth but early nurturing persons. Our metaphors—whether earth mothers, sky father gods, nations, or workplaces—are descendants of our developmental pasts (Diamond, 1984, 1988; Diamond & Allcorn, 1987, 2009; Stapley, 2006; Stein & Niederland, 1989). Organizations are not families. Yet in them we represent and reenact our earliest familial experiences, fantasies, and roles. People externalize and reify these in their perceptions of organizations; much of the social construction of reality is projective (Berger & Luckmann, 1966). Organizations feel like families even when we know they are not.

Mourning is the fulcrum of change (Freud, [1917] 1957; Pollock, 1977; Mitscherlich & Mitscherlich, 1975; Diamond & Allcorn, 2009 ; Vivian & Hormann, 2002; Doka, 1989). On one side are the working through, the liberation, and the renewed devotion to life; on the other side are the inability to mourn, the chronic grief that keeps the dead and the lost as if they were alive and killable, the flight from mourning into repetition, and the endless revitalization or restoration of the past. Mourning itself is often taboo since it would be too painful, too fragmenting, too guilt-ridden and shameful, too full of sadness (Doka, 1989). It would remind the bereaved that something has been lost.

Change that triggers the experience of loss and the onset of grief work can lead in turn to responses that allow change or that refuse to permit change so that no future except the past is acceptable. Philosopher George Santayana is famed for remarking that those who do not remember the past are condemned to repeat it. I phrase his wisdom psychologically to read that those who do not mourn are condemned to repeat what they cannot tolerate to relinquish. Volkan (1987) observes that

> when changes are not mourned, the inability to mourn and its psychological effects carry on from one generation to the next, like other grievances; children and grandchildren want to recreate aspects of what is lost, and of events pertaining to the loss in order to complete the mourning. This is potentially harmful, stimulating an unconscious thrust toward political action, a kind of persistent group compulsion toward mastering shared hurts. (p. 925)

Silencing, acting out, and sealing over group trauma occur not only intergenerationally in families and ethnic groups, but also among adult-recruited members of a workplace organization. Consider the new CEO of a corporation who is brought in to quickly and magically "turn around" the organization. He or she may demand of managers and employees to forget the past, to regard the organization's past as all bad and responsible for all of its current problems.

What people are allowed to remember is inseparable from what they are compelled to forget. These are among the first lessons of the informal, implicit "job description" that new recruits to an organization find in their social contract. Through storytelling during "orientation" and beyond, the myth of the past is recreated and reaffirmed as part of the price of initiation into the organization. To be loyal, to become worthy of being "one of us," new recruits must make others' beliefs and convictions about the past their own as well. In this way defense against the hurt of loss and mourning is transmitted to new "generations" of adult recruits. The defense haunts as much as any original insult.

The inability to mourn has dire consequences for individuals, families, organizations, national cultures, and international relations alike. Organizational groups must work through the difficult stages of grieving if a new organization is to emerge from the losses. For all types and sizes of social groups, the inability to mourn poses one of the greatest impediments to change and complicators of change (see, for instance, Freud, [1917] 1957; Mitscherlich & Mitscherlich, 1975; Fornari, 1975; Pollock, 1961, 1977; Volkan, 1981; GAP & Stein, 1987; Kets de Vries & Miller, 1984; Kets de Vries, 2003). Similarly, the working through of grief creates openness to novel solutions and enhances reality acceptance.

I have repeatedly seen how organizations can first recruit and attract prospective workers; make them promises; soon undermine, if not demoralize, these workers after they have become dedicated employees; and finally discard them as expendable waste. This book is in part a memorial for them, my expression of gratitude for our years of association and grief for loss that seems unnecessary. Whatever else this book is, it is testimony. If this book is about organizations and their cultures, it is also about grief's role in haunting them.

If the inability to mourn the past leads to a refusal to accept the past's finality and our role in it, mourning leads to greater realism about and acceptance of the past. It offers the prospect of a future that does not need to restage the traumatic past and make it over anew. Personal and group defenses, unconsciously designed to be self-protective, are ultimately self-defeating. They interfere with perception of the world and with memory in order to exclude the unpleasurable (A. Freud, 1966, pp. 104–105). They further distort judgment and interfere with realistic decision-making. Mourning achieves the opposite of these. It fosters genuine change rather than the changelessness and timelessness of historical repetition (Nedelmann, 1986).

Perhaps needless to say, the organizational researcher or consultant gains access to the experience of each of these five key concepts largely through listening deeply—to others, and to others via ourselves and how others affect us. The ensuing chapters will elaborate on each of these interrelated concepts.

2. Understanding Groups

Introduction

None of the five key concepts stands alone apart from the others. They each are part of a matrix or constellation. The researcher or consultant makes sense of an organizational group through the main instrument of observation, the self. He or she will explore "what it is like to work here," or "what a typical day is like" through group symbols such as central organizing metaphors, often revealed through language, and the nature of group leadership and followership.

Since change—often continuous and traumatic change—is part of every workplace group's experience, the researcher or consultant will naturally explore how the group and its leader(s) respond and adapt to change, whether, for instance, the process of renewal acknowledges loss and grieves it, or whether the leader will insist on short-circuiting mourning and lurch ahead into "progress" and innovation. Clearly, much of organizational life is about the experience and awareness—or the putting of awareness out of one's mind—of time.

In our everyday language, we say people are members or parts of groups, belong to groups, are loyal to groups, and commit themselves to groups. These groups can be workplaces as well as tribes or nations. People experience being "in" their groups (as we say spatially) as if the group were a living organism and had a distinct life and body, even an immortality of its own, one from which they draw a sense of sustenance, cohesiveness, and well-being. In this chapter, I tell several stories that illustrate organizational group life. I relate the organizational consequences of a "perfect computer" that was anything but perfect; the story of a demoralizing downsizing; and an extended story of my work with a medical corporation, the significance that organization played in participants' lives, and the consequences to their morale and functioning of the threat of closure.

No single story can illuminate the entire universe. No two organizations, no two cultures, no two persons, are identical. Cross-organizational, like all cross-cultural, comparison helps keep both science and consultation honest. Nevertheless, just as a poem, novel, short story, or symphony can conjure facets of our lives, likewise a single organizational story can help us *listen* to our own organizations better, to realize that work sites become a part of our emotional tissue, enter into our deepest memory, and take root within the borders of our own souls. When our "organizations" become threatened, so do we.

Before I present and discuss some organizational stories, I want to take time to discuss my own formative experiences that are the foundation of listening deeply. Then I address the crucial relational or intersubjective dimension of storytelling and story listening that help us to understand organizations (Gabriel, 2000). Stories exist in the ebb and flow of storytelling and story listening.

Formative Influences on Listening Deeply

Here, I would like to devote some time to describe two central formative influences on how I approach and understand organizational groups as researcher and consultant. They are my *experiential precursors to the notion, methodology, and theory of listening deeply.* I do this not to provide my "credentials," but rather to give the reader a sense of how I came to "use" my self in organizational research and consulting.

One major influence was the annual convention of the International Psychohistorical Association (IPA), which I have attended regularly for many years since its first convention in 1978. At the conclusion of each day of the three-day conference, one hour or so was devoted to "group process analysis," which was explicitly not a critique of papers presented during the day, but an exploration—always in a large circle—of *what it felt like to participate in the conference* and what the contents of the papers *felt like* to the listeners. Although the IPA was a scholarly society, and the IPA convention a scholarly meeting, both were organizations. I had much to learn about the IPA and the convention *as organizations.*

How novel an idea, I thought, to apply psychohistorical (psychoanalytic, historical) approaches *to our own group(s)* as well as to the groups we officially study in culture and history. We would explore our own emotions, fantasies, desires, and defenses as these were evoked from hearing presentations and in participating in the conference. In short, from the IPA I began to learn *how to listen to a group and attend to group processes.*

As well as participating by offering my own experiences, I observed the group and its (usually) two facilitators (e.g., Lloyd deMause, Casper Schmidt, John Hartman, Henry Lawton). I watched them like a hawk, drinking in and absorbing leadership, group process, and content of the members' often highly emotional sharing. The facilitating leaders would offer observations, interpretations, and point out group themes/fantasies. They would mostly observe and remain silent. Sometimes I experienced their contributions as helpful to the group, sometimes intrusive and heavy-handed. I was in the process of finding my own way. I was clearly enthralled by this discovery of a new universe. I identified with it and hoped to have opportunities to do something like it myself. One of my early roles in my family medicine department where I could "apply" what I was learning, was to cofacilitate, with a faculty physician, intern and upper-level resident Balint groups.

Over time, my role expanded from being a cofacilitator to being asked to coordinate, and lead, all departmental Balint groups: intern, upper-level resident, faculty—and for a while, community physicians who had trained in the residency program where I worked. Further, over time, I developed monthly Balint groups for the three rural family medicine residencies where I taught. Over time, I came to allow the structure and content of the Balint groups to expand from the original focus on the physician–patient relationship. Let me explain.

In my family medicine department, I coordinated and led or facilitated all Balint groups for interns, residents, and faculty at three residency training sites, a role I occupied from the middle 1980s through my retirement in 2012. I led some 2,000 groups during that time. The original Balint group in England, named for psychoanalyst/psychiatrist Michael Balint, consisted of a psychiatrist and about five to seven practicing general practitioners (Balint, 1957 [1964]; Friedman, 1971; Glenn, 1983; Johnson, 2001). Group members were physicians whose professional identities and roles had already congealed. In contrast to the issues and identities of those British general practitioners, there are different issues, identities, and roles among the interns, residents, and faculty physicians involved with Balint groups in U.S. family practice residencies.

Balint groups were originally designed to be specific "work groups" in Bion's (1959) sense of the term, that is, of task-orientation. The focus of the group was the task of *presenting a case* about some difficult doctor–patient relationship, helping members to reflect on and more deeply understand the physician–patient relationship involved, and returning to clinical practice with greater wisdom. The group was not designed to be supportive or to analyze unconscious aspects or emotion-based "basic assumptions" (1959) of the group process itself.

Merenstein and Chillag (1999) document from ethnographic observation, interviews, and focus groups how the actual practice of Balint group leadership in family practice residencies—and hence the group process itself—widely deviates from Michael Balint's original model and from later International Balint Society doctrine. The groups as constituted in family practice departments and programs differ from traditional groups in that they provide support, offer reassurance, provide teaching and guidance, provide answers, are hierarchical, and are willing to give the "right answer" (Merenstein & Chillag, 1999).

In particular, I became interested in what happens when the group itself, and not a patient, is allowed to be the "case." Instead of enforcing "what should happen," I pay attention to what does happen and what can happen when one takes cues from the group as well as from doctrine. Indeed, I question whether Balint orthodoxy is always appropriate, or even possible, for intern, resident, and faculty groups whose members' developmental needs and group boundaries differ from those of the seasoned practitioners in classic Balint groups.

Another way of putting this is, just as I came to understand the IPA and the convention *as types of organizations*, I came also to approach the discipline and department of family medicine, and the Balint groups within the department, *as types of organizations* that could teach me how to respond to them in a healthy fashion. *I was able to transfer my knowledge and approach of listening deeply from my work with these organizations to my work with any organization.*

In the U.S. family practice residency groups, group facilitators readily respond (Buber, [1923] 1958; Winnicott, [1960] 1965a; Bion, 1962; Boyer, 1999) as issues surface, strive to take priority, and ask to be acknowledged and addressed. In these residency-based groups, within the boundaries of confidentiality and respectful listening (which are core Balint values), we learn together what needs to be addressed. Often, *group* goals, issues, conflicts, and other processes must precede the capacity of interns, residents, and faculty to process the human dimensions of difficult or vexing physician–patient interactions. Intense, case-focused discussions may occur in the second part of the hour's meeting, after issues of psychic survival, fragmentation, and self-worth have first cleared the air. Internal and interpersonal issues among interns, residents, and faculty must first be recognized and addressed if participants are to have an emotional reservoir of empathy toward patients.

Several core realities converge in the many Balint groups I have led. First, these groups are one of the few places and times in which interns, residents, and faculty (in separate groups or in combinations) see each other and have the opportunity to meet. Second, these groups have historically been one of the few emotionally safe places in the department and in the health sciences training environment. Third, these groups are one of the few places in the larger organization where participants are able to affirm their identities as family physicians and feel good and competent about it. Over time, Balint groups have increasingly become a kind of rehearsal place or testing ground for presenting and addressing group issues and ideas in wider departmental settings.

During a typical group, either I or the coleader would (1) inquire how the month's rotations are going; (2) listen to the group conversation for a theme or a case that might become the group focus; or (3) directly ask if anyone has a case. Because I had already provided group members with a history of the original groups, and passed out a packet of reading materials about Michael Balint and his early groups, group members know what the call for "a case" signifies. Usually the group would land on a theme, or I will discern one out of the conversation.

Thus, what may appear to be "obstacles" or "deviations" of residency Balint groups from classic Balint groups are actually necessary developmental steps that take place through "learning from experience" (Bion, 1962). By widening and reframing—putting a new "frame" around the same content—the concept of "case," one can foster an atmosphere where all participants' psychic and real-world realities are taken seriously. Balint participants are often able and willing to discuss a Balint-type clinical case once their own experiences are given voice, acknowledged, and validated. As Shapiro writes: "People cannot take care of the 'work' until they take care of themselves" (personal communication with Johanna Shapiro, Ph.D., May 16, 2002, with permission)—until they feel taken care of in the group context. The Balint groups I have discussed are places in which both can occur.

For me, as an "extension" of my many years of work in Balint groups, listening deeply with all clients and organizations becomes foremost *an act of caring so that people feel cared for* (through attentive listening) as an interpersonal (intersubjective) foundation for addressing specific organizational problems, conflicts, and tasks—and perhaps also better caring for themselves and others in their workplace.

To summarize: In all the Balint groups I facilitated for over 25 years, I had an opportunity to "apply," test, and revise all that I had learned from observing daily IPA group process, as well as from other organizational consultations. I grew also from reading those key writers on group process theory, who had greatly influenced IPA group process leaders, especially Wilfred R. Bion, Lloyd deMause, and John Hartmann. Further, with my Balint groups as with the IPA, I learned better how to listen to groups and *how to respond from listening, rather from a preset agenda*. Listening became the most important thing I did in consultations.

Stated another way, I developed ideas, methods, and theory about listening deeply from my having become immersed as *participant observer in organizational fieldwork* (Duncan & Diamond, 2011; Hunt, 1989; Volkan & Hawkins, 1971; Stein, 1982a) both in the IPA and family medicine Balint group meetings, and subsequently in the life of other organizations during consultations.

Consider, then, listening deeply as a form of anthropological or sociological *ethnographic fieldwork* in organizations, either as research or as part of consulting.

Among the methods or tools used are naturalistic observation, participant observation, open-ended interviewing, and listening to people's stories. All these are dimensions of *immersion* in an organization's culture.

One dimension of the quest for objectivity in gathering and analyzing data is the need to not distort data through subjectivity, that is, to be aware of it, to reflect on one's work—to observe oneself observing. This sounds sensible—even though, because of unconscious influence, it is more difficult than one might think to filter out and control distortions.

One way of addressing this methodological conundrum is to cultivate an attitude of "not knowing," of approaching a person or group by suspending the need to know (French, 2001; French & Simpson, 1999; Stein, 2007). As previously explained, it is an attitude called by poet John Keats "negative capability" (1817), the capacity for relaxing into knowledge rather than tense drivenness to know—immediately, if not ahead of time.

Further, all interaction with human beings (e.g., corporate leaders, board members, managers, and employees) is in fact *intersubjective*, that is, attuned unconscious to unconscious, soul to soul. At issue is not *whether* this will happen, but whether the researcher or consultant has *conscious* access to this data as they occur. As George Devereux emphasized decades ago (1967), the ethnographic researcher or consultant cannot directly observe the unconscious in another person, but rather learns about it by examining his or her own physical, emotional, and mental (thought processes) responses to this other person or group. Thus, the intersubjective dance of transference-countertransference (Diamond, 1993; Diamond & Allcorn, 2009) offers crucial information about the "other" mediated by the self of the researcher or consultant, for instance, in the storytelling/story listening dyad.

In listening deeply in organizational ethnographic fieldwork, one is attuned to the other person or group, to oneself, and to a constantly fluctuating common mental area constructed between them (Thomas Ogden's concept of the "third," 1989a, 1993, 1999). Thus, the self of the participant observer can at once contaminate the communication with the other person or group, *and* be the most valuable and reliable source of understanding that other person or group. The self of the organizational researcher or consultant is the ultimate instrument of knowing about the individual client and organization (Duncan & Diamond, 2011).

I turn now from the formative experiences in listening deeply, to the actual process of how storytelling and story listening occur in all types of organizations.

The Dance of Storytelling and Story Listening

Let me here try to describe the conscious and unconscious "dance" of the storytelling and story listening partnership in discussing toxic workplaces. For the storyteller, the starting point is the emotional burden of living with the emotional abuse, uncertainty, anxiety, dread, and despair that characterizes countless workplaces. For the story listener, there is the willingness to be present and to listen and contain all the burdens the leader, manager, or employee shares. What I remember psychoanalyst James Masterson (1983) saying of the role of the analyst in relation to the patient holds for the story listener's central role as well: You are the servant of a process.

Telling one's story of workplace experience is a process of externalizing the toxicity, putting it outside oneself, and trusting that it will be safely received, heard, even processed by the empathic listener. In primitive terms, it is foremost a process of vomiting out the poison (in the vernacular, "spilling my guts").

In the presence of a safe listener, the storytelling helps the storyteller to cognitively and emotionally organize the content, in the service of making sense of all the toxicity that he or she had experienced. Organizing one's story is part of the antidote to inner fragmentation and disorganization. Further, the storyteller does not tell the story only once, but instead many times and in many permutations—often to the same person and to different people who are emotionally safe harbors. By turning horrific experience into an "object," a story, shared with others, it is "out there" rather than trapped inside the self, which in turn traps the storyteller. It is as if to say: "Someone is with me with my story. I am not alone." Storytelling is thus both liberating and healing.

For the story listener, through empathy and identification, one helps the storyteller to feel *heard*. The hope is that there will be "good enough" self-other boundaries that the listener will not be overwhelmed by hearing and witnessing the stories. This becomes especially challenging and difficult when the storyteller and story listener share the same or similar trauma—such as happens in downsizing, and as happened in the 1995 Oklahoma City bombing and the 2001 terrorist attacks on the New York World Trade Center and the Washington, DC, Pentagon. One surely did not have to be physically on the site of the catastrophe to be deeply emotionally wounded—even devastated.

Consider this brief story: Around 1996 I was consulting with an organization in eastern Pennsylvania and spoke with a manager who seemed highly anxious and worried when I met him. He knew that I was from Oklahoma City, where the bombing of the federal building had recently occurred on April 19, 1995. Although I was not there to discuss the Oklahoma City bombing, one of the first things he said to me with agitation in his voice was: "I know you're from Oklahoma City where the bombing recently occurred. Tell me, Howard, I'm frightened for our children. *How are we going to be able to protect them* here in eastern Pennsylvania? What do we do?" I could feel his horror and sense of helplessness. I also felt his merger of Philadelphia with Oklahoma City, a spatial or geographic collapse, as though it were the same place, as though "there" was "here," and that danger in his city was imminent.

I sensed that he was inconsolable and that any reassurance I might try to offer would be false. I sat there with him and listened, and served as a witness to his raw feelings. Maybe I nodded my head. I shuddered with him. Through identification and empathy, I felt boundaries blur between what I had experienced after the bombing in Oklahoma City both as a resident and as a group facilitator, and his dread far away—but not emotionally far away—in Philadelphia. I vaguely remember saying something like, "These are scary times," to acknowledge his feelings. He nodded his head. I had no "answers." Shortly thereafter we began to discuss the subject of my visit to his company.

I thus know from personal experience the difficulty of maintaining personal boundaries from my role as long-term group facilitator for first responders to the April 19, 1995, bombing of the federal building in Oklahoma City, and in my equally long-term role as "humanizing" consultant in 1995 and ensuing years to the downsizing of the University Hospital in Oklahoma City. Fortunately, at the time I was in weekly psychotherapy, although my therapist insisted that I focus on "personal" issues as opposed to "community" or "social" issues—as if the two were not inextricably entwined (Volkan, 1997, 2004). Clearly I did not have the luxury of the emotional distance that "usually" separates the therapist and patient, or consultant and client.

In our technologically highly interconnected world (Internet, e-mail, Facebook, Twitter) where communication is virtually instantaneous and visual images and videos give immediacy to distant events, consultants, psychoanalysts, grief therapists, and all people who help others need to be better prepared to emotionally be a part of the storyteller's world. In many instances we do not have the "luxury" of the traditional emotional distance between consultant and client, or psychoanalyst and patient. In a sense, we all are participant observers in a largely shared culture. At the same time, empathy and identification can become overidentification, and instead of one standing with feet firmly planted as the stream rushes by, one can be toppled over by the swift current and potentially drown, an image from Seth Allcorn.

Here is where *self-reflection in the moment*, monitoring one's countertransference in the midst of action, is essential for the story listener. After all, the listener is listening both to the storyteller and to oneself experiencing the storytelling—as the storyteller and story reverberate within oneself. Further, it is wise for the story listener in a case involving trauma to have a person or group in which he or she can safely tell the story of the experience of listening—and thus avert what has come to be known as "secondary trauma" (Vivian & Hormann, 2013).

I begin with the brief story of the role listening played in storytelling about an organization in which the story falls under the category of "You couldn't make this up."

A Story: The Perfect Computer

This is a story of how, while listening deeply may not "fix" organizational problems, it can help people feel heard, understood, and contained. They feel less alone, less imprisoned. Around 2005, I consulted with a subsidiary company of the multisite Global Health Systems Corporation (GHSC). The subsidiary company was located some 200 miles from corporate headquarters. The CEO of the overall corporation had implemented a corporation-wide computer system that was designed to integrate all units and functions through a centralized computer. Members of the local GHSC told me countless stories of how the system which worked perfectly "in theory" and "on paper" often failed in practice, but that the failures had to be denied. Managers and employees had to design ingenious, novel solutions to compensate for the many lapses in "integration." Meanwhile, the CEO proudly touted his vast computer matrix as paperless, entirely electronic.

At the local level, employees often found that the distant computer was down for a day or more, or for inexplicable reasons was too slow to be of use. Eventually, in order to perform their tasks and deal with customers, clients, patients, and physicians in a timely fashion, they had to create an entirely *parallel* paper-and-file-based system. So, instead of paper being obsolete, it *rescued* the people at the local company and was essential to their performing their tasks and keeping the place running. This entirely compensatory system was hidden from the CEO, whose self-image and reputation as an innovative, successful corporate leader was at stake. At most it could only be acknowledged that there were occasional "glitches" in the system that required visits from headquarters to fix.

As if these complications were not enough, both the main computer and local computers required frequent software updates to keep the company at state-of-the-art-level computing and competitive in the marketplace. Employees found that, no sooner had they learned one new software program, they had to learn another—that nothing could be taken for granted. The ground was constantly shifting beneath them.

Further, neither the local organization nor headquarters could afford to shut down day-to-day operations so that employees could learn the new computer software. People had to learn the software while they were using it to conduct ordinary business. The level of stress and anxiety was high, and it grew higher each time new software was introduced. Employees were ever vigilant for the next sudden change. Yet they had to put on a mask that "all was well" and the computer system was working perfectly.

Although I could not fix the computer problems, nor could I change the CEO's need to "look good" far and wide, managers and employees repeatedly thanked me for taking their situation seriously and *taking time to listen to their stories*. To them, what I was doing was valuable to them, that I was not merely "doing nothing." They told me that they looked forward to my visits (consultations) and said that they felt better after telling their difficult stories and clever solutions. In short, listening deeply is not a quick-fix-it modality, but helps people to feel heard, understood, contained, and respected—to feel treated as human beings and not as mere functions. Employees and managers expressed gratitude to me that, when we visited, they did not have to pretend that everything was fine and lie about reality.

I turn now from listening to the story of a computer that was not magical, to listening to the story of a demoralizing downsizing that took the form of a management ambush.

A Story: The Walk Out

This is a story from a conversation I had with a colleague and friend who was working in an organization undergoing large-scale downsizing around 2008. She told me the following story. The day began like any other Friday at Consolidated Telecommunications (CT, a multinational corporation). People greeted each other, got their morning coffee, spoke of their weekend plans, and set about their usual tasks. What all but a few could not know was that earlier in the week the board of directors and upper management of CT had met and decided on a large-scale reduction in force (RIF), in order to make CT more productive, profitable, and competitive. It would take place at 10:00 a.m. Friday. Rumors had circulated lately that "something" was about to happen at CT, but no one knew what or when.

As if perfectly choreographed, managers from throughout the corporate site showed up at 10:00 a.m. on Friday, each with a large, empty cardboard box, at the work sites of those designated to be fired. The managers simply notified them that their employment was terminated effective immediately, and that they were to fill this box with their personal belongings, turn over all their keys and other corporate property to the manager, be escorted by the manager to their vehicle in the parking lot, and to not return. Few words were spoken. The managers politely told the employees not to take this personally, that it was just a necessary business decision. It felt like an ambush. There was no way the targets could prepare for it.

From the moment they were notified of their firing, the employees' every move was carefully monitored, and the office door (if they had one) and the parking lot gate were locked behind them. Management was afraid that those who were fired might try to sabotage the computer system or steal equipment. Those being fired were notified by the manager that they would receive their final paycheck in the mail within a week. The RIF was executed so flawlessly that many of the remaining employees did not realize it was occurring as they worked. They only noticed during afternoon breaks and later that many people were no longer there and that their work areas or offices were empty.

The event became known in the vernacular as a "walk out," named for managers "walking" the fired employees out of the building to their cars. This was the third RIF in four years. The remaining employees were resigned to their fate, grateful that no manager had shown up this time at their workstation. They kept to themselves, staying very busy, trying not to think about what had just happened and what could happen at CT. Many thought that if the managers saw them working hard, they might be spared in the next "walk out." The term spread quickly at CT, becoming a metaphor of the trauma that had happened—and could happen soon again. Morale plummeted, and a heavy air of gloom pervaded CT. The company became yet another inconsolable organization in which survivors tended to their jobs and "kept under the radar." A place once brimming with conversation became deadened.

Let me return to *how I came to know* the story of "the walk out." This story is the *product of a process, of a relationship*, one a story listener and the other a storyteller. The story itself would not have come into being apart from the moment it was created had it not been for my colleague's eagerness to tell me her eerie story and my eagerness to stay put and listen. The story was in fact cocreated by the shared moment in which the conversation took place in the shadow of the recent wave of firings. The "eliciting" of the story went beyond data collection; it was the fruit of listening deeply. I sensed my colleague's urgency in wanting to tell me her story. My experience of her storytelling was that she had been liberated from the prison of secrecy—that the secret was finally out and safely housed in the story listener.

In a similar vein, my third story also deals with the experience of downsizing, specifically with the idea that *organizational downsizing* might be considered to be a form of *atrocity*. From countless stories I have been told by those terminated by downsizing and those who at least temporarily survived it, the language of their stories is the *language of atrocity*.

Organizing Atrocity in Organizations

I would like to relate a story—in fact, a condensation of many stories—on downsizing in organizations, based on Seth Allcorn's interviews with people in General Hospital that was undergoing downsizing in the mid-1990s. But first I would like to offer some thoughts that will set the stage for the story.

At first glance, the word *atrocity* might seem odd to associate with *organizations*. (Stokes & Gabriel, 2010). Yet a moment's reflection on history will call to mind the KGB under Stalin in the Soviet Union, the SS or Gestapo under Hitler in Nazi Germany, the Inquisition in Catholic Spain, and McCarthyism in the United States. Although atrocities occurred in radicalized nation-states, they were themselves in fact carried out by *organizations* (Stokes & Gabriel, 2010). Organizations as well as the larger groups (religions, ethnic groups, nation-states) in which they are embedded, can commit atrocities that kill the spirit as well as the body. Indeed, atrocities occur in many social forms. One contemporary organizational form in which atrocity occurs is *downsizing*.

The link between organizations, atrocity, and genocide should by now be obvious. The reason that it is not self-evident but rather a lacuna comes from the fact that, in the West, we have long thought of organizations and management as guided by rationality, objectivity, realism, and enlightened self-interest. Stokes and Gabriel (2010), if anything, reveal the heavy *rationalization* of brutality, atrocity, and genocide that justifies and masks evil toward fellow human beings. Whether literal mass murder or *symbolic* genocide, it requires considerable *organization* in order to be carried out. And the organization is, in turn, *managed* by people, many of whom have boundless conviction about the rightness—the morality, the sacredness—of their deed.

It turns out that the impersonal "banality of evil," "obedience to authority," and modernity's bureaucratic rationality thesis of Hannah Arendt (1963) and Zygmunt Bauman (1989) that has prevailed since the early 1960s is a kind of intellectual seduction. Countless scholars and readers have been seduced by it because it was an ideology that they *wanted to believe*. Even though in 1980 Robert McCully's re-analysis of Adolf Eichmann's Rorschach revealed that Eichmann was masking his aggression and lively imagination, McCully's work did not succeed in overturning the widespread belief and wish that the Nazi organizational apparatus consisted primarily of petty bureaucrats who would not wish to hurt a flea. More recently, Steven Aschheim (2014), in a *New York Times* essay, "SS-Obersturmbannführer (Retired)," similarly refutes the petty-bureaucrat theory.

The enigmatic Eichmann, then, turns out to be both a pivotal *ideologically driven figure* in the Nazi Holocaust, and a *metaphor* for the widespread fantasy that organizations are more driven by compliance than desire. The metaphor belies the enduring *wish* to believe that Eichmann and other Nazis were really not as brutal as the results of their acts might suggest. This in turn reveals more about the scholarly and reader community's denial than anything about Eichmann. Or put differently, Eichmann's self-deception and Arendt's complicity with this deception (rationalizing it with a theory of bureaucratic behavior) *resonated with* scholars and readers' wish to believe that Nazis themselves were really not that evil, even though their acts were. As Richard Koenigsberg has argued in numerous books and essays since 1975, Hitler and countless Nazis and their followers were driven by a messianic zeal to save the sacred body of Germany from infection and death by the Jews who embodied disease, that the Holocaust was a vast public health enterprise implemented by an industrial model.

Stokes and Gabriel (2010) take the entire argument a courageous step further and explore *symbolic* organizational genocide as well as literal physical mass murder. Since the 1980s, tens of millions of Americans, and countless people elsewhere under the spell of globalization, have been the casualties of human destructiveness that goes by such euphemistic names as downsizing, reduction in force (RIF), redundancy, rightsizing, restructuring, reengineering, deskilling, outsourcing, offshoring, managed health care, and many more. The sheer ruthless fervor, if not sadism, with which CEOs such as Albert Dunlap, Jack Welch, Dennis Kozlowski, Joe Nacchio, Kenneth Lay, Jeff Skilling, and many others approached the radical change in the organizations they led—with the blessing and admiration of boards and shareholders—makes it obvious that they were anything but benign, methodical bureaucrats.

It did not matter to them that hard-working, dedicated employees were simply tossed out into the street, abandoned. What only mattered was inflating the next quarterly report and saving the organization by destroying it. If this metaphoric genocide was bloodless, it nonetheless ruined millions of lives, including the families and communities of disposable employees. The resulting atmosphere of waiting for the next wave of firings, the uncertain future of organizational "survivors," and the pervasive feelings of depression and despair, has aptly been named *miasma* by Yiannis Gabriel (2005, 2006, 2008, 2012). Since the early 1990s, I have spoken with and interviewed countless people involved in downsizing, victimized by it, or who at least temporarily survived it in their organizations. Their stories told me over and again how *personal* downsizing, restructuring, and reengineering *felt*. Their stories told of psychological brutality, callousness, indifference, disdain, on the part of those who designed and implemented these euphemized forms of "managed social change."

Precisely how *personally* driven much of the physical and symbolic atrocities are leads to efforts to make them increasingly *impersonal*, depersonalized, so that those who engage in them are able to be emotionally detached and less affected. The evolution of Nazi killing from brutal pogroms (e.g., the SA; Kristallnacht,

9–10 November 1938) to industrialized mass slaughter is a "model" of this. Early in the process, the SS would have Jews lined up at the edge of, or in a long, deep pit, and execute them with guns (Babi Yar, the ravine outside Kiev). As time went on, many of the SS men felt revulsion over how personal this killing was, and the death camps, gas chambers (Zyklon B), and crematoria were the industrialized, mechanized, impersonalized result.

Further, another distancing mechanism was that people came to perform small, circumscribed roles in the process and were thus spared the emotional trauma of directly killing people. The bureaucratic and industrial model was perfect for creating the illusion of impersonality, and protected the person in the role from feeling any kinship with the victims, or remorse over their deeds. To borrow from American downsizing, it was held to be "nothing personal, just business" (Stein, 2001).

A shared set of stories is the multiauthored 1996 book on downsizing a hospital, *The Human Cost of a Management Failure: Organizational Downsizing at General Hospital* (Allcorn, Baum, Diamond & Stein). This was not the original title proposed by the editor, Seth Allcorn. He initially recommended "Death and Downsizing at General Hospital," but was overruled by his staff for placing *death* in the same title with *hospital*. This change in itself is significant in terms of covering up the editor's experience of reading the manuscript. Bureaucratic administrative considerations won out, and he changed it.

This book, a longitudinal case study that covered a year of interviews of over 20 hospital executives and managers, conducted every four months, revealed the nature of the experience of downsizing. Allcorn "collected" the stories by being an *attentive listener*. The "work" of downsizing was outsourced to a consulting company (distancing from upper management, who could appear untainted) that located the nonessential workers and set in place a removal process.

This process included guards gathering up the victims and marching them and their box of personal possessions (Jews carried suitcases of their possessions to the death camps) to a large room where they filed down a row of human resource professionals who processed their termination. Once in the room, they were not allowed to leave. When they were processed they exited directly onto a parking lot, never to return. There were no actual bodies left, but the people who survived walked around with the memories of those lost. There was no blood in the hallways but it felt like there was. Those who were left were then expected to carry on as though nothing had happened, absorbing the workloads of the departed. Hospital operations were now ostensibly more cost-effective.

Many who survived downsizing and those who did not, sometimes, when encouraged to reflect aloud, speak of loss of personal meaning including roles as breadwinners, and of the organization gradually having "its heart cut out" by repeated downsizing events (one wave of terminations is seldom enough). The trauma can span years, and employees feel that no one is an essential worker. Everyone one has a target on her or his back, not unlike a yellow Star of David in Nazi Germany. Certainly mass murder is not downsizing, where the terminated live for another day. Still, there is also deeply embedded in these social and organizational dynamics an intensely similar experience that destroys the body on the one hand and the human spirit on the other.

There was an unbearable quality to this work for a mere book. The four authors, of whom I was one, had all experienced downsizing themselves or the pressures of downsizing, making the "story" in the three sets of interviews all too familiar. Sometimes one can bear witness to too much. Downsizing was everywhere, making it distressingly clear that the methods used by leaders to remove unwanted workers or ethnic groups are all too similar and all too familiar—surely a depressing realization. Nonetheless, collaboration on this book was an intense, personal education in listening deeply.

I have been engaged to help organizations "humanize" downsizing since the mid-1990s. I have listened to a countless number of people tell me their stories. I learned to listen to the unbearable. (I owe much of this story to conversations with Seth Allcorn.)

My fourth, final, and extended, story is about listening over time to members of a company talk about their frightening experience of living under the CEO of a distant "parent" corporation who was envious of their success and was sabotaging them.

A Story: How Long Can We Circle the Wagons?

This is the longitudinal story of several years in the history of Managed Care Affiliates (MCA), one of several subdivisions of a large medical corporation whose headquarters are located in the Midwest. I served as ongoing internal consultant for many years with MCA. Corporate headquarters and its several regional subsidiaries are in the business of providing many areas of patient care: clinical and preventive care; hospital (inpatient) and clinic (outpatient); geriatric, family, adolescent, and pediatric medicine; wellness programs for the healthy; rehabilitation programs; screening, referral, and consultation. At corporate headquarters, major programs together with funding are devoted to projections of future health trends, efforts to "capture" the market, development of health policy statements, design of medical practices based on cost containment and increased profit, and development and implementation of clinical decision trees based upon probabilistic analysis.

Organizational Change

The board of directors of the main corporate office recommended, and the share-holders overwhelmingly approved, the hiring of a new corporate chief executive officer (CEO) in the early 1980s, a time during which a new national consensus over cost containment, corporate competitiveness, and privatism were congealing. It was a time when corporate medicine became explicitly profit oriented and less avowedly service oriented. Harry R. Kormos (1984) labels this era as the industrialization of medicine. The new CEO, in tune with this emergent spirit, was seen by the board that hired him as a person with a "grand vision of the future," a person who "flew high above everyone's heads, in the clouds, looking for megatrends of the future to capture the medical market." He had been chosen because he showed the most promise of expanding the company into greater profit, visibility, stature, and power in corporate medicine. From the outset, he heavily invested corporate money and personnel time in a proliferation and succession of building plans and models, architectural drafts, and high-technology acquisitions involving multiple computer systems, all of which were expected to interface flawlessly with each other. Many of these had disappointing and costly results.

Soon after the installation of the new CEO and his staff, proposals, policies, and practices began reflecting a new set of dichotomies or polarities and, underlying them, values. Among them were the corporate center versus the periphery (subsidiary companies); urban (or metropolitan) centers versus rural areas (where most subsidiaries were located); income generation and cost containment versus service; medicine as product line versus medicine as skill and service that in turn generate a livelihood; the new executives and managers versus the old ones (young blood versus old blood); centralized authority versus local autonomy; and high technology versus personal medicine. In talks and reports, the CEO favored certain recurrent metaphors or images of medicine: "the automated physician" (emphasis on high-technology-mediated, depersonalized care), medical practice as a "product line," and the physician as a "product line manager"; patient care as "managed care" given by "producers" of health care to "consumers" of health care; "patient volume" enumerated in computerized "production reports"; "the bottom line" as "cost containment" through "managed care systems." Within these perspectives, one rural subsidiary organization, MCA, was devalued despite the fact that it continued to be a reliably high-income generator utilizing the old ways of a family, service-oriented, moderately low-tech, and hands-on approach to patient care.

A large turnover of junior executives and midlevel managers occurred with the installation of the new CEO. Nearly all the inherited "old guard" were forced to leave. This turnover was quickly explained and justified by a polarization of images. The old-timers were viewed as inadequate, if not bad, contributing little or no value to the corporation; whereas those brought in by the new CEO were admired as fresh and new, capable of helping the CEO revitalize the corporation by implementing his vision. By contrast, MCA continued to be run by the old guard. When, after several years, many of the disillusioned and disgruntled new blood at corporate headquarters began to leave as well, this was further rationalized in terms of their having been poor team players. For several years, many members of the corporation did their utmost to sustain their idealization of their "visionary" leader, upon whom they had become increasingly dependent. After several years, however, many began to realize that his personal aggrandizement and the grandiose vision of the organization with which they had identified themselves were purchased at their own and the organization's expense.

After the transition in leadership at corporate headquarters to the new CEO, numerous small events set the stage for an atmosphere of doom within MCA. Representatives of the subsidiary were often overlooked for notification of scheduling for such various corporation-wide meetings as marketing sessions, strategic planning, and the development of philosophy, policy, and goals. MCA members were rarely solicited by headquarters for ideas about decisions affecting their company's internal functioning. In contrast with past leaders, spontaneous visits to MCA by home office executives, and telephone calls from them, diminished markedly. Those few personnel from the home office who regularly consulted with, gave seminars at, or did troubleshooting for MCA found that executives in the home office consistently "forgot" to credit this time spent. They tended to define "100 percent time" only in terms of that spent at the home office. In short, MCA personnel felt they had gradually become the target of discounting or of "death wishes" on the part of the larger corporation.

During the middle to late-1980s, MCA saw an outflow and depletion of virtually all those precious commodities necessary for its survival, including a "rainy day fund" of a million dollars. Through the gradual centralization of all major decision-making and financial management, a sense of local autonomy about MCA's activities and about its fate atrophied and was virtually lost. In some respects, members of MCA felt increasingly isolated and abandoned, but in other respects, engulfed, swallowed up by the central office. Leaders, managers, and employees at MCA tried to remain optimistic about their future and believe that their work was valuable, but this attitude gradually wore down from disparagement from the home office. The CEO of MCA tried to rally his "troops," as he called them, with the slogan of "Onward and Upward." But even he gradually lost his enthusiasm, though never his devotion to MCA.

Gradually, all important medical, administrative, and financial information about the organization was computerized for management from the main office. MCA personnel had to obtain from the home office virtually all "their own" information. Boundary issues abounded: Sometimes members of MCA felt violated, at other times absorbed into the home office, at still other times abandoned by it. Promotions in rank or replacement of vacant positions became notably rarer and slower at the MCA office than at the main office.

Rewards for job performance were likewise far less frequent from the home office for MCA employees. In 1989, not only did the CEO from the home office "forget" to bring plaques for an award ceremony to MCA, but also some months later on a visit to MCA, the chief operating officer (COO) likewise forgot to bring the awards plaques for presentation. MCA was consistently asked to make layoffs and cutbacks and to endure hardships that the main office did not sustain for itself. The chronic experience of unequal sacrifices made MCA suspect that the home office was growing and thriving at the expense of the affiliate.

Reputation likewise diminished in MCA during this time both in the eyes of local and regional supporters and vendors, and in the eyes of the main office. Local businesses, health agencies, government, and the local medical community that had long supported MCA enthusiastically began to wonder whether MCA would survive. They wondered whether the main office was truly behind its local affiliate and began to question whether the main office would honor MCA's commitments. Over time they withdrew their support, and stood on the sidelines to see what would happen to MCA. With local confidence in MCA's future undermined, many businesses and health agencies also adopted a wait-and-see attitude. Similarly, fewer managers applied to train and work at MCA. Prospective employee and trainee applicants heard via the grapevine that MCA might not live long and that the main office had been in keen competition with MCA. With the decline in prestige, the credibility of MCA began to decline both in the local organizational community and within the applicant pool on which MCA relied for its record of success and excellence.

The Experience of Sabotage from the Home Office

MCA personnel experienced this progression of events as keenly felt, unrelenting death wishes from and abandonment by the home office. At one poignant moment, the CEO of MCA speculated sadly, "I think that they [the home office] just wish we would fade away and die." MCA's initial persistent response was the even more unrelenting pursuit of excellence and success to prove to itself and others that the affiliate was indeed doing its job unsurpassed by any. Yet as D. Wilfred Abse (1988) writes, "The very thought of having to justify one's existence is already expressive of a doubt about the right to be in the world" (p. 90).

The CEO of MCA said to me with exasperation a few years ago, "We do the job we're supposed to do, and we're punished, rather than rewarded, for our accomplishments. What do they want of us?" The simple, frightening, and intolerable answer, which could only be gestured rather than spoken aloud, was "disappearance." During this period, the central office did not act effectively to deny or disprove this growing conviction. Both the main office and MCA acted as if extinction was the central agenda, to which MCA responded (for the most part) by striving to demonstrate all the more its quality, if not indispensability. Yet MCA could not perceive and accept that even "doing better" could not prevent its dissolution.

Ironically, MCA's local and regional success was good for one thing for the home office: It was the most profitable unit in the entire corporation. At least the CEO of the corporation needed MCA for their money—which was not altogether theirs.

Throughout the latter years of my consultation, a recurrent phrase used at MCA was the frontier image of "circling the [Conestoga] wagons," a turning inward to protect the internal integrity of the organization. Members, feeling as if their existence was under prolonged siege, wondered how long the encircled wagons could survive the onslaught. Moreover, the anger, resentment, rage, and sense of chaos they felt dared not be directed externally—to the main office or to vendors in the local community upon which they also depended. Instead, members redirected these sentiments internally in the form of organizational infighting, schisms among sectors of the organization (caregiving, laboratory, business-administrative, public relations–marketing), increased incidence of MCA personnel illness and accidents, and widespread demoralization.

In the late 1980s, I noticed from seminars and workshops and from individual supervision of trainees and consultation with managers that employees were much less interested in and capable of devoting sustained attention to problem patients or problem families or to the community they supposedly served. During ordinary clinical seminars and workshops and in informal hallway conversations, I began to notice—or to think I was noticing—the emergence of new patterns. Using such techniques as participant observation, open-ended interviews, and naturalistic observation, I conducted fieldwork while doing my job. I began to keep detailed notes to document and make sense of the pattern I thought I was discerning and to provide additional observational data to test and revise earlier impressions.

I gradually concluded, and corroborated from work throughout MCA, that preoccupation with apprehension of doom and with "survival" made all but the most routine clinical and educational activities lower priority than in previous years. This took place with some of the same managers and staff that had once been ardently devoted to psychosocial and community issues. From cues such as demoralization, greater infighting, and diminished empathy toward patients, I began to pay greater attention to and inquire into (both in the subsidiaries and in the home office) the reality of the threat and fantasies associated with this growing sense of fatalism.

Ironically, in this corporation's nearly two-decade history, MCA had been consistently regarded by the home office and by other admiring and envious subsidiaries as the "flagship" of the institution. MCA was envied as the most consistently productive, successful, and enjoyable work site within the corporate system. Since MCA's inception in the late 1970s, its virtue had been its vice. Envy-based disparagement by other components of the organization had eaten away at MCA. Its successes had become the home office's and other branches' failures. Everything that MCA did well "made" the others look bad. Thus, in order to make themselves feel good about themselves, they had do devalue MCA. At one home office executive meeting at which manager recruitment was discussed, an executive told the following story about how he thought MCA succeeded in its recruitment: "They send one of their cute secretaries to take him [a management candidate] to a drive-in and give him a good time [the implication being that of sexual favors]. That's why they get them and we sometimes lose out."

It is unlikely that there had ever been an official written edict or explicit decision by headquarters to close MCA. Rather, members of MCA, and myself as well, inferred and frequently reconfirmed this conclusion through the home office upper management's acts of omission and commission; through its euphemisms, metaphors, and other turns of speech; and through its acts of mystification. Not-so-benign neglect long characterized much of the home office's practice toward MCA. In 1989, the headquarters published a lavish, multicolor, glossy brochure describing and marketing all facets of the company. The brochure "accidentally" omitted any mention of the MCA subsidiary, even though at a managers' meeting I had urged planners to include MCA in the public relations brochure. The two most common responses I received from executives and managers at headquarters was "We didn't have room" and "We forgot."

Furthermore, at corporation-wide workshops and managers' meetings (at which I was usually the only quasi-MCA spokesperson present), I often reminded the group of MCA's existence when input from, or strategic planning for, the entire corporate "family" (as many members called it) had been the ostensible agenda. Several midlevel managers and junior executives approached me after meetings and said, some with chagrin and embarrassment, "You know, it's easy to forget that MCA even exists, they're so far away, and you never see any of them down here." Forgetting was frequently tantamount to the wish that MCA would disappear. Action at corporate headquarters often seemed commensurate with the conclusion that this wish had been activated.

Consultant Roles

In my roles both at the home office and the subsidiaries, I strived to serve as an advocate for psychosocially informed medical training and medical care and for group morale founded on reality acceptance and on a concern and respect for one another's welfare. I attempted to help members of the subsidiary acknowledge perceptions and feelings they were dreading, while at the same time I attempted informally to document to the corporate executives at headquarters the consequences of actions and policies they would not openly acknowledge. My written documentation and privately spoken expressions of concern to executives at the home office were characteristically met with reassurances that their flagship affiliate continued to have their unwavering support—or with discounting, incredulous smiles. Nevertheless, I staunchly urged executives from the home office and MCA to make more frequent contact through visits, telephone calls, or letters. In sum, my advocacy was less for one "side" than it was for greater reality testing and emotional inclusiveness on the part of both.

My unstated function at MCA became increasingly *to listen to their storytelling*, and insofar as it was possible for me to do so, to compare members' stories with realities or official stories available to me from the home office, to help members listen to each other with less condemnation and greater attentiveness and compassion, and through these to help empower them to do whatever problem solving and decision-making were within their compass. In my rescue fantasy, I had once wished to be able to "sound the alarm" or "blow the whistle" at the main office. However, neither alarm nor whistle was audible at top levels of the organization and even outside of it. The fate of MCA, and of its members' mental and physical health, thus rested entirely upon the members themselves. Our individual and group discussions gradually helped diminish their need for projection, which decreased infighting and increased group morale and productivity. These discussions helped them mobilize the courage to look at reality as directly as they could bear. Labeling me "the listener" and then identifying with this function, they partly began to listen to each other.

In 1990, various MCA members stopped me in the hallways and began to tell me about serious or terminal illnesses or deaths in their families. Although during my 17 years at MCA I had consulted and counseled many MCA members on a wide range of professional and personal subjects, never before had there been such a groundswell of thoughts on death. Our conversations often drifted onto the fate of MCA, suggesting to me that real as these family events were, they also served as displacements for the dread of MCA's organizational dissolution (cf. Yalom, 1970, p. 115) and loss of friendship networks and MCA identity.

Subsequent History

The dispirited leader of MCA did his best to rally from time to time. He always vocalized mottoes such as "Onward and Upward," "Steadfast and Determined," "Bowed but Unbroken," and "We'll Make It." However, his actions—passivity, lack of follow-through regarding the home office's promised policy change, together with his increasing absences and emotional unavailability—expressed the opposite. Junior executives, managers, physicians, and medical and administrative staff of MCA frequently told me that they thought their leader was depressed and that they had to assume increasingly large numbers of his decision-making functions, which he had passively ceded to them.

In the form of demoralized leadership and group morale, the enemy was now as much within as without. Over a period of several years, during which the head of MCA had clearly and repeatedly announced his wish to retire and leave MCA in good hands, both the home office and local MCA junior executives did virtually nothing to secure a replacement and continuity of leadership. This made MCA a further captive of its collective sense of imminent calamity. I spoke on several occasions with senior executives of the home office, and I even wrote letters and memoranda to them as a subtle form of pressure (documentation), urging the central organization to assist in the transition, to make more frequent contact with MCA leadership, and to show a greater interest in the affiliate's future.

Yet even when home office executives made a site visit and created a momentary stir of enthusiasm and hope, MCA leaders could rarely sustain enthusiasm for saving the organization. They immediately mistrusted the sincerity and follow through of their visitors and fell back on the nostrum (and metaphor) that the "handwriting [had been] on the wall" long ago. Feeling tired, burned out, helpless, and hopeless after having led his organization for a decade through almost eight successive years of corporate economic and political tumult, the CEO of MCA now disbelieved that the home office could or would provide any help to turn things around. Taking little initiative and giving fewer pep talks to his workers than he had once done, his refrain now became "Too little, too late." While not verbally giving up on MCA, and still wanting to have a successor take over "a ship in full sail," he hastened the very fate he feared by his actions and inactions. "If they really mean business, they should come up here and talk with us. You know the old saying, 'Don't tell me; show me.' I'm waiting for them to show me their intentions." He felt overwhelmingly discounted and disillusioned. His increasing passivity, dispiritedness, and fatalism unwittingly played precisely into the hands of those executives at the home office who had been passive aggressively undermining all of MCA's functions.

At all levels of the organization, day-to-day work continued perfunctorily. Partly through identification with the depressed leader, many, if not most, members of MCA gave up on themselves as an organization. They gave up a sense of we-ness because preserving it, if not reconstructing it, was too painful. If the demise of MCA became a fulfillment of the tacit wishes of the home office, it would be for many MCA managers, trainees, and staff a partly self-fulfilling prophecy, one in which they had unwittingly colluded.

Over time the group became more resilient and rallying than regressed. Increasingly MCA members expressed to one another (as well as to me) their feelings about living with a foreshortened sense of time. These episodes of rallying attested to genuine creativity and even intimacy rather than to a "manic denial" of reality through frenetic activity. What could not be changed at least could be openly acknowledged. The taboo that had kept the dread shrouded in secrecy had been lifted. MCA managers, trainees, and staff began to talk openly about group death, about the possible limits to, if not futility of, their still-valiant efforts. They allowed themselves to be openly sad.

The inability to plan for longer than a several-month stretch, the style of short-term, rather than long-term, planning, became more openly accepted. The idea that MCA could dissolve within six months or a year was still profoundly distressing to all its members. However, they now showed greater resolve and commitment to "give it their all" for as much time as remained. Genuine sadness—rather than frantic efforts to seal over the unspeakable dread—began to show. There was a sense among MCA employees that they had somehow managed to take at least part of their fate into their own hands while also facing their common situation more realistically.

Countertransference Issues in Consulting with MCA

My years of work with MCA, its home office, and its other affiliates were emotionally wrenching and illuminating. They coincided with the protracted terminal illness of my mother, who died during the early days of MCA's difficulties. I would often blur the image of my dying or deceased mother with MCA. A fervent wish to rescue, if not revive, MCA alternated with the uncomfortable, although no less potent, wish for MCA to die and the agony be over once and for all. In the spirit of the Great Plains, I often wished I could get a gun and just shoot MCA! Then I would feel guilty for so terrible a thought. I learned more than I bargained for about how to ward off grief and how difficult it was to grieve. For in order to grieve, I had to accept the reality of loss.

Much of MCA's history in the 1980s rekindled my memory of my mother's chronic depression and numerous suicide attempts during my childhood and adolescent years. Dread of loss and abandonment vacillated with the horrible wish that MCA succeed in its self-destruction by "complying" with the delegated role assigned by the home office. With respect both to my mother's last years and to the latest period in MCA, I had difficulty knowing whether I should commence mourning for a beloved "object" or rally myself to hope and action (feelings shared by many families for a chronically ill or long-dying member). At times I felt myself holding on for dear life; at other times I found myself letting go in various ways—indifference, sarcasm, avoidance, sadness.

Unconscious family and ethnic issues all blurred for me into my experience of MCA. This sometimes helped me feel to an almost intolerable degree what MCA was going through, and sometimes interfered with this assessment. I realize now that I felt as if I was symbolically living out Jewish history in the European Holocaust of World War II. It was as if my people were in danger of being wiped out again. I had identified MCA, mostly unconsciously, as those many Jewish relatives who had perished and as the entire Jewish people, whose existence was threatened. The home office had come to represent for me the loathsome Nazi persecutors. Perhaps—only now can I exhume my driving fantasy—I could avert and prevent my family and ethnic tragedy, this time through defending MCA. Magically, I could help the Holocaust to un-happen.

The wager was that maybe I could revive the dead through MCA. If I could not literally revive the dead, then I might magically prevent death from happening again (which, alas, I had not been able to do with MCA's "sister" subsidiary company, which had been dissolved several years earlier). One of my abiding family roles, missions, was to be a redeemer of Jews, a person launched into the world to save the Jewish people from ever suffering their harrowing history again. Clearly, I was in danger of blurring past and present, fantasy and reality. At the same time, lifelong familiarity with catastrophic feelings and fantasies allowed, if not prepared, me to withstand and absorb the terrible feelings that members of MCA were having and to be of some help to them.

Although throughout the MCA ordeal, I knew intellectually that I was alive, I often felt as if I was being asked to die or was momentarily numb and dead. Furthermore, in the drama of MCA and corporate headquarters, it was easy for me to projectively identify the beleaguered satellite company as a victimized mother and headquarters as a bad, abusive father who sexually possessed, yet rejected my beloved mother. A wide gamut of my own pre-Oedipal, Oedipal, and ethnic issues was clearly condensed in this vocational drama. I came to realize that my noble mission of saving MCA and reconciling it with corporate headquarters, thereby preserving both, was at least partly driven by a sinister internal threat: "If I can't make it work, I'm not only bad but also abandoned and dead."

To these issues must be added my often ambiguous role in MCA, the home office, and its other corporate affiliates. The structural, divisional splits between headquarters and satellites, together with the divided loyalties they induced in me, corresponded to and rekindled a host of still-haunting inner divides from my early years. Among these was a split between the household in which I was reared, consisting of my father, my mother, and myself, and my maternal grand-father's household, which was located in and reigned from the apartment across the hallway. In family conflicts between my parents, and between my father and grandfather, I was constantly pulled to be an ally of (if not a spy for) one and an enemy of the other.

Other splits included one between my family ghetto of the apartment building and the remainder of the world, and one between the mostly Gentile world of the small Pennsylvania town in which I lived and the Jewish world of the syna-gogue in Pittsburgh, 20 miles away, in which I received my Hebrew education. To achieve even a crumb of personal cohesion and to fend off perpetual fears of annihilation and abandonment, I took on the role of mediator and mender, healer of splits. In my family of origin and in this subsequent work setting, I was "in the middle."

In my work with MCA and (to a lesser extent because of narrower role defini-tion) the home office, I attempted not only to stay aware of these powerful emo-tional currents, but also to use my emotional reactions as a diagnostic tool and as a key to how and when to intervene. I did not assume that all personnel—many of German, English, Irish Catholic, and Protestant ancestries—had childhoods, families of origin, religions, and assumptive worlds identical with my own. How-ever, I quickly found that although our idiosyncratic experiences differed widely, many core unconscious issues and their defenses were remarkably similar (Stein, 1987e).

I could thus—and this is the whole point of introducing countertransference into this long story—*use* my own developmental experiences and those reawak-ened inner "presences" still alive from the past, to help members of MCA tol-erate, and to a degree accept and work through, materials in their (as in my) persecutory anxiety, the feeling of falling to bits evoked by the chronic, menacing circumstances of their workplace. In short, I sought to place those regressions of mine that were genuinely therapeutic at the service of MCA's grief work, reality acceptance, group morale, and task productivity.

Organizational Adaptation

The organizational effects of adaptation to a sense of doom in the preceding story were numerous, pervasive, and indelible:

1. Increased infighting and factionalism
2. Increased discrepancy between the group's self-expectation to perform at 100 percent efficiency and responsibility, and the group's inability to fulfill its expectations because of an absence of sufficient personnel and financial support
3. Episodes of group despondency, apprehension, self-blame, helplessness/hopelessness, resignation, and outrage
4. Rallying periods of resolve and hope through the infusion of "new blood" (new junior executives, successful marketing, annual new groups of medical managerial trainees)
5. Constant "patching things up," as with trowel and plaster, while feeling pulled apart and falling apart (continual negotiation with local and regional subcontractors and vendors for new corporate markets and community support to shore up what had been withheld and lost from the main office)
6. Sense of abandonment, conviction that MCA was the victim of an outside plot, and belief that annihilation was only a matter of time, that members' fate was out of their hands, that the main office had no place for MCA but was not saying so
7. Decrease of reality testing and further regression
8. Discreet search for outside jobs by apprehensive executives, managers, salespeople, and staff so as to "jump ship before it sinks"
9. Sense of impotence on the part of MCA leadership
10. Merger of feared destruction with group self-destructive behavior by members of MCA
11. Proliferation of and vulnerability to rumors about firings, resignations, and omens, together with a magical "watching for signs" in facial expressions and attitudes of MCA leaders and/or home office management personnel

Many widespread feelings of distress within the corporate main office—aimlessness, the CEO distant from the daily affairs of the members, lack of clear roles and expectations, demoralization resulting from unacknowledged members' contributions, fear of abandonment, and spasms of accountability for problems beyond any individual's control—were induced in the MCA affiliate office. Mechanisms of defense such as displacement, projection, projective identification, splitting, and isolation, which are familiar in individual psychology and family relations, can be used to regulate *organizational group* cohesiveness, identity, aggressive and sexual impulses, and status anxiety (De Vos, 1966). Families, corporations, whole societies, and international (-group) relations can be, at least in part, governed by an emotion- and fantasy-based division of labor (Stein, 1986). Roles can be based on the complementarity of inducing and embodying "bad," if not catastrophic, feelings, fantasies, and wishes (Devereux, 1980).

In the story under discussion, the sense of integrity and safety in the home office was purchased in part by depositing the parallel sense of disorganization and danger in MCA—in fact, by provoking feelings and realities of endangerment in MCA. Through MCA, the home office could divest itself of frightening, disorganizing feelings while "managing" them at a distance in a subsidiary that was simultaneously a part of itself yet apart from it (Stein, 1987a).

Furthermore, home office personnel experienced considerable ambiguity over their ideal professional identity—that is, regarding values of medical care giving and training versus profit-making and hierarchy-maintaining roles. MCA served as a container (Bion, 1963) in which to dump and house devalued aspects of the home office, attributes that were nevertheless still touted as its official ideals. Home office executives and managers continued to profess the continuity of physician–patient relationships, consumer-oriented medical practice, consumer-friendly medical products, and contextually based medical and business relationships rather than financially and technologically dictated corporate values (see Stein & Hill, 1988). Their actual practice was the opposite. I constantly struggled to believe what I was seeing, hearing, and feeling.

Over the years, the unconscious psychological foundation of MCA gradually shifted from what Bion (1959) calls the group's basic assumption (fantasy) of dependency to the group's basic assumption (fantasy) of fight/flight. Interestingly, Bion's third basic assumption, pairing (finding a magical redeemer), only intermittently and briefly appeared, as did the hope for new, young, permanent leadership. MCA culture lived mostly in the present, focusing on day-to-day operations and short-term planning. A more remote future was too dismal to imagine.

In short, my role (one among many) as story listener could not save their company, which depended on the whim of a distant executive. I could not protect them from the reality of their long-term situation. What I could do was, through deep listening, help people live under conditions they could not alter. I could *bear witness* to their tribulations, courage, and struggle for dignity. In doing so, I believe that I was able to help them feel less fragmented and confused, and more integrated; less disorganized and more whole.

For both them and me, it turned out to be good enough.

3. Use of the Self

Introduction

Of all five key concepts, the use of the self is the methodological key to unlocking a deep understanding of the other four. How various dimensions of the workplace affect the self of the observer, participant observer, and interviewer shape what he or she will understand about the group, its core metaphors, the relationship between leaders and employees, and the experience of change.

For instance, the researcher or consultant does not directly observe employees' (in part transferential) inner experience of a leader as an abusive or emotionally unavailable parent. Likewise, the researcher or consultant cannot directly know how much of organizational life can be understood and explained by key, recurrent metaphors (symbols) such as a leader's espoused "open door policy" that is its opposite, or explicit mission statements and strategic plans that supposedly point to the real world, but in fact mask a leader's underlying agenda of self-aggrandizement and exploitation of employees' dedication and good will. A researcher or consultant's daydreams, physical reactions (a tight gut, a headache, a twitch), fantasies, and emotions can go a long way to understanding how and why leaders and employees flee from the experience of loss and grief during and after a massive downsizing.

How do we know what we know? When we conduct organizational consultations and workshops, how do we know how to be of help—what words to use, when to say something, when to be silent? How do we even know that the terms *intervene* and *intervention* are appropriate? Is a consultation a *military* action? How do we know where a case begins and ends, when we are or ought to be starting to gather data? Our usual answer to such questions is to look more carefully outward, to do a more thorough environmental scanning, to gather more data from the people in the organization, from the procedures manual and brochures, from the use of space. In this methodological chapter, I offer several stories that illustrate how we understand others, and know how to answer these questions, *via ourselves*. Some of our most crucial organizational data, and data about when and how to respond, come from what we as consultants are feeling and fantasizing during the course of the consultation. Seemingly extraneous, personal thoughts and feelings, and body reactions are crucial, indispensable data induced by the process of consultation. To ignore or discount these is to omit, if not to repress, an entire level of knowledge about the organization, to seal off awareness from ourselves and our clients.

Whenever the biologist looks at a specimen under the microscope, whenever the astronomer looks toward some distant galaxy through the telescope, whenever the consultant gazes out upon an organization whose members he or she is trying to help solve some problem—in all such instances we tend to find ways to subtract the self of the observer. With our British-science-derived horror of subjectivism, our insistence on empirical, observable, touchable truth, we forget that it is the eye, and the life behind the eye, that peers into the microscope, the telescope, and the corporate organization. What we see is part of how we see, what we need to see, and what we dare not see. What we hear is part of how we hear, what we need to hear, and what we dare not hear. In the natural sciences no less than the social sciences, in the applied as well as the pure sciences, the self of the investigator is always a key part of the subject matter. Some of the most bitterly fought current debates over human history and astrophysical theories of the universe are conflicts between deeply personal theologies.

Empathy, Identification, and Listening Deeply

Two instruments of the self are key to understanding and helping others in organizations and beyond. Listening deeply is fueled by *empathy for* and *identification with* another person or group. Both consist of ways of emotionally turning toward others. In empathy we turn our concern and compassion toward another human being or group of people and their situation. Colloquially, we say we "walk in another's shoes," we "feel for" them. We reach with our selves beyond ourselves. *Empathy for* is a *movement toward*, not a static emotional condition.

In empathy (*em* = "in, into"; *pathos* = "compassion"; *Einfühlung* = "feel into," German) we project ourselves into another person or group in order to better understand and respond to them. We use our imagination to strive to experience their emotions as our own. We "extend ourselves" to them. In empathizing with others, we not only try to comprehend and experience what it is like to be them, to have their feelings, but we also have concern for their well-being as a distinctive, separate person or group. We extend boundaries, but do not dissolve them. The other person or group becomes, in a sense, more real to us as a result of empathy.

In listening deeply, identification complements empathy. In identification, at least momentarily, we take the other person or group into ourselves and our minds (more correctly, our representation of them), make a comparison between oneself and the other, find some resemblance of the other with our own inner and outer experience, and discover a common bond—and shared humanity. The movement of identification, paired with empathy, is two-fold: a taking in and reflection upon what we have taken in; and (2) a reaching out with empathy, compassion, and concern toward the other person or group. This second part is using what we have learned of our common ground to enhance our relationship with the other person or group.

With identification and empathy as our principal instruments, I am thus interested in what happens "methodologically" when we place the self of the observer at the center of "knowing" in a consultation rather than at the periphery. Our received and taught scientific wisdom is that we learn and help despite ourselves rather than through ourselves. I emphasize that both are true and that some of our most effective organizational interventions are based on our inner experiences as we listen and watch during our consultations.

In this chapter, I reverse the usual order of the foreground and background, or the usual subject and context. I focus on the role *my own feelings and fantasies* played in two extended stories toward the end of the chapter, the first complex story dealing with the closing of a corporation, the second long story dealing with the crisis created by a manager's angry public outburst.

First, I offer several brief stories. I emphasize that our very selves mediate the consulting process and that we are always a part of the field in which we conduct fieldwork. This chapter is thus a part of ongoing conversations about observer and consultant *countertransference* and the influence of the inner world upon the outer world in all human interaction (Devereux, 1967; Hunt, 1989; Boyer, 1989, 1993; Allcorn & Diamond, 1997; Duncan & Diamond, 2011).

The consultant's use of the self is most trustworthy as a diagnostic and problem-solving tool when the consultant can feel most able to *play* with the emotional responses that percolate to consciousness during a workshop or consultation. The spirit of playfulness, in contrast with compulsiveness and the quest for control (such as coming up with expertise, with the right answer, with the correct solution), helps the organization lower its shield because the consultant has first taken the risk to do so. The greater access the consultant can have to his or her own unconscious during a consultation, the greater access he or she can foster in the client organization. *When both can play, they are less compelled to repeat.*

Playfulness in Organizational Consultation

Let me explore this seemingly strange juxtaposition of organizational research or consultation and play. What does it look, sound, and feel like? Here, the work of pediatrician/psychoanalyst Donald Winnicott (1971) is central. Winnicott ([1954] 1958) proposed the psychological reality of a "transitional space" that mediated between the baby's earliest experience of psychological merger with the caretaking figure (often the mother) and reality. The baby creates a "transitional object" such as a blanket or soft teddy bear to serve as this intermediate object. If the caretaker is hostile or hateful toward the baby, this space will be felt—now and in the future—to be persecutory. If the caretaker is comforting, nurturing, and accepts the baby's rage and tantrums by not retaliating, this space will be felt to be open to much creative possibility. The caregiver literally holds the baby in a comforting, reassuring way, so that the baby's physical experiences of annihilation and death are averted. Winnicott called this the original "holding environment."

Translated into adult experiences, in listening deeply as organizational researcher or consultant, one creates with the client or group an atmosphere of safety and of *symbolically holding* and *containing* the client or group, resulting in an *emotionally safe transitional space* in which play with ideas and reflection on them can take place without anxiety. It is a creative, emergent space in which something new might happen without censure, shame, or punishment. Emotionally, the climate of play is opposite that of an oppressive, threatening, persecutory space, common to the menacing tone and behavior leaders set in countless workplaces, dominated by fear, if not terror, the need to be right, and the enforcement of rigid, party-line thinking.

In nurturing the spirit of serious play, the researcher or consultant helps participants to let their true, authentic selves come out from hiding behind the mask of a false, defensive, rigidly compliant self. Only when clients can be their true selves, feel alive and real, can they play, and spontaneously offer new, creative ideas, without fear of shaming or punishment. The spirit of play releases the spirit of discovery. One can discover and try on something new rather than feel compelled to cling to the old. Without having to be "right," one can learn from experience (Bion, 1962). Mistakes are acceptable, even necessary, stepping stones to learning something new. The researcher or consultant, and ultimately the leader, who nurtures a playful environment, unleashes boundless group spirit—and the accomplishment of workplace tasks.

Two Contrasting Brief Stories
Strategic Planning, Its Discontents, and Its Redemption

Consider two contrasting brief stories about common *strategic planning* meetings and retreats in organizations of all types and sizes. I have participated in many. In the *first* story (or conglomeration of many years of similar stories), group members anticipate the strategic planning sessions with apprehension. They dread that this will be a long, boring, even scary, empty ritual in which the leader will impose his ideas top-down about how the future of the organization is to be planned.

Although he or she says that this is an open forum and solicits ideas from the participants, most are afraid of saying anything counter to what they think the leader wants to hear. They know that their role is to sit still, listen, and approve the leader's roadmap for their organization. Their past experience of his or her harsh authoritarianism has taught them to keep quiet. They fear his or her ire, punishment, or even worse, being fired for daring to differ from the leader. As a result, the predictably uninspired meeting turns out to be uninspiring. If the leader listens to members' suggestions (if they dare), it is mostly perfunctory listening.

The human geography is a metaphor for the process. Invariably, the leader sits and presides at the head of the long, rectangular table, and other people sit on the sides of the table, or he or she sits in the midpoint of a large square of tables. Likewise, the leader often makes a PowerPoint presentation of his or her plans. It becomes obvious that PowerPoint slides are far more fixed than writing on a white board, blackboard, or flip chart.

The group members experience themselves as "yes men and women," who are there not to brainstorm, but to mirror and echo and ratify what the leader wants. Participants leave the several-day-long meeting feeling that they have wasted their time, but that since this was a "command performance," they were compelled to attend. When I have attended strategic planning meetings and retreat like this, I have felt afraid that something terrible might happen, and as if a heavy weight were on my shoulders. Through empathy and identification, I felt both "my own" feelings, and what it was like for other participants as well. I felt a huge sigh of relief when it was over—like a weight lifted from me.

Let me offer a *second* story that contrasts with this first strategic planning story (or conglomerate of stories over the years) in which group members' experience hostile, persecutory space by a leader who would not listen. Even though this alternate story certainly occurs, it occurs far less frequently than the one above. It is story about a departmental meeting in which participants feel free to offer ideas. The leader attentively listens and truly does want to hear what his or her group members think ought to happen. The leader fosters a climate of No-Fault Change, or No-Fault Brainstorming.

He or she has the qualities of what Seth Allcorn and I (2014) have called a "good enough leader" or GEL. For the GEL, making hard decisions and implementing them is an open, inclusive, transparent, collaborative, trusting, and respectful process, rather than a unilateral, top-down and not infrequently poorly informed process. *The GEL listens deeply to the people in the group because he or she cares about and values them as distinct human beings.* Because the GEL seeks others' perspectives, he or she does not self-isolate and is not "alone at the top." The GEL makes decisions *with* employees, not *despite* them.

For the GEL, there are no dark secrets, no "black boxes" to which only a few are privy. Everything is put "on top of the table." The GEL encourages storytelling and is a willing listener. He or she wants to know how employees experience their organization and its leadership. The GEL does not treat fellow executives, managers, and employees as *objects* through which to impose one's will, but as *experiencing subjects* with whom the leader collaborates.

If I may use Seth Allcorn's image of the process once again, the GEL is able to stand solidly in the rapid stream of organizational process—often chaotic—and let the stream flow around him or her without toppling the leader into personal disorganization (personal communication, 2015). Continuing the metaphor of *standing*, in many of the strategic planning sessions like this, the leader often stands in the middle of the space created by a large rectangle of tables, or alternately stands to the side with a flip chart, and writes down what group members are saying. When I am in strategic planning meetings like this, I feel safe, energized, inspired, invited to stretch my imagination. I feel that the leader is "one of us" rather than against us or above us.

The emotional atmosphere of the first story was heavy with fear. The emotional atmosphere of the second story was light with a feeling of safety and possibility. The first story was mostly one-way talking by the leader. The second story had an air of excited interaction. Finally, the first story had no room for imagination, only decree, while in the second story, imagination had free reign.

A Second Brief Story: The Little Man with the Blue Book, Learning to Play Again

This brings to mind a story of *how I relied upon my imagination, playfulness, and creativity*—my countertransference—to help solve a problem in a consultation where my client was and felt "stuck" when nothing that he tried was working (Stein, 2007). Decades ago I worked with an internal medicine resident (trainee) in a large city's training program. I was his behavioral science faculty member.

We both loved classical music and poetry, and we enjoyed visiting about them; he often consulted with me about patients with whom he was having difficulties. One day he approached me with the story of an entire category of patients: indigent patients for whom he had tried in vain to link up with services at the local Department of Human Services (DHS).

I sensed that he wanted to tell me his story, his experiences, and his frustrations, and then see if I had any ideas of doing it a different way. I *listened* to him intently. He said that he was exasperated that most of the time when he phoned DHS, or when one of his patients did so, because they ended up being shunted from one office to another, or put on interminable hold. Ultimately, they got nowhere, and were rarely connected with the service the doctor was trying in vain to get for them. They all tried doing the same thing over and again, and nothing worked. They felt afraid, intimidated—and still sick.

What could I do? How could I help? My mind wandered. I told him that I heard his consternation that he felt defeated over something that should have been simple. I also said that I had no magical solution, but instead invited him to think aloud with me. Maybe we could come up with something new together. I relied on my imagination, an instrument of my countertransference. I offered him my free associations, my imagination, and countertransference to his (transferential) request for help. We *played* with ideas.

My point of departure was that since nothing was working, he was clueless as to how to make things work in order to help his patients. He (or his patient) was at one end of the telephone line, and someone at DHS was at the other end, and he was most times frustrated. I *thought out loud* that I could "feel" his sense of paralysis and entrapment. I then tried on an idea. I said that *perhaps* if he went to DHS and spent, say, a week with them, conducting applied fieldwork, he would learn more about the organization, and would be a real person to other persons, and not merely an anonymous, and maybe threatening (since he was a doctor), voice at the end of a phone line. He would be a participant observer and an open-ended interviewer.

I reminded him that I was an applied anthropologist (which he knew), and suggested that, if the medicine residency program director and the DHS director approved, he might spend a week of his community medicine rotation doing *ethnographic fieldwork* (including participant observation and informal interviewing) at DHS. Fortunately, both the residency director and head of the local office of DHS agreed. During his week there, he spoke with many people, some of whom referred him to speak with yet other people. He asked questions about how things worked there, what it was like to work at DHS, how one went about getting information about how to get services for patients.

He was finally told about "*the little man who had the Blue Book*," a mysterious, rarely seen person, working in a little room somewhere, who was the absolute person of last resort, and who knew the rules-behind-the-rules, and who knew how to make things work. The trouble was, virtually no one on the outside of DHS knew of his existence, and among the functions of the many DHS people between him and the outside world was the function to protect him from them by serving as a barrier, and keep most people from getting to him. The doctor was actually able to visit with "the little man with the Blue Book" in the supervisor's small office. Instead of the man being a phantom of the doctor's imagination, he was now a real person. He learned that the famous blue book referred to a policies and procedures manual which the supervisor knew a lot about, and also how to use or get around the policies and procedures. It was the ultimate nearly mystical source of "how to get things done around here."

The doctor explained to him that he was an internal medicine trainee in a program in town, and was there to learn how DHS worked, and perhaps together to figure out a way that he could better help his patients get the services they needed. Could the official help him? Most specifically, the question was how people on the Outside could talk with the keeper of the Blue Book and find out how to proceed and solve their problem. Surprisingly to the doctor, everyone was friendly and brainstormed with him a way to solve this problem. They actually were willing to help, and acknowledged that theirs was a cumbersome system which they just didn't know how to fix and in which *they* felt stuck too—until the physician showed up for his fieldwork and got people to talk with one another who rarely spoke with each other.

As a result of his fieldwork, he left with an agreed-upon plan for patients who called: for the patients to say that they were patients at the internal medicine clinic and that they wished to speak with Mr. X, who had the Blue Book that specified how things were supposed to work. Soon not only was there a better outcome for the doctor and his patients, but there was also an unintended positive outcome for communication and morale among the DHS employees. Unwittingly, my medical colleague became an agent of culture change in the organization he had visited.

In the process he learned more about organizations than either of us had bargained for: First, it had been impossible to get things to work because it was impossible to get to the person who knew how things worked and was the guardian of that information. A second lesson: Through getting to know organizations by studying them from the inside, such as by ethnographic fieldwork, one can occasionally help change the organization at least a little.

Alas, although my vignette has a "happy ending" (problem resolution via the achievement of greater organizational functionality and improved patient care), most of the time such success is elusive, and bureaucracies remain bogged down with their sacred rituals of "red tape." In the story, part of what helped create the atmosphere for the successful outcome was that I took an interest in the doctor's predicament, *listened intently* both to him and to the reverberations in me of his struggle, and created an atmosphere in which creative play with ideas and options could emerge. We both were not trapped in and by the past.

I turn next to a story of a *longitudinal* consultation I had with an organization in which I came to notice that the subject of loss and grief reappeared every year at about the same time. My eerie sense of the uncanny "reappearance" of this issue in my clients triggered in me an inquiry into its significance, and the significance of repetition in the organization.

A Complex Story: The Anniversary Reaction

For seven years, I did consultation and managerial supervision at a southwestern community-based medical corporation, Community Medical Corporation (CMC), which eventually folded in June 1985. CMC was one of a half-dozen subsidiaries of a larger company. My official role was to teach, facilitate, and supervise midlevel manager trainees in the group. However, my unofficial but increasingly valued and time-consuming role became helping the entire "permanent" chain of command and staff of 25 go through two painful, protracted years of uncertainty as to whether CMC would continue, and eventually help them grieve over the loss of their local corporation. Following the closing of the company, five employees (office manager, executive secretary, computer specialist, nurse, medical transcriptionist) were transferred to the main corporate office. In the years following 1985, we discussed and worked through what I later came to experience as a recurring "anniversary reaction" to the painful loss of not only a job but also a way of life that had meaning for those who felt robbed of it.

Around May and June of each year, these colleagues and I found ourselves reminiscing about CMC, still agonizing about "why it had to fold." At first, we did not realize we were grieving for a lost "object"; for lost intimate—not coldly professional—relationships; and for the social cause of community-based medical training. Only after two or three years did we realize our subject was traumatic loss and difficulty saying good-bye to an era, not only to a job. While I was talking with the former business (administrative) manager of CMC five years after the organization folded, she said to me out of the blue:

> I don't think that we ever told you how much we appreciated your continuing to come out every two weeks and visit with us, even after everyone knew that we were closing at the end of June. We were all having lots of strange, uncomfortable feelings during those months, and you were interested in

what we were going through. It's not that you had any official information or could do anything about our situation—we were all in the dark for a year or two as to what our fate would be. But you stayed in there with us, down to the very end. I just wanted to tell you we're grateful.

Although she was sitting behind her large wooden desk and I was seated at a chair across from her, I felt I had just received a huge hug. I felt affirmed for the continuity of our personhood and for my commitment to a common struggle to preserve our humanity, one I had imperfectly tried to provide over those harrowingly uncertain final years. If I had (not having yet the words, the theory) tried to provide a holding environment to help the group through anticipatory mourning, I now felt deeply acknowledged, as if my own loss and grief were contained, held, and caringly returned by another person.

I had driven twice a month (for a while, once a week) to CMC, offering seminars, consultations, and supervision to the eight manager trainees. I also had rapport with medical and administrative staff, and wider medical community. I could scarcely see myself working exclusively with the "targeted learners" (to use educational jargon) and not more inclusively with the entire clinic, which was, after all, the educational environment for two years of the trainees' lives. Officially, I presented a behavioral science conference, seminar, or workshop for an hour to an hour and a half beginning around noon; "shadowed" clinical trainees with their patients in examining rooms (that is, observed as unobtrusively as possible the interactions and privately afterward commented briefly on physician-patient-family communication); consulted with residents on "difficult" patients; offered limited counseling/therapy to trainees, upper-level managers, and staff on personal/professional problems; and, in a quasi–public relations or networking capacity, helped integrate CMC with the larger community by inviting local speakers for conferences. Unofficially, I helped with organizational problems and morale (I had not called such activity by these terms until more recent years). It simply made sense from anthropological, ethnographic, group process, and psychoanalytic viewpoints to know the "whole culture" of the workplace.

It was upon such a foundation that I began to give even greater attention and sheer time to the personnel of CMC in 1984 and the first half of 1985. I say with hindsight that I was helping the organizational group to ventilate rage and sorrow (catharsis), give feelings and words to anxiety (organize feelings of fragmentation), deal with mounting uncertainty over CMC's future, prepare to relinquish an organizational identity, feel affirmed that no one was going crazy, and express confusion over knowing whether to "knuckle down" and get ready to "hold on" to the organization or start to "let go" and "distance" from it. In the morning, I would enter the multipurpose break room-kitchen-library and see several staff members with masklike faces sitting silently or talking in a hush, a scene so different from the animated, even loud din of earlier years. Instead of simply saying a perfunctory "hello" and walking through the group to the seminar room beyond it (where I would conduct the formal conference at noon), or instead of going directly to the hallway of exam rooms where physicians were likely to be, I would sit down with administrators and staff, take a cup of coffee, often say nothing, and listen.

People at CMC would try to maintain an optimistic, upbeat, business-as-usual demeanor. They acted as if, so many rumors to the contrary, the corporation would somehow make it through. At the same time, they would foreshorten their former long-term view and talk mostly about making it month to month, and, later, day to day, afraid to think too far in advance, afraid to invest themselves emotionally in a future from which they and their program might be absent. They filled the immense void of official information with abundant fantasy and suspiciousness. They learned apprehensively of their future mostly by rumor, sometimes via an article in the local daily newspaper.

Radically divergent views of the situation existed in the central office and in the community program. The vice-CEO of the home office tried to reassure the employees and listen to their concerns. Yet several staff members told me that he gave them a stern lecture on "toughing it out" and being loyal during hard times, and that he did not listen to their worries at all. Meager information from the home office and its most senior executives inflamed and intensified rumor, gossip, and suspiciousness among the program personnel. The CEO, vice-CEO, and other senior administrators of the main office emphasized to me over the final two years of CMC's existence that they did not want to impose unnecessary emotional burdens on the staff, managers, and trainees of the subsidiary corporation by telling them every detail of what was taking place. One administrator reminded me of the "no news is good news" aphorism. He later expressed exasperation to me that people in the program would be so "paranoid."

During all these behind-the-scenes demands and negotiations, physicians, staff, and trainees of the program felt confusion, abandonment, betrayal, rage, and frightening feelings of imminent annihilation. Many said to me repeatedly, in fact and in essence, "The administrators at the main office keep reassuring us, telling us that nothing is happening, but they're not telling us anything. If nothing was happening to us, why all the secrecy and silence?" They could only hear echoes of their worst fears and fantasies. Early on, when I had first sensed something was amiss and began sitting with them and listening to their concerns, I talked with them about "stress reduction" strategies popular in psychology and organizational consulting. I soon realized they benefited most not from special-ized tactics of stress reduction (such as tightening and relaxing all muscles, one part of the body at a time) but from the simple fact that I was willing to sit among them, listen attentively, care, occasionally interpret, and help them feel acknowl-edged rather than lectured at or reprimanded for not being loyal enough.

To the end, CMC personnel remained committed to their mission—to train clinicians and deliver medical services. Although the Great Plains economy had been reeling since 1982 from the low prices of oil, land, wheat, and cattle, and although many secretaries, laboratory personnel, medical assistants, transcrip-tionists, and midlevel administrators worried about what type of jobs they might have available in the future, they mostly referred to their program as far more than just a job. They talked about how much they enjoyed working with each other, about being part of a larger corporation they wished they could admire more (as they once had), about how they had the opportunity to serve their state at their job. They compared the status and wage of their present jobs with the supermarket cashier they feared they might have to become ("downward mobili-ty" only euphemistically captures the deflation in self-image that such demotion and devaluation entail).

Around June 1985, several physicians at CMC, including the former director, took me to a local restaurant for a farewell lunch. They thanked me for sticking with them to the end, for not bailing out, for not abandoning them. At the time, I could not have verbalized why I continued going there twice a month (beyond generalities such as the importance of continuity in human relationships and my caring as much for those who ran the program as for the trainees).

Only toward the end did it dawn on me that I was really helping them get through a chronic crisis, anticipate and grieve for the eventual loss of an identity, and deal with deep feelings of catastrophe while they continued to function with trainees, patients, and the larger community as if everything was impeccably in place. Not only did this profoundly affect them; it also affected me. I relished—even as I occasionally resented—my biweekly drive to the east through swaths of scrub oak, cottonwood, and gnarled maple; the change of seasons; the emotional closeness of rurality and its counterpoint to my urban drivenness; and the com-mitment of many employees to a mission I also considered important. None of us could ever conclusively know why the closing happened or whether it had to happen. I could only help them, and myself, make peace with a past we had been unable to avert or restore.

In late June 1991, six years after the closing of CMC, I asked its former medi-cal director whether he would be willing to let me interview him about the clos-ing of the corporation. CMC was still on both our minds, although now in the background. Current events in our present workplaces frequently resembled and rekindled the horrible feelings still not laid to rest. The talk, lasting an hour and a half, was therapeutic for both of us. Significantly for my physician-administrator colleague, as for many at CMC, it was far simpler to reconstruct external events and to remember symptoms (marital conflicts, physical sickness, increased use of double entendre humor) than to recall what those last years *felt* like. I told him that the former clinic manager had (as if a kind of grace out of nowhere) generously expressed appreciation for my having continued to come to CMC all those additional months. I asked him to tell me what he and they thought I had done that had been so helpful. My contribution had not been an official act or anything that dramatically fixed the situation. Yet that "something" felt real for both of us, for all of us. Today I label that "something" a holding environment and container that allowed the hidden grief to surface.

> You were the *communication* with the home office. You were a *contact, a physical presence* of the home corporation, a *continuity*. You were here since the start of the subsidiary corporation through the end. You provided that *contact*, that *support*. It was kind of like *brick and mortar*. [He laughed.] If they started taking away the building, that would be bad. They [the executives at the home office] took the midlevel managers away. Equipment was starting to be taken away. The junior managers made off with some of it. Things were getting packed up. Patients were leaving our corporation. They were being notified that we were going to close the clinic. There was a front-page article in the town newspaper that we were leaving. Patients who came to us were upset. They knew the medical community of our city had run us out of town.

I asked him what feelings he recalled having or recalled that others in the company had: "Abandonment, loss, grief. You know, I'm having a hard time remembering specific day-to-day feelings. I liked being in the clinic. Maybe it's amnesia. But I *liked* being *inside* the clinic. I liked seeing patients. It's enjoyable. I liked the people I worked with. To me it was fun. When I got into the hospital it was a bit more tense." During this long interview I first became aware of the sequence of events at CMC. For my physician friend, I sensed that his retrospectively constructed chronology was a working through via memory and emotion, and not a strictly cognitive exercise. The loss of the clinic was the loss of *close relationships*, of *meaningful work*, and of *psychological as well as physical boundaries that contained the people and their work*. During the protracted time of great uncertainty and anxiety, members of CMC and I had something of a shared surface that held them together amid the threat of dissolution, and of being torn apart, exposed.

Around the middle of 1984, the CEO of the home office demanded that the local medical community dedicate significant financial resources for the training and support of managers at CMC. Shortly thereafter, in July 1984, the larger of the two community medical corporations voted to withdraw support from CMC. The smaller followed suit in October 1984. In that month, the upper-level medical and administrative managerial trainees at CMC were transferred to the home office to complete their clinical and managerial apprenticeships and receive further corporate training. In late 1984, the CEO of CMC was removed and demoted to a midlevel manager. The local county medical society voted in January 1985 to discontinue support for the organization. CMC closed in July 1985.

Most members of CMC had little inkling of these dates or markers. They knew only how they felt living and working in the wake of these events. To use a different metaphor, they lived in a world of shadow but had little idea of what cast the shadow and no knowledge of how to find out. When CMC closed, many executives, physicians, and staff felt that the CEO of the home office had been unsupportive, uncommunicative (for example, he often did not return telephone calls), equivocal in decisions, unavailable, and unwilling to provide any guidance about how to navigate these troubled medical-political waters. The CEO of CMC, a person who preferred to avoid direct confrontation, was often blamed and ridiculed by people at the main office for being a "poor leader," "a poor communicator," "ineffective," "unable to make the hard decisions." At the same time, these supposedly fixed "personality" traits were intensified by others' failure to inform him about the circumstances of his organization. Even if CMC had not been consciously targeted for destruction by the main office, CMC members nonetheless felt unwelcomed, abandoned, and discounted.

Interestingly, while writing this chapter I exhumed from my seven years of notes the preparation for a conference I gave one year before CMC closed. For several months, I had felt increasingly frustrated at my underutilization by trainees and managers at CMC. In contrast to earlier months and years, they no longer brought medical cases to me for consultation or for seminars. Nor did they now involve me in seeing their patients with them (such as for feedback on physician–patient relationships). I sensed they did not want to deal with anything "psychological," "familial," or "cultural," only with strictly medical issues. I felt more than neglected for my skills and interests. I often felt strangely, even uncannily, useless and unwanted. I sensed something was amiss: Although my behavioral science conferences and supervision could always be improved upon, they were not that bad! I felt that I was the focus of something else that I could not name. In my notes for June 11, 1984, I wrote, "The feeling of being unwanted, abandoned, is one of the most painful. In feeling your rejection, I wonder: Are you also feeling rejection, abandonment, a sense of being unwanted? If I am more the *focus* than the sole *cause*, then perhaps your helpless feeling at CMC might help explain your reaction to me as target."

I remember no resounding affirmation of my speculative interpretation at the conference. Many managers and staff members sought to reassure me that I was wanted, that my presence was welcomed and appreciated. They acknowledged feeling considerable "stress" about the uncertainty of their organization's (and their personal) future, but they apparently ignored the deeper chasm of emotion I had felt within myself. I say apparently because over subsequent weeks, months, and, with several people, years, they repeatedly referred and returned to these same images and feelings that had been consciously less accessible to them, more fended off when I had first made my early interpretation. My own feelings, induced by experiences at CMC, constituted crucial data about CMC.

This case was my first occupational "teacher" as reluctant consultant in organizational change, loss, and grief. Its on-the-job training by fire attuned me to issues of anticipatory grief, grief over actual loss, and the inability to mourn. It further taught me to trust those often catastrophic feelings and fantasies evoked in me as I consult. They serve as valuable, if seemingly ineffable, measures of "something" an organization is going through that its members cannot yet put into feelings, let alone express in words.

This case also taught me not to ignore my own developmental, emotional tasks, for they are inseparable from my "work" as a consultant. If this 12-year-long story has enabled me to help people at CMC truly say good-bye, it has also helped me do likewise.

I turn now to a second elaborate story about repetition in an organizational setting, one which came about through what started out as a straightforward discussion of a *medical case* with a physician trainee at a medical conference. As the story unfolded, I had the strange sense I had some unstated unconscious meaning for this physician, and the process of unearthing that significance played a decisive role in addressing the "case." It is a story in which the use of my self was at times the only thing I had to help make sense of what was unfolding.

An Elaborate Story: Enuresis and Its Organizational Reverberations

On the surface, this story is about a child's bed-wetting (enuresis). But beneath the surface, this story is about what enuresis represents, about enuresis as a personal, family, and organizational symbol—metaphor. The account goes far beyond biomedicine into the emotional life of an organization and that of a physician who angrily brought up the topic at a clinical conference.

All workplaces have often recurrent, stylized symptoms that in one way or another express discontent: alcoholism, drug use, chemical dependency, absenteeism, accidents, identical physical complaints by the workforce, large-scale resignations, to name but a few. To understand and attempt only to fix them concretely and literally (to take the symptom as the entire issue) is to miss the depth and breadth of meaning and feeling they possess. Organizational crisis occurs when one such symptom (or several) surprises and overwhelms the calm routine. At issue for organizational consultation, as for clinical teaching and practice, is whether we can tolerate our own anxiety, ambiguity, and uncertainty long enough to inquire into the larger picture—as mentioned previously, what poet John Keats called "negative capability" ([1817] 1974, p. 705; see also French & Simpson, 1999; French, 2001). Can we approach a problem or task with the attitude of not knowing what we need to know? If we can, we stand the chance of surprise, astonishment, of learning something we could not previously imagine.

In businesses, industrial plants, government agencies, and hospitals, extreme situations often make us painfully aware of what we would not really care to have known in the first place. The crisis itself is the lightning flash that defines, if only momentarily, what has all along been hidden in business-as-usual. It is a catalyst, not the cause, of change. It often also requires the reflective presence of another person—therapist, organizational consultant, or even friend—to help us know what we are trying hard to fend off. This story illustrates that how a crisis is resolved depends in large measure on the nature of the group's leadership; its members' style of response as a group, including the availability or absence of group members who are willing to help the group understand the meaning of the crisis; the timing of the crisis; and the often volcanic eruption of feelings in its wake. In the story, I served both as outsider (participant observer) of an organizational group and as insider (trainer, facilitator, consultant) (Duncan & Diamond, 2011). I did not consciously set out to listen deeply. Rather, as the story unfolded, it taught me who and what I needed to be in order to be of help.

The Explosion

In the mid-1980s, I was a participant in a medical clinic's weekly morning meeting at which the list of hospitalized patients was reviewed, with special attention given to diagnosis, laboratory tests, treatment plans, and cost. The conference was attended by primary care faculty physicians, residents, behavioral scientists, and other medical personnel. After the last patient had been presented and discussed, the senior physician leading the conference asked matter-of-factly, "Is there anything else?"

In a tirade of castigation, Dr. Don Bradley, a resident physician, exploded. He expressed dissatisfaction with the program curriculum. He complained that there was too much emphasis on geriatrics, occupational medicine, and presentations from local community organizations. He demanded to know why he had not received a lecture on enuresis/encopresis in children and on other topics specifically suited to preparation for residency training exams. His rancorous complaints were filled with accusations against individuals and against the entire organization. I felt personally attacked.

Taken aback by the barrage, I haltingly and initially sternly responded that I had made sure there were a number of volumes, encyclopedias, and journals in the clinic library to cover topics such as enuresis. I made a mental note to myself about my defensive sternness, and began to wonder what it was about. What unconscious personal drama was I playing in the physician's life to evoke such anger? It seemed misplaced, and felt as if some *parent* were yelling angrily at me, scolding me that I was a bad boy. Although I then promised to give the presentation on enuresis in the near future, I also reminded him that he, too, could research this topic as well through local hospital and university libraries and computer searches of medical literature, and that he was not as helpless and dependent on me as his grievances seemed to claim. Emotionally, I felt devastated, as though I had just been beaten up. I wondered what lay behind his rage.

I was also haunted by a long history of events such as this. Ten years earlier, I had arrived at one clinical teaching site only to learn from the program director and his administrator that the residents had staged a kind of *coup d'état* on the behavioral science curriculum that I coordinated (Stein, 1983a). Earlier that week, they had collectively approached the medical director and the administrative manager, complained about numerous components of my curriculum, and demanded that these "irrelevant" topics and seminars be immediately dropped. I arrived to find a fait accompli, which the medical director quietly and considerately explained to me. "What could I do?" he asked. "I hope you'll understand," he said apologetically, as if he had not made a choice but instead was entirely a victim of circumstance. "They felt that they really weren't getting what they needed out of those conferences, and besides, we both know that attendance was dropping. So we might as well try something else anyway," he reassured himself and me.

It felt like a rebellion, and I was the target. I felt not only sabotaged by the trainees but also undermined and discounted by the program leadership. What devastated me—and I still bristle at this 30-year-old memory—was that neither administration nor residents even considered including me in the discussion and decision-making. I felt that the curriculum was at least partly my own (it was published in 1985 and for many years was updated annually; see Stein & Grant, 1993); that I was a colleague of theirs, not a servant; and that I had already gone far out of my way to tailor a clinical curriculum to their program, community, and cultural needs.

I began to feel that nothing I did could be good enough; I began to doubt my own adequacy as a medical educator. I recall protesting meekly to the director about the way the decision had been made. The best he could say was that he understood how devastated I must feel and that they decidedly wanted me to continue coordinating their behavioral science program. Despite his conciliatory effort, I was filled with rage, depressed, and humiliated, as if I were a small child being unjustly accused of wrongdoing by a wrathful father. I sensed that some unconscious drama was being played out and that I had become woven into it as the villain. Some part of me was free to wonder what that was all about.

Now, 10 years later, I was in a similar situation, experiencing similar emotions. Later the conference chief told me privately that the resident, Dr. Bradley, was dissatisfied with his own performance on a recent written medical exam and was now blaming many people and the program for his failure. This senior physician then added that Dr. Bradley had actually fared well in comparison with national scores on the test but that he had fallen far short of his own expectations. Shortly thereafter, I photocopied several review articles and placed them upon his office chair.

From Victimhood to the Beginnings of Mastery

Four weeks later, I was surprised to find myself in a conference that Dr. Bradley had volunteered to lead on enuresis. After hospital rounds were over, he had come to me, saying he would like me to sit in on a conference he was about to give. He had said no more. I walked into the conference room where the residents were seated, and I sat down. He began by saying that he had been very upset about the omission of this particular topic from our conference schedule because he had just had a case that he could not fix. He said that he had read the material I had put in his office and found it useful. He alluded briefly to some *personal familial* issues on enuresis, but he quickly turned to the two medical cases he wanted to present.

The first case, from more than a month earlier, had been a five-year-old boy, son of a rich, local family. The boy had recently developed bed-wetting. Dr. Bradley did some laboratory tests and confidently announced to the parents that he had ruled out diabetes. He felt that he had performed his job in having assured the parents that their son did not "have anything serious." They left and did not return. He felt humiliated. He now realized that he had been scathingly critical of me and the behavioral science curriculum because he had not had the answers himself. He had rebuked me in order to avoid blaming himself and finding himself lacking.

Dr. Bradley then briefly described the second case of enuresis, which he interspersed with some autobiographical material. The second case was of a 12-year-old girl, daughter of a woman diagnosed as schizophrenic who had another infant girl. Dr. Bradley complained to the group that the clinic nurse had grabbed him before he had gone into the exam room and excitedly said to him, "She's schizophrenic!" Dr. Bradley said he wished she had not told him because no matter what he did or what the mother said, he would automatically think "Schiz," meaning "crazy" or "weird," "somebody you didn't know what to expect from." He said that neither mother nor daughter was well educated and that they pretty much expected him to tell them what to do (a doctor–patient style he in fact preferred).

Dr. Bradley then awkwardly interjected that part of what had so upset him about these cases was that there had been "some enuresis in my family." He stopped; there was dead silence in the room. He continued, saying, "My father was the accuser, and someone was the accused." Shortly afterward he added with embarrassment, 'Well, I was the accused." I immediately remembered that *I had felt accused* during his earlier devastating criticism of the medical behavioral science curriculum. He went on to say:

> My dad just flat didn't understand. He never abused or beat me. But he said I was lazy. No! That wasn't the problem. I just slept too deep. I still do, although I don't wet the bed. I was cured in four to five years. I'd have nocturia two times a night. I still have a small bladder capacity. During high school, I'd try holding it [urine] during the day to increase my bladder capacity. My dad was a football coach. He was a great dad, but he just didn't understand.

I commented that he and his dad were both "pissed off" about this (associating anger and the urination in bed) and that he wished he had been better understood when he was younger. Dr. Bradley downplayed the conflict and insisted that it was no big deal. He said, "My grandad gave me a salt pill every night and that cured me. One of my cousins was encopretic. We once lent him one of our sleeping bags, and he pooped all inside it. [group laughter] We never lent him a sleeping bag again." He went on to say that his father may have been enuretic when he was a child. I said that I thought it was courageous for him not only to make these connections about enuresis but also to discuss embarrassing subjects in the group.

Dr. Bradley continued with the second case:

> Mother and daughter were ready to put an end to enuresis. They had enough of it. I found out that the girl has a big glass of Gatorade every night at 10:00 or 11:00 p.m. before she goes to bed. Then she urinates in the bed during the night two or three times a week. I told the mother to wake up her

daughter, but [to give her] no punishment . . . I read about Tofranil in the resources that Dr. Stein had suggested. I put her on Tofranil [imipramine hydrochloride]. They're [the patients] easy to treat [on Tofranil]. Just tell them what to do. The question is what to do the *next time* they come? What if the bed-wetting hasn't stopped?

I urged that the first thing he do was not get angry and upset and not get in a battle over control with the mother and daughter. He emphasized that he had discussed with the mother issues of bladder training, no caffeine, sleep interruption. Several physicians then discussed whether the mother or an alarm clock should wake the daughter—the latter to enhance her sense of personal autonomy and responsibility. Group participants speculated about mother–daughter enmeshment (overinvolvement, maternal intrusiveness); the possible significance of the mother also having another, infant girl; or the possible sexual significance of the bed-wetting. Dr. Bradley said, "To be honest, I can't think like that. That kind of thinking makes no sense to me."

I encouraged him to approach the problem and the mother–daughter relationship as a detective rather than trying to have the answer before he next saw them. For instance, was there a pattern to the two or three nights per week? A certain hour? Recurring dreams? Was mom acting crazy at these times or sane? Was there anything to which the bed-wetting could be connected in the daughter's thinking or feeling or in outside events? Dr. Bradley responded, "I get excited about certain cases. I like cases that are fixable, *so you won't be a failure.*" He had only begun to connect emotion-laden, family-of-origin issues to his practice.

Over the ensuing weeks and months, Dr. Bradley and I continued talking about his enuretic cases. He scoffed at genograms (the construction of multigeneration family trees in which patterns of relationships are mapped out) (Pendagast & Sherman, 1977; McGoldrick & Gerson, 1985) as being too "touchy-feely" for him. Our discussions of his patients' families and his own family were informal, ad hoc, and brief. They rarely had the status of official or scheduled consultations. He kept coming back for more.

At first protesting that we had made far too much of his own family situation, he later said to me that his difficulty with the two cases "made me feel bad about myself the way I did back home, like I was visible to everybody, with nowhere to hide." I imagined that the second patient's mother's diagnosis of schizophrenia did not increase his self-confidence and that it harbored some unstated danger or menace and the prospect that he would lose control of both her and her daughter, not to say of some frightening facet of himself.

The Past in the Present

The two cases of enuresis occurred around the time Dr. Bradley received the results of his performance on the written examination. His response might be seen as at least partly understandable in terms of the "return of the repressed." That is, he felt unjustly accused and exposed by parent surrogates and by the parentified institution (reified, as if now the entire organization was sitting in judgment of him) that had let him down, if not betrayed him. He experienced me and others in the program as bad, judgmental authorities who symbolically had caught him again peeing in his bed, revealing him as a failure who had now *lost control* of his professional performance.

Interestingly, in his first year in the program, while he had acquired the reputation of being a superb biomedical diagnostician, the nurses and medical assistants feared him as a perfectionistic tyrant who would ridicule, if not self-righteously accuse, them when they failed to perform up to his exacting standards. In this recurrent scenario, he had "identified with the aggressor," his father; his medical assistants projectively embodied his vulnerable, imperfect child self. As the months went by after the "crisis," the nurses', medical assistants', and laboratory technicians' complaints about his imperiousness dwindled to nothing.

In organizations, blurring of actual individual differences commonly occurs through pressure to be team players, to achieve productivity goals, and to reach consensus around a common view of reality (especially of what company leaders represent). In the organizational upheaval I have just described, the angry physician likewise temporarily obliterated differences (the boundary) between his family past and his workplace present. He carried his internalized or introjected family conflict within him like a time bomb. When the right fit between current and early circumstances (trauma) occurred, he exploded in a shame-denying and shame-defying rage. Searles (1965) writes similarly that "one of my schizophrenic women patients once gave me to realize that, in the midst of a furious upbraiding of me, she was misidentifying herself as her mother, and me as the mother's son. She thus beautifully revealed her prior introjection [mental internalization and representation of a person or relationship] of the conflict between her mother and her brother" (pp. 324–325).

Dr. Bradley had projected onto me (our relationship, and, more broadly, his relationship with the organization) an intolerable emotion and self-image that he could not have recognized as a part of himself without conflict at that time (Searles, 1965, p. 331). My emotional reaction (countertransference) to his scathing attack (transference) was complementary to his. My reaction provided crucial information to me about how to respond—and how not to respond, as in defensively or offensively—to him. I had to separate my real self from the enemy target-image he had attacked, even as I personified and felt like that enemy. In turn, I quickly had to use my own emotions and fantasy to imagine in myself what the battle was about. What Searles writes—once again discussing his work with schizophrenic patients—of the therapist applies equally to the organizational consultant: "The therapist's capacity to endure such a barrage of fragmentation-fostering experiences, from both within and without, is essential in his helping the patient to become better integrated through identification with the therapist whose personal integration can survive this onslaught" (p. 343).

Caught off guard by Dr. Bradley's onslaught at the conclusion of hospital rounds, I tried to be crystal clear in the alternatives I offered him. I attempted to place considerable responsibility—and opportunity for mastery—in his hands, while avoiding a judgmental or condemning tone. Months later, he gratefully thanked me for not "hammering" him or berating him, for giving him the opportunity to prove himself. When he had first exploded, I certainly felt unjustly accused and enraged myself. I tried—insofar as I could at so volatile and vulnerable a moment—to imagine myself as a screen or target for his projections of unacceptable parts of himself and likewise to imagine feelings welling up in me "like" those of some earlier figure (later identified as his father) toward him. That is, he had induced in me a "complementary transference" (after Kernberg, 1965), so that I felt toward him the way he as a child had experienced his father acting toward him. Only as the months went by could I talk with him at this level and he not dismiss it with "I can't think that way."

Together, he and I and his program learned that diseases, problems, patients, families, teachers, administrators, and entire institutions can embody and play out early childhood dramas opaque to memory. The best supervision or advice I could give him about management of his patients was to help him acknowledge and unravel his own presence in their story. By not accusing him and instead by attempting to understand his "unjust" accusation of me and of the program, I helped him gain greater access to the story behind the official clinical or programmatic story. Through the empathic, respectful, inquisitive attitude I had toward him, he internalized my observing ego and took a more compassionate, less savagely cruel attitude toward himself. Gradually, he was able to be more self-critical without being self-accusing.

There is yet another layer of emotional sediment to this clinical and organizational story, namely, my own. *Why* does this matter? Simply put, we listen and respond to others' stories and lives *through our own*. Our subjectivity is Janus-faced: It can be both tool and impediment (Hunt, 1989; Duncan & Diamond, 2011). We not only bring our biographies to our current situations in some general sense, but we can also be triggered to repeat old feelings, if not deeds, by situations that most resemble emotion-laden early ones. This is true in clinical and teaching circumstances, in workplace organizations, in larger political and historical processes—in all we do and for all participants.

When new circumstances make us feel "raw" emotionally, exposed all over again, the question is whether we can recognize how the emotional character of the present event is shaped and intensified by our own life experience (transference). Then can we use our own emotional response to be of help in the present? If we cannot tolerate the feelings, fantasies, and meanings that are evoked in us, we will not be able to help others do likewise with what arises uninvited in them from the depths of their lives. We can use our own reaction as vital data not only about ourselves but also about others (as if we take a reading of others' emotional fever by placing the thermometer in our own mouths).

Here is where *my own story* enters the picture and becomes a part of the case. I had *identified* with him. When Dr. Bradley exploded, verbally evacuated all over the organizational group, and directed much of his ire at me and my curriculum, my feeling of being under attack reawakened some of my own family and Jewish ethnic experiences. Although I had not been a bed-wetter or soiler beyond my infancy, my father would often erupt furiously and unexpectedly. He was a stern, often emotionally aloof taskmaster, one whom I strove to please but whose ideals I could never achieve. Often he would verbally "chew me out" in a rigidly controlled manner. I would stand paralyzed at the kitchen table listening to his self-righteous lectures about my report card grades. It was years before I could begin to allow myself to reexperience the murderous rage and dire helplessness that I felt at those moments. Guilt and shame entwined to make me feel inadequate much of the time as well as bad for having violated some unknown rule.

How do I know that my emotional response to Dr. Bradley revealed something about him (and his past) rather than only about me (and my past)? When I can tap quickly into those feelings, wishes, fantasies (including disturbing ones, such as revenge, murder, abandonment), and memories from my own childhood and be able to move from my inner world to the world of the client or workshop, I can trust that I am using myself rather than being stuck in myself. My own life did not distort my perception and assessment of this immensely volatile and threatening situation because I could *then and there*, as I experienced his barrage, bring in my own mental associations with the past as a tool of understanding and interpreting the present.

It turns out that in all organizational research and consulting, listening deeply is sometimes an echo chamber. In turn, attending to one's own echoes might be a key to understanding what the other person is saying, meaning, and feeling, and, further, a key to how one might be of help. The self of the organizational researcher and consultant is a valuable instrument that needs to be constantly fine-tuned. If listening is one of the most important things we do—and not only in organizations—then the *self of the listener is one of the most important instruments of listening.*

4. Metaphors

Introduction

Some personal history seems appropriate here: It turns out that metaphor has been a central organizing theme throughout my over 45-year work life in many disciplines: from the evil eye among Slovak Americans, to the us/them split in Soviet-American relations during the long Cold War, to alcoholism and technology in American culture, to the symbolism of technology in the United States, to the doctor–patient relationship, and most recently to organizational downsizing and political-economic deregulation. I coauthored a book with Maurice Apprey called *From Metaphor to Meaning* (1987), and metaphor was the foundation of my work in psychogeography, that is, the projection of the experience of the human body and family into the experience of space and politics (1985b, 1987a).

Virtually anywhere, group metaphors are a "royal road" to group images, feelings, and behavior—including in workplaces. The question of "What is it like to work here?" is in large measure answered by the metaphors that pervade and organize the workplace, metaphors that leaders, managers, and employees "live by" (Lakoff & Johnson, 1980, 1999; Diamond, 2014). Far from being limited to "literary" subjects, they are everywhere. We just fail to realize it, mistaking the concrete for the symbolic. Metaphors are profound figures of speech in which one object, person, group, or place is compared, connected, and equated with another. "A" is the *same* as "B" (unlike with simile, where "A" is in some characteristics *like* "B."). The connection is not always simple, direct. The connection is often unconscious, and, as Lakoff and Johnson (1999) show, is ultimately rooted in the human body.

Richard Koenigsberg (1975) long ago wrote an exemplary book, *Hitler's Ideology*, in which he studied the metaphors Hitler used in his speeches and writings (for example, Jews as vermin, cancer, disease, and so on, that were infecting and killing the German body politic). For Koenigsberg, metaphors, like ideology, are driven by and articulate unconscious fantasies that derive from the human body (e.g., Germany as the mother from which her children are inseparable; the mother as suffering from a deadly disease; extermination of Jews as the prescribed treatment and cure; and extermination as therefore a public health program). Metaphors and ideology are therefore the medium through which the unconscious enters social reality (Koenigsberg, 2016).

Consider the *machine* and the *mechanical metaphor* as applied to human beings in workplaces since the Industrial Revolution. In many workplaces, people are thought of and treated as if they were machines, not experiencing subjects. Frederick Winslow Taylor's famous time-and-motion studies in the early twentieth century (1911) and Fritz Lang's grim 1927 film *Metropolis* long ago attested to the ubiquity of the man-the-machine image. *Efficiency*, once applied to machines in physics, is now casually applied as a prized attribute of workers. Consider, too, the widely used workplace phrase that "we are only a cog in a wheel." The philosophy of the popular Lean/Six Sigma training is congruent with this metaphor. People—workers—are not full-blooded, experiencing humans but are mere machine parts run by someone else (Stein & Hill, 1988)—"parts" that are to be made more "efficient." The mechanical metaphor enacts the fantasy of workers-as-things. Many leaders try to turn their organizations into a "lean, mean, fighting machine." Through the machine metaphor, sentient people become inanimate things.

Michael Diamond (2014) reveals that metaphor rests at the core of human thought, that its role in human groups of all kinds is far more profoundly textured than simply constituting a linguistic device of semblance that links signifier and signified. For Diamond, metaphors take us to the core of an organization's identity. Diamond distinguishes between frozen, rigid metaphors (of organizations and beyond) and fluid, creative, playful metaphors.

For instance, through the widespread spatial metaphor of the *organizational silo*, Diamond explores the experience of frozen metaphors in workplaces such as corporations (Diamond, Allcorn, & Stein, 2004; Diamond, Stein, & Allcorn, 2002). For many who live and work "inside" the silo, it is experienced as a highly limiting, constricting, rigid-surfaced space. (See below for expanded discussion of the silo metaphor of the workplace). As Diamond and Allcorn write (2003):

There is always the danger that bureaucratic, silo-like organizations might foster regression into more homogenized and conformist, authoritarian organizations (Diamond et al., 2002). Shared individual anxieties of group and organizational membership generate a vicious cycle of regressive and defensive responses that reinforce the schizoid dilemma. (p. 70)

For adherents of the frozen metaphor, the metaphor *must* be true, real, not symbolic; for those who use metaphor in a fluid, flexible manner, the metaphor *might* be true, and *might* be a useful, symbolic, contingent tool of understanding. Frozen metaphors straitjacket those who use them; people become prisoners of their own language. By contrast, fluid metaphors are evidence that play is at work. Dictators such as Hitler and Stalin applied frozen metaphors to categories of people they despised and killed. Today, totalitarian business executives apply frozen metaphors to categories of employees they degrade and fire.

Unlike tangible corporate artifacts such as coffee cups, posters, pens, strategic plan documents, mission statements, and retirement gold watches, metaphors that signify organizational identity (Diamond 1993, 2014) are often more elusive. Yet, if one knows where and how to look and listen, they can be easily identified. They can be about leadership names and epithets (e.g., "Neutron" Jack Welch of General Electric; "Chainsaw" Al Dunlap of Sunbeam) and/or the group, or about major change and the tension between loss and renewal (omnipresent *boxes* in downsizing). One can say that the meanings of organizational metaphors lie "beneath the surface" of culture (Stein, 2005).

For instance, in one corporation, the new CEO quickly recruited two senior executives who had just written and published a book (an organizational artifact) that he expected to set the standard for the company and to make it a leader in its industry. All employees and managers were required to buy and read the book, absorb it, and change their attitudes and behavior accordingly. Any deviation from this new doctrine was forbidden and punished if found out. Some employees embraced it uncritically; others mouthed it out of fear. The book quickly became known as "The Bible," a phrase that swept the company like a wild grass fire. It became "Gospel," to cite another biblical term used to describe the status of the book. Clearly this was the sacred corporate text which the CEO made clear was to be regarded as orthodox. No deviation would be tolerated. The term could be used by employees out of fierce loyalty, or sarcastically, but it was clearly a core metaphor that, as all its dimensions became clear, ideologically organized the company. It was a metaphor of power, authority, and control. Its use by corporate authority was intended to induce regression into childlike subservience.

Metaphor as Organizing Workplaces

Metaphor pervades and in part organizes workplace life. We often mistake the symbol for literal reality, as in intense nationalism where the country becomes equated with the flag and the flag embodies the country. However, through "listening with the third ear," as psychoanalyst Theodor Reik (1948) called listening through the unconscious, we can listen to the psychic reality of an individual or group. Consider the following ideas frequently encountered in organizations in the over four decades of downsizing: The company will survive only if we "get rid of dead meat," "get rid of organizational fat," "cut down to the muscle, even to the bone," "get rid of dead wood," to create a "lean, mean, fighting machine." Or, the company must "make great sacrifices" if it is to be saved and turned around.

Business competition is described and often experienced as an act of war, for which battle strategies are required in this "kill or be killed" competition for the "survival of the fittest" (neo–Social Darwinism). War metaphors often fuse with metaphors of oral aggression. "It's eat or be eaten. Where do you want our company to be on the food chain?"

Sports metaphors likewise abound in organizational life. The CEO is often characterized as the "quarterback" who "calls the shots," and expects managers and employees to be compliant "team players." The team wins by "scoring" against the competition.

Beneath the metaphoric business dogma of "rational man," "technocratic man," "objectivity," "profitability," "the bottom line," "total quality improvement," "Lean/Six Sigma Black Belt," "growth and development," and "mechanical efficiency" is a world inhabited and ruled by emotional neglect and abuse, callousness, psychological violence and brutality, remorselessness, waves of fear and psychological terror, and despair. In such a world many employees "keep a low profile" and "stay under the radar" to avoid being noticed—and punished. The trauma can be sudden or insidious—like a cascading waterfall or the incessant dripping of water on stone. Only by listening deeply to the language of the workplace, to how employees actually experience their workplaces, is it possible to elicit stories that portray a world far more sinister and frightening than official fictions and lies.

This chapter is thus about listening and looking for organizational metaphors, and about helping organizations become less oppressed by the power of these symbolic, linguistic, largely unconscious devices. Metaphors are crystallizations in recurrent words, phrases, mottoes, and artifacts of what it feels like and means to be a member of an organization and to work there. They convey how the place "makes sense" to the people there and how a group remembers its history. Metaphors encode a sense of place. Organizational metaphors mediate between, and condense, the seen and the unseen, the avowable and the unacknowledgeable/ undiscussable, reality and fantasy.

We usually take our metaphors for granted as rock solid, real, permanent. We place them beyond criticism because they are (projectively) "us"—even though we become "their" prisoners as well. We often picture our metaphors as existing outside of ourselves, as being real. After projecting them outward, we in turn take them back inside our minds so that they become a part of ourselves. To question them is heresy because without them, we feel we may disintegrate.

In this chapter, I build on the earlier introduction of metaphors and present several extended examples of organizational metaphors, their vicissitudes, and their relationship to space and time. From the outset, I wish to emphasize their ordinariness in workplaces. They are like the air we breathe, not unusual or extraordinary.

Some Brief Examples

Let me begin with several short examples. In one meeting, executives characterized their multinational energy company as a "fat cash cow" and as the "Nile River" when I asked them what image(s) came to mind to depict their organization. They lamented how lethargic, sluggish, often immobile they were in decision-making about petrochemical exploration and investment. All decisions had to be arrived at by consensus. No public appearance of conflict could occur at the highest levels. Endless smoothing out of rough edges had to prepare senior executives for their decisions so that peace could be maintained. The cash cow would become too fat, distended, and unwieldy, if not stopped dead, by its own fear of divisiveness and open aggression. The corporation was in reality a giant, multinational corporation, but many executives could barely feel it move.

A second example: Consider the notion of *the bottom line*. Since the early 1980s, many organizations have invoked the bottom line as an objective, fixed place on a budget printout sheet, as an economic fact, as a First Principle in explanation, much as God was used in medieval theology. Many people worship at the sacred shrine of the bottom line. No one dares dispute the finality, the truth, of the bottom line. It ends conversations. Yet even something so seemingly concrete and real as this notion embodies choices, values, priorities, and attitudes about what counts more and what counts less—what deserves our money and high technology, what merits our thoughts and feelings. Bottom lines are not objective facts but metaphors of choices we prefer to externalize rather than accept as our own. When an executive says, "Let me tell you the bottom line . . . ," he or she is declaring what is most important and saying that he or she will tolerate no deviation from it.

In a similar vein, at medical conferences since the 1980s I have heard many physicians describe the patients seen on a hospital service over the previous month in terms of "production reports" and speak of health care as offering "product lines." The discussion at these meetings covers the total number of people seen, types of medical diagnoses, deaths, procedures, and the like. Why is all this called a production report? A hospital is surely different from an automotive assembly line. But perhaps we are coming to view people as machines, as commodities. This is a metaphor of increasingly depersonalized medicine, what many in recent decades have described as the *industrialization of medicine* (Kormos, 1984). People become products and commodities, health care becomes production, particular methods and procedures become product lines, and so on.

Let me turn briefly from words and phrases to tangible things, objects, artifacts, as metaphors in workplaces. Something as seemingly only tangible and utilitarian as a coffeepot can embody deep symbolic organizational significance. Many years ago when I first came to work at one medical organization, I was not allowed to obtain a cup of coffee from any of the coffeepots in the several units where I worked. Although I worked for these various divisions and my paycheck was assembled from their various budgets, I was not allowed to take coffee; nor was there a "mechanism," as they called it, for me to give money (cash) for coffee on a regular basis to any one of the units. Secretaries and executives told me there was no way to enter this set of miscellaneous dollars on their printout.

The only way I could have coffee was for me to purchase my own coffeemaker! My sense of rejection and outsiderness informed me of boundaries between inside and outside. I quickly realized that something as ordinary as a coffeepot could serve as an organization metaphor for belonging and not belonging, for inside and outside, for boundaries. By knowing who had access to which coffeepots, I learned important facts about the culture I otherwise would not have been told.

As the coffeepot scenario illustrates, many metaphors are subtle, unofficial, and unannounced. Others, however, are given great fanfare. (At one airplane engine refurbishing plant where engines were baked in giant ovens named by employee vote, the entrance was heralded by a bright silver jet engine with the caption "Bertha's First Baby.") Quiet metaphors are rarely recognized for the symbolic crystallizations and distillations that they are. They come not only as words, phrases, and mottoes but also as artifacts and things. Occasionally, the group recognizes, interprets, and even transcends its own metaphors.

A Story: Lotion as Group Metaphor of Comforting

For instance, in 1993 I conducted an all-day workshop on hospital culture and identity for one state psychiatric hospital's nursing executives and staff. Outside, the temperature was 10 degrees Fahrenheit, and an average of 10 feet of snow lay on the ground. Inside, the 30 or so participants were talking about frequent, major changes in top management (hospital and statewide), an endless onslaught of budget and personnel cuts, increased responsibility for a growing number of chronically mentally ill patients in a vast region, and their commitment to care for people whom no one else wanted.

Early in the morning as we began, several participants rummaged through their purses and briefcases for hand lotion or Vaseline to lubricate their dry, broken skin. I had brought a large plastic bottle of hand lotion on this trip since outdoor cold and indoor central heating always leave my own hands dry, cracked, and bleeding. I offered the group the bottle of lotion and left it on the table, saying participants could use it as they needed. At the time I did not think of it as a symbol, although I wondered what its odyssey would be over the next nine hours.

Early in the afternoon as group members were talking especially candidly about their sense of chronic uncertainty, anxiety, and abandonment, they passed the lotion counterclockwise around the table, each person taking the lotion bottle, squeezing it, rubbing the lotion in, and passing the bottle on. As this was happening, we kept talking about our "subject" (change, rage, loss, responsibility, feelings of boundarylessness). Suddenly, several members in a row in the group burst into spontaneous laughter, looking at themselves and at one another, saying, "Look at us! We're all *comforting* ourselves and each other with your lotion. We must really be pretty stressed!" Later one executive characterized the passing around of the lotion as "communion"!

I did not need to interpret much about the hunger for nurturing, for a kindly touch, for a soft, soothing skin to bound them individually and collectively, during these stressful times. By the end of the nine-hour workshop, the lotion had made (to my count) at least three complete circuits. It was a metaphor for the organizational sense of deprivation, neediness, and longing to receive—and ability to receive—the beginning of succor from one another. Their skin could now absorb the nurturing from others. They could lower the protective armor that they had put up over the siege of change. The lotion was a thick metaphor that condensed many meanings and feelings.

Although the lotion was "mine," it quickly became adopted, incorporated as theirs, as ours. It was intersubjective, relational, a bond between us. It was part of the restoration of a sense of goodness among people haunted by their own sense of badness, inadequacy, and violability. It was a testament to our relationships and to their willingness to allow themselves to be touched symbolically. They used the lotion as a metaphor for the holding environment they were creating for themselves. It said far more than words could about deprivation and consolation. At the same time, they recognized in words, that lotion, in addition to being a skin softener, was also a group metaphor.

A Short Story: Black Holes in Organizations

Before I turn to more extended illustrations of listening and looking for metaphors, I offer one final brief story: the metaphor of "black holes" in an organization. Over the past four or so decades, the popular imagination has seized upon developments in astronomy and astrophysics around the concept of *black holes*. These are hypothesized, powerful, unseen forces from which no light can emerge and into which everything is sucked in, disappears, and is annihilated. Nothing can resist their deadly force. Black holes are ready symbols of personal and group catastrophe: annihilation, separation, dissolution of boundaries, boundless rage, ferocious aggression, and oral devouring, among others.

People in medical departments, hospitals, universities, and corporations all reeling from financial and employee cutbacks, downsizings, restructurings, leadership transitions, corporate mergers and acquisitions, and other massive changes, often describe their experience of this disruption and loss as harrowing, inescapable black holes over which they are powerless, helpless, and hopeless. Anxiety over separation and annihilation (violent death) are part of everyday life at work.

One university hospital department, for instance, lost 40 faculty members during the course of constant turnover and upheaval over a decade. One faculty physician said to me, with a protest in her voice:

> You never see people around here anymore. You see them once a month at faculty meetings. The rest of the time they disappear. Where do they go? Each one goes onto his or her own service, teaches his or her classes, and is never seen again. People disappear down a *black hole*. Gone! The same with faculty who leave. They announce they've taken a position somewhere else, are going in two or three months, and you never see their faces again. They're here three years, then, down the black hole. Maybe they're swept to another universe. Who knows? Just when you get used to them, the black hole sucks them out, and you never hear from them again. It's like there is some evil force around here that swoops down and sucks people out. This place is one big black hole.

We do not need to be committed Freudians to see and hear in her words the condensation of separation, anxiety, annihilation fears, violent devouring rage, horror at being swallowed alive, and other deeply disturbing, primitive feelings. In sum, then, organizational metaphors are treasure troves that take us to the heart of the experience of identity in a workplace (Diamond, 2014; Stein & Apprey, 1987). The consultant can use knowledge of this wealth to determine how to intervene. It is a matter of paying attention and listening for words, phrases, and images that are not necessarily part of some explicit, official agenda.

A Story: Space as Metaphor

Groups encode in metaphors who "we" perceive ourselves to be as an organization and how "we" experience trauma. Metaphors can be tools by which we plumb our environments more deeply, or they can be self-imposed prisons whose truth we in turn impose on all who enter our doors. Organizational metaphors take us beneath the genteel veneers to the undisclosed heart of organizational life. The study of metaphor in all organizations is a new frontier for consultation. It promises to help correct distortions that unexamined metaphors inevitably introduce into, and impose upon, their workplaces.

Knowledge of how organizational space is symbolized is of great use in consultations. Metaphors can often be found in any organization's use and relative valuing of *space*. At deeper levels of meaning and feeling, these areas express group psychogeography (Stein, 1987a; Stein and Niederland, 1989), areas that are mentally safe and areas that are emotionally hot and avoided. For instance, for countless decades on many hospital wards, patients who are dying are often relegated to rooms at the end of a long hall. They are put literally and metaphorically at the end of the line. Death is magically separated off from the central goal of patient care: healing and restoration to life. Many health professionals, as well as countless patients and visitors, do not wish to be reminded of the presence of death. With dying people put out of sight, and often out of mind, there is the sense that death cannot contaminate life.

In one medical setting, my office was located near the clinic conference room, administrative offices, and reception or waiting area. These were at the other end of the halls from examination rooms, laboratory, and nurses' station. Although I occasionally used my office (which I shared with a faculty physician) for resident supervision and counseling, most family medicine residents and faculty did not come to "my" area to talk about a patient or about personal problems. They talked much more comfortably and spontaneously—often publicly, around the nurses' station—on their own clinical turf instead of mine. Space served as a metaphor for emotional safety and control.

During one clinic visit, for example, a physician had just learned that his 60-year-old patient had been diagnosed with metastatic cancer. After ushering his patient out of the exam room, he came over to the nurses' station railing and visited quietly for nearly an hour with me. He traced, among other things, his considerable anxiety and sadness over his patient's fate to his new concern for his recently retired, albeit healthy, farmer-teacher father and to the reawakened memories of his horror and grief at his younger sister's drowning 20 years earlier.

During the two years I served as his teacher and supervisor, we never once talked *in my office*. Rather, all our meetings were unofficial and impromptu and conducted either in his office or quietly in the hallway around the nurses' station.

This way, for him, as for numerous other physicians, our discussions could not be construed by anyone as "therapy" or "counseling" (which are associated with "being crazy" and with my office). Instead, they could be called "just visiting," "BS-ing," or "consulting" (a legitimately medical activity). For him, space was a metaphor for safety with its many meanings. I took my cues from observing him—and practiced participant observation with an individual. I listened deeply to him on his own terms.

I turn now to yet another story in which space served as a workplace *group* metaphor.

A Story: The Front Versus the Back

At a family medicine clinic meeting, the recurrent, unpopular topic of Medicare rule changes was under discussion. Doctors and nurses wanted to treat patients, not drown in paperwork that not only took their time but also told them what they could or could not do clinically. Here are some excerpts from the meeting:

> I don't like their authoritarianism at these Medicare meetings. . . . I rebel against it. . . . Send the front end [business office] folks to the meetings to get the information for us, digest it for us. [Another physician:] I don't want to deal with this; just tell me what to do. . . . [Another physician:] Don't be confrontational with Medicare. They have a bigger hammer than I have; they've got the bigger penis! [group laughter] They have a bigger computer than we have, so they can spit out facts we don't even know are there. So if we fight em on their terms, we lose. . . . [A receptionist–business office staff member:] The physician should go and hear it [at Medicare] for himself. [The business office manager:] Do you think we could *tell* the docs what Medicare tells us? They'll kill us!"

Here I ventured an observation and interpretation, stimulated by my long history with the organization, and my unconscious, even physical, response to the meeting. Through my own sense of agitation, I had felt the group frustration building. The hidden metaphor, I suggested, was the unstated distinction between "the back" of the clinic where medical care was given and "the front" where the business office was located. I said something like the following:

> The "front end" people who go to these Medicare meetings are in a double bind because they're faithfully giving physicians [who work in "the back"] information that physicians really *don't* want to know about in the first

place because it's not about medicine but finance. . . . This recurrent front–back problem won't go away so long as health care practitioners can't or won't include discussing or thinking about financial issues in the practitioner role. As it stands now, you're setting each other up for bad feelings. Everyone might feel better if we realize that *nobody* here really wants to have to know this Medicare stuff. [Heads nod in assent; the mood of the room becomes more relaxed.]

Without discounting the reality of their situation and the seriousness of the discussion, I noted that an undiscussed deadly "ghost" sabotaging the group's task and morale was the spatial metaphor of *front versus back*. This was difficult to talk about publicly because no one wanted to be "bad," to fail to do his or her job well, to be seen as slacking off, I said. Yet the division of labor represented by this distinction ensured that those in the "front" would embody system-wide "bad" feelings that involved demanding money rather than rendering service (Stein, 1983b, 1990b).

The group felt understood. People relaxed and talked with, rather than accused, one another. A toxic issue had been identified, and everyone was able to save face. Some were in tears of recognition. We could begin to find a solution in which someone did not have to be branded as bad, deficient, or flawed. I could only offer useful help after I first listened attentively to them.

The next story shows the multiple levels that a workplace spatial metaphor can have.

A Story: Bifloral Splits

In an eight-floor office building housing a medical corporation for which I did consultations over many years, organizational and clinic personnel had offices on the second, seventh, and eighth floors. Despite the reality that physicians and nonphysician professionals were officed on *both* seven and eight, there staunchly persisted an organizational myth and group fantasy that only "real doctors" (physicians) were on seven and that nonphysicians (mostly Ph.D.s) were on eight. Over the years, several newly hired physicians adamantly refused to accept offices on eight.

Many managerial clinician trainees would not walk up the stairway to visit members' offices or hold conferences on eight. Over the years, several trainees told me they "knew" their fears were irrational, but eight somehow seemed to them to be a "leper colony," a place "out of bounds even though it's an important part of the organization . . . a place we're afraid to venture to." It was associated with mental, psychological, family, and psychosocial issues that not only fell outside their professional or academic boundaries but were also often personally intimidating. This fantasy of endangerment was reinforced by physician managers, with whom they identified as "role models" and who could not comfortably navigate between seven and eight.

Many years ago at a corporate-wide meeting, one physician manager who had regularly appeared on *both* seven and eight was facetiously labeled a "*bifloral floater.*" The term elicited anxious laughter from the group. The label stuck indelibly, branding him as different, even alien. The sexual or gender overtones of the bifloral metaphor were patent. To be bifloral was to be, in others' fantasy, both us and them, bisexual, male and female, a merging that was intolerable because it was anxiety evoking.

To try to make sense of it, I relied on my sense that this language was eerie. Implicit in this metaphor was the fantasy that people on seven were physicians and, whether in fact male or female, were all "real men." Those on eight, the non-physicians, were quasi-women: Ph.D.'s who did not perform manly medicine but who conducted research and did talk therapy or counseling rather than diagnosing, ordering procedures, and prescribing medication—the work of "real doctors," "real men." Despite considerable boundary ambiguity between floors and the presence of multiple programs on each floor, *the group's need for a boundary made group fantasy or myth override reality.* Organizational space, including meanings and feelings associated with that space, can be imbued with powerful group metaphors that affect relationships among group members and tasks performed. This affect-laden division of labor between spaces can be referred to as emotional geography or psychogeography (Stein, 1987a; Stein & Niederland, 1989).

Within this same organization, members of programmatically isolated units on the second and eighth floors described themselves in identical terms: "orphan," "stepchild," "stuck up (down) in a corner by ourselves," "out of the mainstream." Years ago one unit member said to me that his group had learned to turn "benign neglect" to its own advantage in pursuing internal interests. Nonetheless, this turning of passive abandonment into active mastery, this reclamation of initiative, rested upon a sense of having been cast out, or at least excluded, from legitimacy and honor in the organizational "family." This latter image and fantasy served as a widespread metaphor throughout the corporation.

One emergent facet of my consulting work with the organization was to help members understand the meanings and feelings that kept "everyone in his or her place" and thereby enable a less rigid role structure to emerge. I made myself available for meetings and consultations throughout the building and clinics outside the building. I constantly raised questions in clinical groups about the consequences of *where* we were conducting some activity for the activity itself.

I also tried to unearth issues that lurked behind ostensibly geographic ones: the need for control, the fear of helplessness, anxiety about gender identity, and the unacceptable wish for dependency in this medical profession and in this organization. Without careful listening, none of this would have been possible.

This brings me to a longer, more complex story. It begins with the *fact* of the resignation of several managers from a corporation within a short time span. The *significance* or *meaning* of the resignations only emerged slowly, and proved to be a powerful metaphor for life in the corporation. I acknowledge that the story is long. But to simplify it for the sake of brevity would be an injustice to the psychological and group reality that took place.

A Story: The Resignations

At a medical organization, Threshold Limit Value (TLV) Corporation, with which I consulted for nine months, seven mid- and upper-level managers had submitted their resignations all within the same month. TLV, a health care corporation that also served as a clinical and administrative training facility, employed approximately 150 people. It was a subsidiary of a larger corporation and itself had several smaller divisions. Frequent turnover of officials and staff, one or two at a time, had characterized TLV throughout the CEO's rigidly top-down decade of leadership. These latest departures felt different because of their quantity.

Shortly after the announced resignations, I facilitated two managerial support groups back to back the same day: the first, a mid-to-upper-level management support group, was followed by a junior manager-trainee support group. Both were officially scheduled as case conferences built around difficult human relations management issues. Each group consisted of 11 or 12 participants. The junior managerial group was joined by three senior managers who had volunteered to discuss what they knew and felt about changes at TLV.

In both groups, participants freely acknowledged they were reeling emotionally from the resignations and impending loss of leaders, whom they respected and admired and to whose work styles they had adapted. The metaphors people used, together with their associated emotions, were similar in both groups. One manager said, "Did I make a mistake in coming here [to TLV]? I thought I'd be working under Dr. A. He's out! Then we started getting close to Dr. B. Now *he's* gone! Now Dr. C is interim COO and he's so new. Does he know his way around enough to be our advocate? It feels like sinking sand."

The first group, attended by eleven managers and medical personnel as well as nonphysicians, began with a presentation by an upper-level manager, Dr. Joe Frager. With the "severe magnitude" of changes at TLV, he wondered "what will survive." Because he was about to leave TLV for a new job, he said he felt himself to be an "unwitting accomplice" to the turmoil by having recently recruited some new managers. Then he felt "like a deserter." He felt conflicted between being "truly happy" for others' career advancement and having a "morbid satisfaction" that "the exodus is a demonstration against the current leadership." He said:

> I feel about TLV as if we were climbing a mountain, and were only a few feet from the summit, but then we slipped and now we're falling back to where we were years ago. . . . I don't like to feel I'm getting airlifted off a beached ship that is taking on water fast, only to leave many of my friends still on board trying to bail it out. But there is absolutely nothing [emphatic] that I can do about it. [Then, with surprise] I just had a revelation: I've been treating the corporation [TLV] as if it were a separate entity. My training and work really came from the people—and they still exist, just in different spatial coordinates.

He described how outsiders he knew spoke of TLV as if "a floodgate had been opened." We discussed his and other group members' feelings of abandonment and guilt. Another manager spoke of "sadness at losing people . . . lots of discussion about leaving versus staying [at TLV]. A feeling is that this is a sinking ship. . . . We have an eerie floating feeling, a vague uncertainty."

I felt that group members were trying to tell and retell their story in order to make coherent sense of what was happening to them and somehow master it. I considered this a clue that organizational grief was taking place in response to great loss. Individuals and organizations suffering loss engage in a review of their history as a part of grief work. Reintegration of the past is necessary before it can be let go and the future emerge.

At times, participants' descriptions of events drew heavily upon the defense mechanism of isolation, wherein details of events are remembered but lack the feelings associated with them. I often asked the group to identify what feelings the stories and metaphors prompted. Discussion followed along the lines of the following composite:

> We liked, loved these people. They befriended us. We learned from them. They're like our mothers, spoon-feeding us, and suddenly they're thrown out of the nest. It's like our parents have cancer. We're the abandoned child. It's like a divorce, no pleasure.

> The CEO has a difficult time caressing and hugging his people. We're left naked. We're leaving home and never will get a lot of adoptions the next few months. You get the feeling TLV is folding under your feet. We've been

asked to help improve TLV. Roll up our sleeves and try to make changes. . . .
Our leadership is lacking this year. When Dr. Holt left last year at this time,
he told us before that he was leaving. Jones said nothing. We feel abandoned
and betrayed.

Toward the end of this meeting, a psychological split or factionalism took place
in the group. On one side were those who had begun to mourn the losses more
deeply; on the other side were those who wanted quickly "to keep production
going," "to get on with things." In the latter camp, one senior manager pleaded,
"When you have a family member die of cancer, there's grieving. You cry; you
have anger, all sorts of feelings. But don't strip the patient or our company of
hope. We shouldn't become despondent or hopeless. . . . Lots of people have an
investment here. We need to rally. We should rally!"

Dr. Frager reiterated that his final point during the presentation had been the
most important *and* surprising to him: "I had thought of the company, TLV, as
an entity separate from people. But I realized that my training came from individual managers. . . . They won't disappear, as if an entire company could. But
there is no such thing as a company." I wondered how much of what he said was
acceptance of his own separateness and individuality and how much was denial
of grief, as if to say, "If the emotional investment in the symbolic object can be
denied, it cannot be lost; therefore I need not feel sadness."

Immediately following this meeting, I met with the group of junior managers–
trainees. Dr. Frager and two senior managers from the previous group had volunteered to discuss changes at TLV with them. Images similar to those of the first
group surfaced repeatedly in the second group. The following metaphors were
spoken sequentially during that discussion:

> Top heavy . . . leaving, that opened the floodgates . . . Junior managers don't
> feel like managers but like students. We feel now on real shaky ground. . . .
> The CEO likes the frog-in-the-water image, to see how you do as he turns
> up the heat to a boil. . . . Get to know another manager to be your advo-
> cate. . . . I don't know *any* [new] managers. . . . We feel we're always kept in
> the dark, but how do we even know when it's dark? . . . Turnover is natural,
> to be expected. Life will go on.

Table 2 lists key metaphors used during these two groups as well as over many
months, thereby offering a cross-sectional view of how this traumatic period was
experienced. These metaphors are part of a single emotional pattern and cognitive
disorganization and reorganization that occurred in response to the resignations

and mass turnover. They can, for heuristic purposes, be enumerated according to three typologies: (1) annihilation metaphors (collapse, falling, engulfment); (2) separation-loss metaphors; and (3) family metaphors (deMause, [1982] argues that metaphors of cracking and collapse also represent birth images). Family roles and feelings were transferred onto corporate relationships at TLV and to the image of TLV itself. TLV had become personified or anthropomorphized as a "bad" family that abandoned and abused, if not annihilated, its vulnerable children, first those who had left and now those who perceived themselves as "survivors" of "the exodus." In groups and in individual conversations, annihilation metaphors expressed feelings of anxiety, if not panic, and rage. Likewise separation-loss metaphors expressed feelings of sadness, nostalgia, anger, and guilt. Family metaphors expressed both.

The metaphor of the exodus is especially illuminating for it connotes more than an exit of former managers. In conversation, several TLV members confirmed my suspicion that a biblical fantasy might underlie the phrase. Some said that those who had suffered under an oppressive leader left to find "the promised land" elsewhere. At TLV, many were left behind to labor under the "tyrant." They created a mental split between inside (TLV) and outside (exodus): Inside was bad, whereas outside (where the others had gone) was good, even idealized.

In the aftermath of the seven managers' departure, the event quickly came to be crystallized in organizational folklore. Alongside the exodus, it became variously known as "the turnover," "the leaving," "the bailout," and "jumping ship." At a corporation-wide managers' meeting held nine months after the seven directors had left, the CEO triumphantly reframed and resymbolized the experience for the organization: "Some people call this an 'exodus'; I call it a 'liberation,' and TLV is in for a great future." The CEO insisted that TLV had benefited from the departure of those who had never truly been loyal or who had contributed little to the organization. Acceptance of the new story, metaphor, and myth became mandatory.

Throughout this nine-month period, the CEO insisted that those departing his company were at "natural" midcareer change points, that another organization had greedily staged a corporate raid on TLV, that those who had left were not high-quality supervisors anyway, and that the "best" had stayed or recently joined. It was taboo to mention the names—especially if favorably—of the seven who had resigned. The process of working through was made complicated (at times, I despaired, impossible) by upper management's insistence that there was nothing to grieve; that "if you can't take the heat, get out of the kitchen"; and that TLV was better off without those who had left. The attitude enforced from above was in essence, "Be more productive; we don't have the time to dote on the past and mourn."

TABLE 2. Recurrent Metaphors of Trauma at TLV

Annihilation metaphors	Separation-loss metaphors	Family metaphors	Other metaphors
Climbing a mountain . . . slipped back	Survivor	Mothers, spoon-feeding us . . . thrown out of the nest. . . . Our parents have cancer. . . . We're the abandoned child . . . divorce . . . adoptions.	We're always kept in the dark. . . . How do we even know it's dark?
Beached ship taking water fast	TLV as a separate entity versus individual people who will still exist		
TLV folding under your feet			
Earthquake . . . no firm ground under you	The exodus		
Opened the floodgates	I feel abandoned by the CEO.		
On real shaky ground	I feel like a deserter · (said by a management trainee about to leave TLV).	TLV as family falling apart	
Waiting for the aftershocks			
Anxiety provoking, but horrible twinge of satisfaction at things falling apart			
It feels like sinking sand.			
Eerie floating feeling			

The CEO dissolved long-standing structural divisions and committees of people who had been regularly working together. He demanded that different departments at TLV swiftly develop new statements of strategic plans, goals, objectives, evaluation procedures, and marketing protocols. Those managers who stayed on acquired more responsibility, yet they were often asked to perform roles for which they were unfamiliar (a characteristic also of survivors of organizational reductions in workforce, or downsizing; see Tombaugh & White, 1990; Stein, 2001).

The CEO scathingly criticized his subordinates' performances. Nothing seemed to please him. Morale at TLV plummeted. "Triangles" proliferated as he engaged in special deals with executives at all levels, setting one against the other. This promoted further organizational divisiveness, isolation, and fragmentation. Although ostensibly attempting to rebuild his company's morale, he could not tolerate group life to exist apart from *his* active and autocratic participation. Fearing group consensus as sedition, he seemed to do all in his power to disenfranchise, rather than empower, large and small work groups within TLV. Except for the two managerial support groups I led twice a month throughout this trying time, managers and staff mostly withdrew and tried to be seen busily performing their tasks. They tried to "keep under the radar" of the CEO. Often they made themselves unavailable or hid geographically from scrutiny by others.

Over time, various individual TLV members, relationships, and subgroups became temporary metaphors for large-scale loss and unresolved grief. Several months after the departure of the seven managers, one executive briefly became the focus of the enormous sense of loss when he failed to show up to supervise trainees. He seemed emotionally distant even when he was present. At one trainee meeting a manager described him as

gone. . . . He didn't even show up. . . . Rude . . . unfair. . . . We're left up in the air. . . . Taking care of everything by myself. . . . We're never told. . . . It makes me angry to work so hard and get no return. . . . He has no idea how hard you're working, oblivious. . . . He's not emotionally available. . . . I thought he was an ogre. . . . I don't think you care about me. . . . Talking to him is like talking to a wall. . . . How do we deal with people who aren't meeting our needs?

As the trainees voiced their disappointment and anger about this manager's absences and unavailability, I wondered why he had become a subject now. What was the *timing* about? I speculated aloud to the group that, although this physician-administrator had worked at TLV for six or seven years, and although his style had been consistently distant emotionally, he and his apparent aloofness had just now become a poignant metaphor for large organizational losses and the feelings associated with them: unfairness, injustice, emotional unavailability, remoteness, abandonment. I suggested that

the subject of our case conference is not only about our dissatisfaction with Dr. A, but all the issues associated with him also bear the weighty burden of the upheaval over the last six months. Dr. A's emotional distance is more difficult to bear with the absence of so many managers we cared for, and with the depersonalized managerial style of our CEO, who made life here so difficult for them. We're angry with Dr. A, but we're also angry and sad about the seven we lost and angry at our CEO for creating a situation they'd want to leave.

In short, Dr. A had become a metaphor for TLV's pervasive underlying mood.

The biweekly support groups (managerial case conferences) had acquired the additional burden of expressing (in words and feelings from raised voices to tears) what was taboo elsewhere in the corporation. Given my lack of access to and influence in higher management (except for highly structured, bureaucratically standardized meetings, those in which the CEO and his closed circle of upper-level administrators retained control over the proceedings), the support groups were the best the participants and I could do under the difficult circumstances. In the aftermath of TLV's crisis, the support groups (usually consisting of six to eight people) became massively attended refuges, participation ranging from 25 to to 30 people.

During this same period, a new account of the earlier turnover spread vertically from the CEO and then laterally throughout the organization. It was, I believe, an attempt to fend off anxiety, guilt, shame, rage, and the grief of mourning. According to the new, rewritten, revisionist history, those who had left a year earlier had been "problems," not loyalists who had struggled on behalf of the organization to the very end: 'We're glad they left. Things have gotten better since they left," became the new, and enforced, myth. Those who stayed reversed into active rejection their vulnerable feelings of having been abandoned and betrayed by these largely parental figures who had left. It was as if to say, "Since they abandoned us, we'll abandon them; we don't need them." Further expressing the denial of grief was the widely articulated belief that "The good people stayed. We brought some good people on board. We got rid of the bad people." In short, to protect themselves from feeling themselves to be the victim of the CEO, they identified with the aggressor and his reality-denying organizational mythology.

Nevertheless, people felt that some catastrophe was imminent, that their organization was falling apart, that they were being abandoned, that everyone was "dropping the ball" (a widespread metaphor) of responsibilities on them. Yet people remained loyal to the CEO. They lived in fear of him because of their feelings of dependency on him. They accepted and perpetuated the new history of the previous two years. They purchased personal and organizational self-esteem at the price of disparaging, if not altogether writing off, those who had left.

Over time, TLV became entombed in its own myths. Except in support groups, mourning could not take place. Officially, nothing had been lost. To grieve would be a sign of disloyalty, a belief that the myth might be flawed. Endless denials and rationalizations further repaired and validated the myth. They conferred security and self-esteem at the price of distorting the perception of reality past, present, and even future. Those who remained behind, or who were hired on after the waves of resignations, separated themselves from those who had left. It was as if to say, "Only those who are flawed, disloyal, would leave or think of leaving. Therefore, I, those who are here, and the organization itself are sound."

Loss and dread of loss, grief and defense against grief, badness and goodness, continued to plague the group. Group members feared to speak up. In history and in fantasy, outspokenness led to expulsion. To speak was to be called disloyal. "There's the mystique of 'Open your mouth and you have to leave.'" To speak up was to have one's emotional valence in the group changed from being one of the good people, to being one of the bad ones. Many struggled with how to become good, to feel pure again.

This conflict surfaced at one managers' meeting in the following dialogue:

Manager 1: "I don't like the image of 'if someone leaves, it's because something's wrong with us.' They're not loyal to us. It's not our fault that people leave. It has to be okay for people to leave. [They leave because of good job offers elsewhere,] not because of us."

Manager 2 [fervently]: "They *looked* for a job. It wasn't just that the jobs were available. There was something about here that made them want to look."

Manager 1: "You're angry. We're still *good*; we're not bad because they left."

Manager 2: "Can't it be *both*? People I came to work with are *gone*. That's hard for me."

Manager 1: "Is there a family that's *not* dysfunctional? I'll admit that we are. . . . But let's stop wallowing in it. We have to have something we like to *stay* here for."

Manager 3 [flippantly]: "I can't sell my house!"

The group struggled between demythologizing and remythologizing the past, between feeling good and bad about itself, between compartmentalizing and integrating good and bad feelings and persons, between maintaining secrecy and embracing openness. To the CEO in this organization, the ultimate act of disloyalty was to become a distinctive self (to separate, to individuate, or to differentiate a distinctive self from the corporate self). Stated differently, the ultimate offense was to acknowledge publicly that something was profoundly wrong, rather than right, about the system; to leave it or to think of leaving it; or to remain, yet become a distinct person, rather than subordinate one's values and critical, independent judgment entirely to the system. The CEO and upper management demanded that everyone be a "team player," by which he meant to submit their thought and will to his.

As a group process consultant, I tracked and processed the emotional significance of the choice of terms such as "darkness," "earthquake," "sinking sand,"
"exodus," "survivor," and "deserter" via their emotional reverberations in myself
as an instrument of the group feeling. I used my own affective response to inquire
what group feelings attached to these metaphors. From experiences such as these,
I believe that what Bion (1959) argues for treatment in small groups applies as
well to organizational consultation, at least in the foregoing story: "In group
treatment many interpretations, and amongst them the most important, have to
be made on the strength of the analyst's own emotional reactions. . . . The analyst
feels he is being manipulated so as to be playing a part, no matter how difficult
to recognize, in somebody else's phantasy" (p. 134).

The foundation of metaphoric analysis and group interpretation rests not only
upon the consultant's *cognitive* recognition of metaphors in the group, but also
upon the recognition of various pleasurable and unpleasurable *feelings* induced
in him or her by the group. I try to respond both to the group's words (or phrases) and to the emotions I infer through my own. Each response I make is a
hypothesis about the group that I offer. Both the group and I learn much when
my interpretation is wrong. My ultimate goal in metaphor analysis during the
crisis period at TLV was to help the group heal and to improve human relations
and work functioning within an organization where managers and staff did not
feel valued or listened to by upper hierarchy. Although these consultations did
not result in major organizational restructuring, they nonetheless helped TLV
members feel frightening emotions and accept disturbing fantasies they had been
avoiding. This in turn helped them adapt to, if not subtly influence, a bureaucratic structure they could more realistically assess.

Throughout my consultation with TLV, I felt helpless and was helpless to confront the several levels of upper management about midlevel managers' morale
and sense of catastrophe. The CEO, COO, and executives immediately beneath
them in rank insisted to me that TLV was in better shape than ever. My efforts
to bring group issues to the attention of the CEO were met with a blank face,
astonishment, a platitude, or a veiled threat that others in TLV, not the CEO, saw
me as a troublemaker who was dangerously "stirring the pot."

The CEO once congratulated me on being a "survivor" at TLV, not recognizing perhaps that the regime I was surviving was his own. In my meetings with
upper management, I always felt that I was living in the "Newspeak" world of
George Orwell's *1984* (1949). I felt I was being asked to doubt my perception
and judgment entirely and replace both with theirs—precisely the psychological
contract, fueled by projective identification, that the CEO demanded of his subordinates. At best, I used my own sense of tragedy, despair, and shame as organizational assessment data for use in individual and group meetings with midlevel

managers and trainees. I listened. I stood with the managers and employees as witness to what was taking place. They taught me that the only way to be of help was to listen deeply to them.

From an Orwellian organizational story, I turn now to the story of an organizational phenomenon and metaphor that has come to have widespread currency: the silo. It is a story to which many readers can personally relate.

A Story: The Metaphor of the Silo

Perhaps a single, recurrent metaphor conjures up the experience of countless "tall," hierarchically structured, vertically integrated, often autocratically led, structures: the *silo* (Diamond, Stein, & Allcorn, 2002). It is a stark visual image drawn from the countless white grain silos (or elevators) that dot the North American Great Plains. The term became widespread and commonplace in the 1990s. As Michael Diamond, Seth Allcorn, and I consulted with large organizations during the formative years of the term, executives, managers, and employees would often gesture with their two hands in the air, carving two parallel, vertical lines from top to bottom, when asked to describe what their workplaces are like.

We learned about this repeated experience and image by listening to people's stories and observing them carefully. In organization after organization, employees characterized their workplaces as consisting of multiple tall, vertically "integrated" hierarchies which had little or nothing to do horizontally with other divisions or units of their overall organization—whether these other divisions were across the street in different buildings, or spread across the world in multinational corporations.

The silo is not only *cognitively* perceived, but also *emotionally* (affectively) felt. The hard, impenetrable, sometimes inhuman, isolated silo is what the workplace looked like and felt like as a shared mental representation. For many who lived inside of silo-like workplaces, it often felt like what Thomas Ogden called an "autistic contiguous" mode of experience (Ogden, 1989a, 1989b), in which anxiety centers on boundlessness and dissolution.

To be fair, the silo could embody multiple emotions, fantasies, and modes of experiencing. It could alternately be experienced as safe and as persecutory, as reassuring and as confining, and as reassuring and as persecuting, comforting and unapproachably hard. In any event, the mental silo structure became part of one's identity as part of an organization and of group identity (Diamond, 1993).

Moreover, members of each silo commonly mistrusted members of other silos, suspecting, for instance, that the CEO or president or provost treated *them* unfairly, but favored members of *other*, competing silos. Members of one silo often felt that they worked harder than people in other silos. There was little of the sense that "we're all in this together." There was resentment, competition, mistrust, and envy. There was little sense of community, unity, or identity with the overall organization. Instead, the unit of identity and identification was one's own silo. Between silos, mistrust, rigid boundaries, thick walls, protective defensiveness, and even paranoia prevailed.

The world of silos was "us" versus "them," "good" versus "bad." Such an emotional environment made enthusiastic cooperation and collaboration on projects between silos difficult or impossible. Put differently, emotional factors interfered with real world task accomplishment. In short, methodologically speaking, *knowledge of all this would have been impossible had we not listened attentively to employees' storytelling and observed their gestures.*

Permit me to add a historical note. Over three decades ago (1982e), I wrote an essay I called "Autism and Architecture: A Tale of Inner Landscapes." In it I described and discussed how autistic symbolism had come to be the hallmark of much office structural design in American culture. One is immediately struck by the extent to which these buildings are designed to be insular, self-contained worlds with hard surfaces. Many are tall, sleek window-buildings, with tainted or mirrored faces. Those inside can see out, but those outside cannot see in. They house humans, but they are inhuman workplaces. They are, perhaps, precursors of our organizational silos and silo metaphors.

I would like to conclude this chapter on organizational metaphors with a story in which both metaphor and leadership are highlighted, a story in which the client triggers (via projective identification) in the consultant a metaphor that subsequently becomes vital in their relationship and in the consultation. For once, it is a story in which an organizational problem is resolved.

The story illustrates how one can practice psychodynamically-informed organizational research and consultation virtually anywhere. It does not even have to be called a consultation. It is a matter of using one's imagination and listening—both to the client and to one's own unconscious. One often finds that a metaphor uncovers what the story is about and is likewise crucial to helping a client solve a problem.

A Complex Story: The Canary in the Coal Mine

Around 2010 the new chairperson of a large department of medicine in an academic health sciences center asked if I could consult with him. We had been colleagues and friends for years, sharing a common interest in the medical humanities, such as poetry. I had recently told him that my next poetry book would be published by Finishing Line Press, in Kentucky, a state which has much in common with West Virginia, the state in which he had grown up.

He looked tired, weary; he did not have the usual lilt in his voice. He told me that he was just learning the ropes in his department. While acquainting himself with the department's finances, he found several things very wrong. A lot of money was missing. He said to me that he suspected that the administrative secretary was embezzling money from the department. The secretary was very protective of the finance books and refused to divulge any of the questionable expenditures to him.

The administrative secretary had been in the department "forever," and when questioned by the new chair about something in the department's finances, she snapped with her teeth showing, "This money is MINE!" This administrative staff person seemed to hold the entire department hostage, the chair said to me. She consistently kept her office door shut. No one knew what she did in there! She would let no one see her e-mail, so they had no idea of who, she was corresponding with, or about what.

The chairperson had then checked with two prior chairmen of the department, and both of them were very hesitant to say anything about their interactions with their "personal" secretary. Although forthright about everything else, when it came to the department finances and the administrative assistant, they were suddenly evasive. Both of them advised him not to ask further about it. It came out that the assistant had done both of them special financial favors—making major purchases for them and keeping it a secret from the rest of the department.

It became apparent that the unspoken contract was that she wouldn't disclose the shadowy purchases, if they would turn a blind eye to her manipulation of the department's finances, and put their "trust" in her. The new chair was very disturbed by this apparently long history of deceit and special deals, not to mention a lot of missing money. He was preparing to have a meeting with the dean or the medical school's CFO about this. He also brought in an audit team to help with the books.

After he had given me this story, I said to him something like: "I want to share with you a fantasy I have had while you were talking. You're from West Virginia. You know that Finishing Line Press is publishing a book of my poetry and that the Press is in Kentucky, a state well known for *coal mines*. So is West Virginia! *I think that you're the canary in the coal mine*, and I think you're afraid that you'll run out of air and the whole mine will collapse." He beamed and literally "ran with" the metaphor for the next part of the conversation. He affirmed that I had understood in a deep way what his predicament and future chosen role were. He added that the metaphor was applicable to him in ways I could not know, i.e., physically: He had asthma, and in recent weeks his asthma had gotten out of control, and he had to use his rescue albuterol inhaler many times.

So he had literally had come to *embody* "the canary in the coal mine." His department had felt "like" a toxic coal mine in which he was struggling for air. His *symptom* was a key to the emotional and organizational content of the *story*. His *personal* symptom was a symptom and symbol of *organizational* toxicity. He had become psychosomatically "contaminated" with the departmental psychological "pollution."

I stayed with the metaphor. I told him that when I returned to my office I would search the Internet for a couple of photos or drawings of canaries in mines, and send them to him. I did so almost immediately. Shortly thereafter, he sent a brief thank-you note, beneath which he inserted a cartoon drawing of a yellow canary *with a gas mask on its face*, and two bellowing chimneys and some kind of industrial plant (an electricity plant run by coal?) in the background. Part of his note above the drawing said: "Things are temporarily stabilized on the home front—breathing apparatus is in place." He was still a canary in a coal mine—or at least susceptible to bad air from a coal-generated electric plant. But this time the canary protected himself and could both literally and figuratively breathe easier. He could then proceed with his departmental tasks.

The departmental chair was attempting to confront the dark forces pervading his department by having a thorough financial audit, and by supportive meetings with health sciences center leadership. He was, in other words, mustering his forces and data as evidence that would eventually be used to confront the administrative secretary. The last I heard from him, his asthma symptoms were considerably less severe, and he was finally getting some sleep at night—because he could breathe rather than struggle for breath. Subsequently, a supportive upper management conducted an extensive departmental audit. The administrative secretary's illicit actions were uncovered, and she was terminated. The entire department breathed a sigh of relief, and the actual breathing of my client vastly improved.

What sense can we make of this consultation? What had happened? And what is the role of my imagination and of metaphor in this process? Let me briefly discuss this story from the point of view of an applied anthropologist doing an organizational consultation. In our meeting, the new chair felt safe enough to discuss disturbing issues he literally could not bring up with anyone in his department. I functioned as an informal consultant. I think that he psychologically "used" me (in a healthy way) to help him test reality, and to affirm that he was not "crazy." He had said that he felt "kind of crazy" in his department the past weeks after he found out all of these bizarre things. I think that I functioned as a kind of Winnicottian "holding environment" [1960] (1965) to help him to "contain" (Bion) (1970) and process his anxiety and distress at what he had uncovered in his department.

His disquiet and his difficulty breathing finally made sense. In his mind he felt less disorganized and less mired in diffuse anxiety. I hasten to add that, through the use of "cartoon" canaries in our e-mail exchanges, we added further symbolism to our communication via metaphor. In follow-up phone calls, I invariably asked him how the "canary" was doing!

In consulting, I have come to rely upon my imagination, including the images and metaphors that come to mind, "induced" by my interaction with the other person or group. In this instance, I utilized my mental association to try to help him see himself better: *Finishing Line Press = Kentucky = West Virginia = coal = coal mines = canary in a coal mine.* My "evidence" that I had been on the right track was his emotional response to the image.

He then enthusiastically identified with the metaphor and transformed it from something passive and potentially destructive (lethal to him and the "mine" in which he worked) into something where he could continue to function, perhaps prevent an "explosion," and at the same time breathe better himself. Put differently, I think that he internalized our visit and adapted it to his situation. I had trusted myself (my hunches), and he came to trust himself more and to prepare to act on that trust. I would add that, from a methodological viewpoint, psychodynamically-oriented consultants often rely upon their own imagination, associations, and metaphors to help a client identify deeper issues and to problem-solve.

What makes this story widely applicable, if not "generalizable," to many organizations is (1) how widely organizations have been held hostage, even destroyed (Enron, WorldCom, Qwest, General Electric, etc.), by collusive compromises that have silenced countless people in the organization; and (2) by the presence and usefulness of metaphor—including literally embodied metaphor—in understanding, and perhaps helping, leaders and their organizations. I think that the use of my imagination led to the discovery of "the canary in the coal mine" as a fruitful metaphor. Further, the story illustrates the use of the self, of imagination, and of metaphor in organizational research and consulting. Perhaps not so strangely, the exercise worked when I allowed my imagination to help inform my understanding of a story told to me. Listening deeply became the key to the collaboration and the work.

A Concluding Thought: Metaphor and Organizational Consultation
A promising role for organizational consultants is to help group members gain greater access to meanings and feelings that coalesce around explicit and implicit metaphors. Consultants can try to assist whole groups to navigate through conflicts and catastrophes by helping leaders, managers, and employees integrate

painful, sometimes overwhelming feelings, often masked by bureaucratic routine and official ritual (Diamond, 1984, 1988, 1993; Stein, 1990b; Allcorn & Diamond, 1997).

One of those masks is metaphor. It is a group compromise that at once reveals and conceals the group, itself. The role of consultants as facilitators for the telling and reconstruction of group stories, together with the reexperiencing of intolerable feelings, deserves to be expanded. Both during crisis and more ordinary times, metaphor analysis provides a window of opportunity for addressing issues underlying organizational culture.

Metaphor analysis expands the range of knowing and feeling—our own and others'. It offers, too, a natural bridge to understanding the symbolic nature of leadership in organizational groups, for leaders embody their groups, just as groups embody the leaders who speak and act in their behalf. Organizational leadership change and succession can unleash an intense emotional response that in turn becomes part of the organization's implicit structure, including its most potent metaphors. Knowing how to *listen* to this process is itself instruction on how to serve as a consultant.

5. Leadership

Introduction

On the surface, an organizational leader is a person near or at the top of a hierarchy, a person who is in charge of directing and organizing the *work* of the group (tasks), and instilling in employees its purpose in the world—what the organization is supposedly and explicitly here *for*. But a leader is far more than that. An organizational leader has *expressive* (subjective, symbolic/metaphorical, affective/emotional, unconscious) as well as *instrumental* (task, work, reality-oriented, conscious) significance. He or she has meanings, inner images, agendas (conscious and unconscious), affects, defenses, and fantasies that are brought to work. Likewise, the leader embodies employees' projected meanings, inner images, agendas, affects, defenses, and fantasies. Leader and follower constantly project their own unconscious and derivatives of their childhood onto each other. We like to believe that the relationship between leaders and followers is governed by rationality and objectivity. In reality, both leader and follower are caught in a firestorm of projection and transference where the unconscious past suffuses the present.

Leader and follower serve as metaphors for each other. These metaphors are not tangible, but can be inferred and tested through the consultant or researcher's use of the self in trying to understand the significance that leader, employee, and organization have for each other. Different types of leaders exude and embody different kinds of emotions, inner representations, and fantasies, e.g., charismatic, transformational, routinizing, maintenance, and so on. Some leaders try to "ram through" what turns out to be cataclysmic, destructive change, to make radical innovations, while insisting on a complete break with disparaged and despised past. The past is relegated to historical garbage. When a leader resigns or is fired, the experience to the group of loss is often emotionally complicated. In short, leaders and leadership are far from entirely rational matters. We learn about the emotional depths of leadership and followership mostly by listening.

Let me take a step back and link issues in understanding leadership to issues in the history of philosophy. The relationship between process and structure, change and continuity, is one that has challenged thinkers and practitioners in every field. From the physics of Sir Isaac Newton and the celestial mechanics of Pierre Simon Marquis de Laplace in the seventeenth century, we have inherited and perpetuated the assumption of a fixed, mechanical, orderly, regular, predictable, and rational natural and human universe. Even in the anthropology in which I was trained in the late 1960s and early 1970s, tradition and its structures and functions remained the predominant interest, outlook, and advocacy of the profession. The "ethnographic present" was regarded as more or less timeless. Change is still regarded by many anthropologists as more the exception, the anomaly, anathema to the old and "good" traditional ways. The study of social disruption has been unwelcomed among many anthropologists, as disruption is unwelcomed among people themselves. Such disruption is then followed by intense, revitalizing ghost dances to restore the lost (La Barre, 1972; Saffo, 2005).

Yet perhaps Heraclitus will prevail over Plato: Flux and transition, not permanence and order, are at the core of all human life. The same is true for workplace organizations. *Leadership succession,* and the language and feelings that accompany it, are not less significant emotional events to people in workplace societies than they are to tribes, chiefdoms, and ethnic groups. Organizational leadership is as symbolic as it is real; part of its reality—authority, power, finance—lies in its symbolism. A consultant can help an organizational group to the degree that he or she can help group members come to terms with the feelings, meanings, and unfinished histories beneath the symbolism, all of which he or she learns about by listening for metaphors.

This chapter focuses on listening for those organizational events, crises, and windows of opportunity (some lost, some opened) such as occur when work group leaders resign, retire, are fired, are terminated; when there are organizational crises or turning points; and so forth. People in workplaces often use the language of "family." Work might not be family by blood and marriage, but it is heir to the *transfer* of feelings and wishes from years no longer remembered but lived out in transference and workplace dramas. Some of the stories are of relative successes in the consultation process.

I wish to emphasize at the outset that the social power or "charisma" often attributed to leaders is not some distinct, *inherent* property located within that person—although we ardently wish to believe, feel, and experience that aura of strength to emanate from him or her. Rather, charisma is more correctly the property of the reciprocal, unconsciously driven relationship between leader(s) and group or followers—what they hope, expect, inspire in, project onto and into, and internalize in each other. Leader and group create each other. Leadership and its transitions bring out the best and worst in us. This chapter is about learning to listen for the meanings and hidden affects (out-of-awareness feelings) unleashed by organizational transitions and other processes.

G. A. Theodorson and A. G. Theodorson (1969) and Edgar Schein (1985), among others, draw attention to the distinction between an organization's implicit and explicit culture. What an observer or consultant might infer about organizational leadership rules often differs from what leaders or managers espouse. Members of an organization also have many levels of awareness about the assumptions that actually govern their behavior. Some things can be done but never directly said.

In other words, an organization may have leadership norms that are avowed and others that go unacknowledged and are even unmentionable, undiscussable. For instance, executives and managers may claim they are leading according to the respectful, consensus-building management theory Y, when in fact they act and unwittingly speak as if they really believe in the mistrusting, authoritarian theory X. The official group standard might exhort people to be cooperative "team players" (a common metaphor, drawn from sports and military) in order to accomplish group tasks and group cohesiveness, while some leaders might implicitly and dishonestly use the slogan to advance themselves at the expense of the group or to extinguish dissent. Alternately, the corporation might harbor the widespread secret that "the boss really does not want us to be an interactive, interdependent team," while the boss and managers must publicly pretend that their norm is one of open communication rather than invasive, top-down control.

Further, often compounding the group's self-deception is its members' insistence, fueled by leaders' demand that everyone believe, that "there are no secrets or black boxes in this company." Yet there are vast subjects and issues that are unmentionable and undiscussable—even unknowable (for instance, repressed or dissociated). Examples abound: for instance, a leader's deceptiveness, brutality, mismanagement of funds, or alcoholism; or the fact that a past leader actually improved the company, when the mandatory fiction is that he or she was incompetent.

Group members lie to themselves and to each other, partly to protect themselves, partly to express and partly to cover up their self-contempt. What psychoanalytically informed accounts of organizational culture and culture change do is offer other, deeper levels of understanding for these social psychological and sociological processes of secrecy and taboo. Specifically, the relation between implicit and explicit is not one between static levels but is a dynamic process—one more easily recognized by consultant and group alike during periods of disruptive change.

In this chapter, examples of leadership and leadership change illustrate the relationship between implicit and explicit culture. This brings me to consider the *limits* of attending exclusively to the *explicit, manifest* level of organizational life, which is *de rigueur* for much of organizational research.

Limits of Empirical Research
and of the Rational Man Model in Leadership

The virtues of attending to the implicit world of the unconscious in understanding organizational leaders can be shown by contrasting that approach with two dominant paradigms: empirical research and the "rational man" model. Empirical research is perhaps the dominant paradigm in the effort to understand and explain organizational leadership. Empirical research into leadership styles and organizational dynamics is problematic in and of itself, because it neglects the emotional-laden undercurrents that drive much of what one finds in organizations. As a result the approach is compromised. Consider the following statement from the *Encyclopedia of Business*:

> Leadership is probably the most frequently studied topic in the organizational sciences. Thousands of leadership studies have been published and thousands of pages on leadership have been written in academic books and journals, business-oriented publications, and general-interest publications. Despite this, the precise nature of leadership and its relationship to key criterion variables such as subordinate satisfaction, commitment, and performance is still uncertain, to the point where Fred Luthans, in his book *Organizational Behavior* (2005, p. 414), said that "it [leadership] does remain pretty much of a 'black box,' or unexplainable concept." (*Encyclopedia of Business*)

Much empirical research on leadership uses accepted leadership styles that are then compared with organizational outcomes such as organizational performance, learning, and job satisfaction. Consider two typical studies to illustrate this research. The purpose of the first study was to determine how transactional and transformational leadership affects employees' job satisfaction in the public sector in Malaysia.

The results showed that transformational leadership style has a positive relationship with job satisfaction whereas transactional leadership style has a negative relationship with job satisfaction in government organization. For the linear regression test, the finding shows that only contingent reward dimension of transactional leadership has significant relationship with two dimensions in job satisfaction (working condition and work assignment). (Voon, Lo, Ngui & Ayob, 2011, p. 29)

The authors conclude by noting that their research "has shown that transformational leadership style has a positive relationship with job satisfaction" (Voon, Lo, Ngui, & Ayob, 2011, p. 29). As empirical researchers these authors then dutifully note the problematic nature of their research, which is inherent in most, if not all, research that uses an empirical approach.

The major limitations of this study revolve around sampling issues as this study does not focus on a specific target group and the questionnaires were only able to be distributed randomly to the employees of government sector in Selangor. As a result, it may have affected the current results. Furthermore, most of the respondents are confused over the [distinction between] transformational and transactional leadership and this might have affected some of the relations studied. (Voon, Lo, Ngui, & Ayob, 2011, p 30)

A second study by Martinette, 2002, on how to create a learning organization, found that:

These results may indicate that interpersonal skills have less to do with creating a learning organization than do managerial or organizational leadership abilities. In summary, the results would suggest that certain leadership characteristics drive certain types of follower behavior. With respect to our current fast paced working environment, it would seem that the characteristics of a learning organization are more clearly aligned with the behavior of the transformational leader. (Martinette, 2002)

Although it is inappropriate to say anything about the vast number of published individual research studies, I suggest that even if leadership styles are described, defined, and then carefully researched using empirical methods, they will still invariably not provide insight into what the leader *experiences, means, or feels* if he or she tries to adopt a transformational or transactional leadership style or any other—and what employees experience as well.

The experiences, meanings, and feelings (affects), conscious and unconscious, of the workplace are part of the workplace. One wonders: What does this organization *feel* like? What is it like to lead or work here? What meanings, desires, agendas, and fantasies drive the leader? What were/are major turning points in the life of the organization, and what was that like?

In particular, the stresses and anxieties that leaders experience make them highly vulnerable to psychological regression to a very early stage of life, to intense anxiety, and to psychological defensiveness. Leaders in turn become vulnerable to personal disorientation arising from many defensive processes (such as splitting, projection, projective identification, and transference, all of these ways of ridding oneself of unacceptable feelings, fantasies, and wishes) that are omnipresent in organizations. Leaders' sense of reality becomes clouded with anxiety-alleviating efforts that drown the leader in fantasy. Empirical research into leadership is opaque to these core issues.

In sum, an extensive empirical research on leadership and management exists, and I acknowledge that it makes a contribution to the literature in its focus on *manifest* aspects of the workplace. At issue is the *kind* of contribution it makes and does not make. In general, even well-conceived empirical studies consistently do not attempt to evaluate the contribution that unconscious and out-of-awareness intrapersonal, interpersonal, group, and organizational dynamics make to organizations' dynamics, including leadership. Psychoanalytic studies, by contrast, attempt to get inside the "black box" of the mind and intersubjective communication.

If *empiricism* is the dominant *methodological* approach to organizational leadership, then "*techno-rational man*" is the dominant *theoretical* model of organizational leadership and organizational functioning. Its premise is that leaders and groups base their decisions and choices exclusively on rationality, reality-based decisions, objectivity, conscious evaluation of options, technical acumen, and enlightened self-interest. This premise underlies organizational mission statements, goals and objectives, strategic plans, total quality management (TQM) controls, Lean/Six Sigma management practices, and the like.

Total Quality Management and Lean/Six Sigma Black Belt

Since the 1980s there have been two, sometimes converging, organizational movements the goal of which is to make the workplace more efficient, productive, and ultimately customer-oriented: *Total Quality Management* (TQM, which originated in the 1950s) and *Lean/Six Sigma Black Belt* management and production processes (which began in the mid-1980s at Motorola), the latter of which is at its zenith of influence. Executives of all types of organizations have embraced TQM and Six Sigma and have urged it upon subordinate leaders, managers, and employees as the ideal way to run a workplace.

As an organizational philosophy and ideology, TQM involves all of its employees in a continuous improvement process in all business operations. Six Sigma is a data driven, disciplined process that improves process by minimizing variability and eliminating defects (to six standard deviations from the mean). Consider the following as an example of the advocacy and adoption of Six Sigma.

On February 1, 2016, the Human Resources Department of the University of Oklahoma Health Sciences Center sent an e-mail flyer to all employees announcing forthcoming "Lean/Six Sigma Certification Workshops." It was sent on behalf of Dr. B. M. Pulat, Lean/Six Sigma Master Black Belt. To be offered were certification workshops on "Lean Six Fundamentals," "Lean Processes/Office," and "Six Sigma" skills. The flyer described what was offered as follows:

> "Lean" primarily focuses on process efficiency, and "six sigma" on process effectiveness/quality. In combination, they can be used to make any process, and its outputs, predictable/in control, and capable (meeting/exceeding customer demands). . . .

> "Lean" and "Six Sigma" are the best known process design/improvement approaches to meet the challenges of maintaining efficiency while meeting increased compliance requirements and customer demands. (http://webmail.ouhsc.edu/owa/?ae=Item&t=IPM.Note&id=RgAAAACOAnByH27yT pgb6 . . . Accessed 2/1/2016)

Let me put TQM and Six Sigma into a wider and deeper framework. As management and leadership *ideologies*, they trace historically and methodologically to the industrialization of workers by Frederick Winslow Taylor (1911) in the early twentieth century. In this image, people not only utilize machines in their tasks, but also *are* machines. For instance, when corporations use the language of "retooling," not only are machinery improved, but employees are taught how to be more effective machines themselves. TQM and Six Sigma began as management "cults" and have by now become established, doctrinal "churches" and mainstream "religions."

Traced back some 10,000 years, advocates, leaders, and trainers of TQM and Six Sigma can be seen to be cut from the same cloth as shamans. As shamans, such leaders and trainers begin with emotionally vulnerable employees who have anxiety about keeping their jobs, and offer them magical ideology and ritual to salve their anxiety. These leaders and trainers rely on the psychological regression of managers and employees, and in turn offer them authoritarian solutions. It is as if leaders and trainers now say, "This is the way," to people who are now all too eager to say, "Tell me what to do to diminish my anxiety."

To return to the metaphor of religion, TQM and Six Sigma doctrine become the new, secular, management "Bible" that is to be unquestionably obeyed. It is no wonder that Michael Hammer and James Champy's 1993 book, *Reengineering the Corporation: A Manifesto for Business Revolution*, became not only a best seller but also a management "Bible" that still exerts a powerful influence. The word "manifesto" makes it clear that this book is an ideological tract!

Despite these hopes, claims, and promises, the ultimate success of TQM and Six Sigma and similar management ideologies is limited if not doomed by the fact that its adherents ignore dark, unconscious forces in individual and group life that undermine the creation of a totally controlled, rational workplace. One need only consider the disastrous consequences of the ideology of deregulation (Allcorn & Stein, 2012; Stein & Allcorn, 2010a, 2010b, 2010c), and the 2008 near-depression in the American economy due to the implementation of untrammeled fantasy.

The model of organizational rationality that infuses these leadership ideologies has been criticized by psychoanalytically oriented theorists, researchers, and consultants since Sigmund Freud. Although there are many models of mental functioning and of unconscious processes, psychoanalytically oriented organizational writers agree that beneath the crust of techno-rational culture is a dark side, rooted in unconscious processes and in early childhood experiences that profoundly affect leaders' and followers' choices and decision-making in later life.

Beginning with Sigmund Freud's *Group Psychology and the Analysis of the Ego* ([1921] 1955a), these authors include Seth Allcorn and Michael A. Diamond (1997), William Czander (1993), Michael A. Diamond (1993), Michael A. Diamond and Seth Allcorn (2009), Larry Hirschhorn (1988), Manfred Kets de Vries (1984, 1991, 2006), Harry Levinson and colleagues (1962), Shelley Reciniello (2014), Howard Schwartz (1990), and Howard F. Stein (2001). These authors show how the *absence of self-awareness, self-reflection (mindfulness), and self-knowledge* in leaders wreaks havoc on organizational missions, visions, strategic plans, productivity, profitability, morale, and the ability to adapt to ongoing change. Stated differently, these authors in various ways show how psychological reality shapes and drives organizational processes such as leadership, followership, and adaptation to reality.

For instance, what could be called "hard" organizational leadership (see below for greater detail) thrives on a lack of self-awareness and unconscious enactment. Hard leadership is characterized by pervasive narcissism and arrogance, vindictiveness, if not emotional brutality, and top-down, command-and-control action. These become instruments and psychological "hooks" for the leaders' and followers' projective identification. This commends what Seth Allcorn calls a "balloon theory" (personal communication, 7-19-16, used with permission). "It might be a 'balloon' theory in the sense of how big the balloon is (expansive, narcissistic, attention-seeking, size of over-inflated self). [It] has a very thin skin the bigger the balloon gets, and will blow up if the expansive self is in any way punctured by criticism. [The leader uses] perfection in the solution to be wielded against others to cut them down to size so to speak—deflate them," even as they try to deflate and puncture the leader.

Ironically, the grandiose leader's vast self-aggrandizement (inflation) is inseparable from the group's sense of demoralization, loss, neediness, and dependency (deflation). They project redemptive greatness into the leader to provoke him or her to great self-inflation in order to save them from their fears and restore their organization and themselves to success, prominence, and greatness. Consciously, and in the short run, they feel revitalized and significant, themselves. Alas, this is emotionally purchased by them through ceding (projection) all their competence and power to the leader. They are, in fact, depleted by the leader's exorbitant greatness. Ultimately, in the long run, the leader's insatiable appetite for inflation—an identification with their projection—is turned against them, and they become their leader's victims rather than beneficiaries. Narcissistic, self-aggrandizing leaders thrive on lack of self-awareness and on total dependency from their group. Theirs is a world driven by *action*. This brings me to a recent distinction between hard and "good enough" leadership.

"Hard" and "Good Enough" Leadership

To take the issue of self-awareness (and its lack) further, there is yet another distinction between types of leadership, one that Seth Allcorn and I have called "hard leadership" and "good enough leadership" (Allcorn & Stein, 2015). The style and personality of *hard leadership* is widespread and well known in organizations of all kinds. Hard leadership is characterized by a constellation that includes qualities of: forcing top-down/hierarchical; drilling down his or her will into the organization; telling, rarely listening; imposing decisions unilaterally; acting ruthlessly, emotionally abusive and brutal; treating employees as exploitable pawns and disposable objects, rather than as whole, valued, real persons. Hard leadership usually lacks self-awareness and discounts its value.

In contrasting the two leadership styles, I hasten to emphasize that the "Good Enough Leader" (GEL) is not "soft" in the popular images of indecisive, wishy-washy leaders, searching more for approval than for completion of tasks, and incapable of making hard decisions. Rather, the GEL makes difficult decisions, but *how* he or she works toward the decisions is what distinguishes between the types of leader and leadership. For the GEL, making hard decisions and implementing them is an open, inclusive, transparent, collaborative, trusting, and respectful process, rather than a unilateral, top-down, and not infrequently poorly informed dynamic (a list of virtues I owe to Seth Allcorn). The GEL is a careful, attentive listener—one who does not compose his or her response while the other person is talking. The GEL creates a playful while serious space in which ideas and solutions may safely be offered. The GEL sees and utilizes self-awareness as a virtue.

Unlike the "hard" leader, the GEL does not have to be right. Being even approximately "right" is the outcome of a reciprocal, respectful relationship between leader, manager, and employees. Instead of projecting anxiety and trying to control others through raw power, the GEL is aware of the seduction of anxiety, regression, and power and is thus not compelled to act on it. The GEL *reflects before acting*. In short, in his or her approach to organizational change, the GEL can be decisive without needing to be command-and-control, often even brutal. In the turbulent sea of change, the GEL can be *with* employees, not *above* or *against* them.

Furthermore, not all organizational change, even in our capitalist, market-driven society, is equivalent. The cultural mood of the 1980s through the present (2016) haunts the organizations described in the stories that follow. If there are lessons here for consulting at anytime, anywhere, there are also lessons for consulting with the ongoing casualties of our cultural era, a time of temporary leaders, temporary workers, temporary corporations, adjunct professors, downsizing, mergers and acquisitions, and a dashed work ethic (Castro, 1993).

I turn now to four stories that will illumine the importance of listening in consulting to leader and leadership in organizations, and to the role the unconscious plays in the least suspected of places. The *first* story is about the experience of a leader's resignation, of loss, and of organizational adaptation—and the role that listening played in humanizing the process.

A Story: The Chief Resigns

For nearly a decade, I served as a behavioral science consultant to an urban-based medical corporation, Midwestern Medical Consortium (MMC), and to its subsidiary, Regional Health Center (RHC), located some 150 miles from the main corporate offices. RHC employs 25 people. Early in the 1980s, the administrative manager of the rural subsidiary resigned from his position and was replaced. This former manager, who had helped found RHC in the mid-1970s, was a retired captain from the United States Navy and had run "a tight ship," as he and everyone called it. People thought of RHC as a "vessel" and him as their "chief." He was beloved, respected, and at times feared and hated. He was always approvingly spoken of by his RHC colleagues and subordinates as putting the success of the "mission" over personal gain, of putting his "men" (and women) first. Although at times stern in his reprimands and regarded as an "authoritarian" leader, he was appreciated for his directness and integrity. He was consistently regarded as subordinating his "ego" for the good of the group.

The resignation occurred a few years after a new corporate executive had come to power in the main corporate offices. The RHC administrative manager had come to feel increasingly compromised in his standards and in his ability to protect his employees and their work. Within three years, following one final attempt to come to an understanding with the new administration at MMC headquarters, he resigned. A younger man, a seasoned hospital administrator, was hired to replace him. The new manager accepted a brief transition in which he apprenticed himself to the chief. Both wanted an orderly transition and not to have the ship (an enduring metaphor at RHC) feel abandoned. The previous three years had been especially tense ones at the subsidiary. Many of its physicians and staff had come to feel that they were losing local autonomy and that the flow of money and decision-making authority was primarily in the direction of the centralizing MMC.

With the change of administrative managers at RHC, a split image between the old and the new managers rapidly took shape. The former manager was idealized as having the unit at heart, while the new manager was quickly evaluated to be an "inside man," a corporate "plant" for the executives at the MMC headquarters, not really "ours." The older manager, although judged by his subordinates as having been at times harsh and unfair, was admired for his devotion to RHC, his selflessness, his altruism. ("The troops come first" was among his most tenaciously remembered mottoes.) The new manager was regarded as something of an egoist, an administrative incompetent who always had to be right even when he was wrong, and a person sharply critical and berating of others in subtle ways. He was seen as self-aggrandizing and as less concerned with the welfare of the group or of its task than with "looking good to the bosses in the main offices." In short, the former manager quickly came to represent much, if not all, the group held to be "good," while the new manager was sized up as a symbol of everything "bad." The old manager was fondly remembered as one who could do little wrong. The new manager was ill-spoken of as one who could do little right.

As the months went by, RHC doctors, nurses, medical assistants, receptionists, secretaries, and business office personnel often privately shared with me their suspicion that the new manager was really a "spy" for the corporate headquarters at MMC, a kind of "fifth column" whose job it was to betray those inside RHC in order to control them better. Occasionally, they acknowledged the unfairness of their comparisons. "He [the chief] was a hard act to follow," or "It would be difficult, if not impossible, for *anyone* to fill his shoes," many said. The more glowing the idealization of the former boss became, the more sinister the image of the new boss appeared. Increasingly, they saw their erstwhile boss's departure as a result of a plot to have him "forced out" or "killed off."

As this pattern unfolded over the months, I came to see it as a group form of delayed mourning of the loss of the old administrative manager. He was too idealized to be let go when RHC employees needed him the most. He was too needed as a nurturing figure for them to acknowledge the ways in which he had been frustrating and humiliating (see Volkan, 1981, 1997). Employees displaced inexpressible anger (toward the distant corporate executives, whom they vilified, and toward the retired manager, who had departed and abandoned them) onto the manager's successor. Grief was blocked, replaced by chronic anger and accusation (at times a patently paranoid response).

On several occasions, I asked RHC employees whether they had discussed their feelings about the new manager with the RHC medical director (the administrative manager's clinical supervisor). They said that over the years they had talked with him about various organizational and personal problems, that he was an attentive and compassionate listener, but that now he had so many other problems in running the organization in these difficult times that they did not want to burden him with more. A kindly, silver-haired physician in his mid-60s, he was regarded by organization members as understanding, generous with time and advice, wise, easygoing, benevolent, and eager to avoid "rocking the boat" or "making waves." They felt called upon to protect this beloved medical leader from conflict, not to give him "bad news." He became the idealized "wounded" leader whom the group had to insulate from further vulnerability—from within and outside the local organization.

In my official job description with MMC and RHC, I consulted on other issues (physician–patient communication). I possessed no formal authority with respect to the issue under discussion. Nevertheless, several RHC members approached me for brief counseling sessions to discuss problems perceived to be caused by the young manager. Some personnel were angry, some tearful, some hurt, some bitter, but all recited the same litany of mistreatment at the manager's hands and frequently compared him with the former manager.

I first asked them the (perhaps obvious) question: Had they discussed their grievance(s) with the administrator who was bringing them so much grief? Horrified, they replied they could never confront him with these complaints. They feared he would just berate them more, demand even more work from them, and probably summarily fire them. I asked them about the possibility of taking this matter up with the supervisory administrator in the MMC home office. The local administrator's managerial (as opposed to clinical) supervisor in the corporate headquarters had made it clear to me, upon my inquiry, that under established policy when problems or grievances could not be solved by local channels in "satellite" corporations, he welcomed contact by phone or letter. He underscored (since I had raised the question) that no one would lose his or her job by raising these very legitimate issues with him.

Although RHC employees appreciated my having informed them of this available official channel of complaint, they were reluctant to use it. First, a widespread communication style among whites in the Great Plains region is that indirectness, face-saving, conflict avoidance, and "peace at any price" are to be preferred (Stein, 1985d, 1987d). Second, children are taught early not to let potentially humiliating "family dirt" out of the house. The sense of being self-sufficient and in total control of one's life is a deeply cherished regional value. Third, despite my reassurance about official policy, RHC employees persisted in their conviction that their job security and the integrity of the group itself would be threatened if they complained (however legitimate the cause) to the supervisory administrator. Their image of this administrator condensed with the image of the corporate headquarters: MMC could not be trusted; *he* could not be trusted. Economic times were Spartan, they reminded me. They insisted their fear of reprisals was real enough to outweigh any gain they might achieve by risking a complaint to him.

Through my own largely unconscious response to them (via empathy, identification), I could sense their confusion over many boundaries, such as between what was real and what was fantasy. I tried to help them sort out what was inside them and what was outside and to decide on a course of action (including inaction) based on a clear distinction between what they were bringing to the situation and what was being imposed by others. I tried to avoid siding with them against the new manager or the distant corporate executives. I frequently sensed in them and commented on their unresolved sorrow and rage over the loss of the chief. They now often talked about their unfinished business with him and his departure. Several RHC employees began to see the new manager and the old one each *as distinct people* unburdened with projections for the first time.

As individual and group counseling sessions with RHC personnel proceeded over time, I shared with them perspectives I had gained from additional discussions with the supervisory administrator in the corporate headquarters, the RHC medical director, and the new RHC manager. I told each of these executives that I sensed a morale problem in the organization. The headquarters supervisor and RHC manager both helped me understand their own sense of vulnerability and isolation. For instance, members often perceive such administrators as ruling with impunity; at the same time, administrative positions in a medical institution are lonely ones, for these workers are neither physicians nor members of the staff. They are expected to meet everyone's needs, while their own needs for being understood are seldom taken into account. Moreover, administrators are often asked to be the "bad guy," the "heavy," to make hard, often unpopular decisions no one else wants to make—only to be accused of being heartless. They, not the head physician, are the ones who bear the "bad news" about financial shortfalls, about the need for cutbacks ("tighten the belt"), and about the need to make sacrifices on behalf of the organization.

In discussions with the MMC managerial supervisor, I mentioned I had observed that when the RHC administrative manager had difficulty with self-confidence, he would harass and ridicule staff members. How, I wondered, might we help him have a greater sense of self-esteem in his leadership role? We agreed that as a long-term procedural policy, one approach would be for the supervisor to talk with the RHC manager more frequently. One nurse at RHC suggested to me that the new manager might be encouraged to be more consistently authoritative. For instance, she suggested he not try to be "one of the guys" while at the same time periodically trying to exercise peremptory authority, which just made him look silly to the staff and undermined his position. Over the months, the RHC manager developed greater self-confidence in his role. He was less haunted by the ghost of his predecessor. His doctors and staff were less inclined to couch everything they said about him in a comparison with the former chief.

At biweekly staff meetings attended by all RHC members, the manager began to take clear charge of the agenda and at the same time foster more open discussion. He would also mete out both criticism and praise. (He was previously known to praise no one for anything.) Instead of reprimanding RHC members for violating rules they had not known to be in force, he began to enunciate formally and publicly those rules. As might be expected, RHC staff members for a time did not know what to make of—or whether to trust—these apparent changes.

For several weeks afterward, physicians and staff had individual confrontations with the newer RHC manager, some angry and loud. But no one was disrespectful toward him. They set limits on him when he could not do so himself. They no longer acted as if he was right about some decision when they believed him to be wrong. They were now less apt to "keep score" against him and sulk about his mistreatment of them. Employees and physicians challenged him about decisions or style at the time rather than brood, circumvent, and gossip. Their jobs were not jeopardized. If anything, their working relationship improved. They no longer needed to complain about limits that he violated but that they had refused to set in the first place. RHC personnel also became more vocal in front of the medical director, who in turn had a "man-to-man" talk with his administrative manager. Everyone in the new situation became a little more "dirty" than they had wanted to be, whereas before they had preserved their sense of "goodness" and "cleanness" by perceiving some members of the local and central organization as altogether bad and dirty.

In subsequent counseling sessions or in hallway conversations, many RHC personnel began to acknowledge aspects of their administrator that they had begun to like and admire. They recognized that he came to work an hour before the office opened. They conceded that he might genuinely be dedicated to the organization's goals and not just be using the organization for self-aggrandizement. After these several weeks of confrontation with him, morale improved greatly. There was notably less whispering behind his back. People looked forward to coming to work instead of dreading each new day, expecting humiliation and rebuke. The retired administrative manager, an occasional visitor and adviser to RHC, was now greeted more as an old friend than as the person who really should still be (or who secretly was still regarded as) their manager.

Throughout this company's transition, I did not try to solve the employees' problems for them. I sensed there to be far more to the conflict than the initial "chief complaint" or presenting problem about the new manager's truculence. As an outside observer I pursued the many strands of the intrapsychic story together with them over many months. I also inquired on site and in the main office as to what the reality might be regarding employees' fears of dismissal and was able to convey accurate information to them. As I became familiar with the changed circumstances at RHC, I was able to help individuals and groups in the dispute hear and understand how each experienced its roles in the corporation. As projection and externalizing defenses diminished, and as participants began to own or internalize their grief and displaced anger, they became better able to confront the new manager as a person whom they included back into the human race. They saw him less as the embodiment of some sinister plot (in part, their own disowned aggression) or themselves as his innocent victims. By listening attentively to them, I helped them listen to themselves and each other.

Gradually RHC personnel realized that their self-protective silence, circumvention, and conflict avoidance had contributed to perpetuating the very conditions they wished to end. In first trusting me, they came to trust themselves more in their relations with one another. As they gained self-confidence and security, they felt they were not totally dependent on their managers and executives or on me. Finding their own voices, they needed less to fear and exaggerate the power of their superiors' voices.

Eight or nine months after this period of confrontation, I heard several raised voices coming from the board of directors' room. The administrative manager and several female assistants were engaged in a spirited dispute, punctuated with laughter. One of the women emerged from the room and gave me a look of exasperation, saying, "We need you to intervene as mediator in our dispute." I declined, saying humorously that it seemed to me they were doing just fine in talking the problem through with one another without me. They continued doing precisely that as I walked down the hall. They eventually solved the problem to everyone's satisfaction.

My *second* story of leadership and listening describes the aftermath of the forced resignation of a corporate leader, and how many employees came to learn that, dictatorial and intrusive as he was, he had also *embodied* what they most could not tolerate about themselves.

A Story: The Dethronement and the Boomerang

I once served as consultant to Medical Consortium (MC), a medical practitioner group that was a subsidiary of Corporate Health Planners (CHP). Around the time of my arrival, the senior executive physician of MC had just resigned from his position, one he had held for eight years. The resignation came close upon the heels of a routine periodic reevaluation of all senior executives by the home office. Dissatisfaction among junior physicians had gradually been building. Their boss was uniformly perceived as authoritarian, paternalistic, and imperious and as a "micromanager" who was unable to delegate power or projects, who insisted on keeping everything under tight personal scrutiny, who favored tried-and-true medical and administrative ideas and techniques, and who frowned upon newer, more innovative concepts and medical treatments. He liked the status quo that was supposedly predictable, and loathed change and its uncertainty.

Many at MC perceived there to be a wide "generation gap" between the boss and his physician and nonphysician juniors. He was a man in his late fifties, whereas most of his coworkers were a decade or more younger. During the review process, a group of medical executives from CHP (the "parent" company) had included a number of junior personnel among those interviewed. They expressed virtually universal disaffection with his style. At a poignant subsequent meeting between this physician-leader and his subordinates, he realized for the first time— as each member of the group was asked to express his or her position—how totally discrepant his own assumptions had been with those held by the others.

An immense sigh of relief among the personnel of MC followed his resignation. Several junior physicians invoked the expression "fresh air" to describe the good feeling and hopefulness about a future with the firm in which they would exert more control. Several managers and staff now openly discussed hurriedly dusted off projects that they had previously felt compelled to "table" and "shelve." They were jubilant in sharing their fresh ideas for medical research, patient education packages, product lines, and community involvement. They felt hope, renewal. A day into the consultation, several began to voice concern about what they would do once the momentary good feelings began to abate. "It is all well and good to feel good about ourselves and the freedom we have, but *what are we going to do?* Where are we going to go with it?" one physician pointedly asked.

Many of the young physicians and their nonphysician colleagues prided themselves on having been "decent" about their boss's resignation. They had tried not to scapegoat him as an evil man, a culprit, or a monstrous tyrant. As the discussions continued on an individual basis and in small groups, many group members began to realize that, despite their wish to be fair and to part honorably with their boss, they had also been participants in their chronically unhappy relationship with their formerly symbolic "primal father," not entirely victims of it. Although structural features of the corporation and personality characteristics of their leader had influenced their fate as colleagues and employees, they slowly came to realize that they had over the years ceded or allocated their own aggressive, "bad" paternal (technically, counter-Oedipal) impulses to the leader, whom they then accused of being heavy-handed and treating them like disobedient, unruly children. By focusing on *his* tyranny, they also averted sibling-fueled rivalry among *themselves*. War with him meant peace among themselves. The dethronement took away their displacement of their own "bad" parts of themselves. What they had projected returned like a boomerang.

The leader's unconscious role had been to serve as their dumping ground. Put in technical terms, the defense mechanisms of projective identification and externalization had come to affect, if not regulate, their perception of their boss's personality and their relationship with him. They felt less Oedipal triumph (that is, the sons' revolt against the father) over their victory, than they felt uneasiness about taking upon or into themselves aspects of the authority and tough decision-making they had disliked. They had retained these aspects at a distance in him and thus could *dislike themselves in him*. These were "him," not themselves, they had insisted. It was emotionally easier for them to feel themselves to be his victims than to take charge of the organization themselves.

They gradually realized that much of what they had disliked about him was what they disavowed in themselves but had relocated in him so that they could distinguish themselves from him and feel superior and pure. They then *provoked* him to enact what they had psychologically projected into him. They remained far from eager to assume a leadership role—let alone compete as siblings with one another directly, or compete with other authority figures within the corporate structure of CHP. Instead they (defensively) sought to prolong the era of good feeling and postpone the question of leadership succession.

Group members and I discussed this as a form of resistance to acknowledging and facing the underlying conflicts that the former boss had both symbolized and enacted for them. They gradually recognized how much they had needed their old boss to do the despised "dirty work" of politicking, making hard choices, setting administrative priorities, and "being a son-of-a-bitch" (in the words of one) so that they could feel more clean, pure, and nice. Up to this time, they had recognized only how much they disliked *him* and *his* style. They now came to realize how much they needed him. If they felt themselves to be his victim, they would never have to own up to their own aggression. His resignation was their emotional boomerang. There commenced a grieving process that seemed to replace the joy and relief—a mourning for the loss of innocence, for the realization that they were far less pure in motive than they had hitherto thought. The mending of good and bad parts of themselves had only begun.

A few days could not undo the psychic work of eight years. But as I left the week-long consultation, I felt I had avoided taking sides with them against their boss but had instead helped them understand what he had symbolically meant to them as a metaphor. I was hopeful that their organization would neither stagnate, dissipate, nor repeat its former pattern. Instead its members had the opportunity to grapple more honestly and with greater self-awareness with the problem of the quest for authority, the issue of legitimacy, the exercise of power, and leader–group relationships in task performance. By recognizing their implicit, unconscious group process, they could succeed in transforming the dislodging of a leader into an opportunity for organizational development and emotional growth, one that had the likelihood of enhancing the maturity and mutuality of all participants (Erikson, 1964).

I had listened to them, and they, in turn, listened better to each other. I had listened to them, and at key moments "told" them what they already knew they knew—at an unconscious level. If I listened deeply to them, it was largely because they "stretched" me into it.

For my *third* example, I would now like to turn to a brief story about the type of energized, productive group process that can occur when a *leader* himself or herself listens carefully to his group, and urges other group members to do likewise with each other.

A Story: A Leader Sets the Tone for Listening Deeply

Since 2012 I have served as group process facilitator for monthly meetings of the American Indian Diabetes Prevention Center (AIDPC) in Oklahoma City. The purpose of AIDPC is to improve the health of American Indians. I was recruited by the leader, the founder and director of AIDPC. The meetings usually consist of 15 to 25 members, and they last one and a half to two hours. The large group is comprised of four core groups, which in turn are constituted by project work groups. The four core groups consist of members who serve as administrators, conduct research, engage in research and training, and conduct community engagement or outreach. There is much diversity in the group: tribal, professional, departmental, university, gender, age, income, and so on.

The meetings are divided, on paper, into two parts: The first half consists of reports to the director and the wider group by each task group on the progress of their projects; in the second hour the interdisciplinary seminar (large-group interaction) takes place. There is throughout both segments large-group interaction in which participants learn from each other and contribute across project boundaries. My main task and role is to facilitate communication and foster a sense of community between the groups, to help nurture a common "Center" identity.

Since my involvement in 2013, there is much more interchange—sharing of ideas, offering suggestions and help between groups, brainstorming, and telling of personal stories—than in previous years. There is much hugging and visiting before and after the group; humor and laughter; and a sense of safety and ease through empathy and identification. I often identify themes and emotional "tones" that pervade the meetings, sometimes asking probing questions, occasionally offering an interpretation, all in the service of reflection, emotional development, community building, and empathic listening and responses *in the large group*.

Toward the middle/end of 2014, it was becoming clear from the work group reports in the monthly meetings that the recruitment of "subjects" or "research partners" was falling far short of the goal necessary to complete valid and reliable research, and in turn to generate publications and reports which are required by the granting agency.

After each AIDPC meeting and often through telephone visits between meetings, I visit with the director to "process" or "debrief" what had occurred during the meeting, and to make future plans based on the consultation—a kind of informal "executive coaching." During one such visit in late 2014, I used the phrase (label) "crisis of the Center" with respect to fulfilling the cultural mission. The director agreed with the term, and we discussed the possibility of devoting an entire monthly meeting or two to sharing and pooling small-group experiences, and in the process coming up with new subject-recruitment strategies. We would ideally learn from each other what had worked and what had not worked. I emphasized that it was crucial to create an atmosphere of safety, of containment, where participants could share their experiences, mistakes, misgivings, anxiety, and disappointments without being singled out for finger-pointing and punishment. I suggested the phrase "no-fault brainstorming," after Seth Allcorn's notion of "no-fault change."

The director embraced the idea, and in fact had the phrase printed in large letters in the following month's agenda, handed out to everyone at the beginning. At the meeting, the director began by saying that the large group would forego core group reports for today and would focus instead on sharing and brainstorming about how better to recruit subjects. He said that the central ground rule was no blaming, no finger-pointing, but pooling collective experience to come up with improved solutions to recruitment.

He then said to the entire group, "I failed in recruitment in my projects. I dropped the ball." He thus set the tone for "blame-free brainstorming." The large group was energized and eagerly shared what had not worked, what had worked, and what might work. The group buzzed with thinking aloud. There was laughter and, after the meeting ended, many hugs. There developed an enthusiastic large-group spirit of serious play, both this day and in the subsequent month's meeting where the process continued. I would occasionally offer a suggestion or identify a theme, but I mostly listened attentively, serving with the director to create and sustain a group boundary in which new possibilities, new solutions, might surface.

The long-term success of this experiment is attested to by the increase of core group recruitment in subsequent months and the ability of the research to progress. Morale improved over the months, as did productivity. I believe that the key ingredient in this process and outcome was that the director set the emotional atmosphere for the large group, saying—and then acting on what he said—that it was safe to be vulnerable and to admit mistakes, that no one would be publicly shamed or punished, that we could learn from our mistakes, as well as from experience and from what had worked. The work of the Center continued to progress into 2015 and 2016. I believe that both the director and I—and our long relationship as friends and colleagues—served as GELs in the process. We learned and worked largely by listening—and by caring enough for each other to listen.

For a *fourth* example, I would like to conclude this chapter on organizational leadership by telling the story of a regular meeting I had with the CEO of an organization over many years, in which my attempt at deep listening was matched by his own hard emotional work.

A Story: The Monthly Visit with the CEO

This is the story of a long-term monthly "visit" with a CEO that was among the most intimate I have had in my career. Although I could never expect what he would want to talk about, I always looked forward to my meetings with him. I admired his devotion to the people of his company and to their mission. He was the quintessence of a "good enough leader" whose style is characterized by values of openness, inclusiveness, transparency, collaboration, mutual trust, and mutual respect (Stein & Allcorn, 2014). I was grateful that he truly worked during our visits.

During the first decade of the 2000s, I had a monthly meeting with the CEO of the subdivision of a large multisite corporation. I had intermittently consulted with the corporate subdivision since the 1980s. The CEO had requested the consultations around 2000, and called it our monthly "visit," although it was in fact a kind of informal executive coaching. In our hour-long meeting, I would begin by asking something like, "How are things going, and how are *you*?" His *experience* of his many roles was as important to me as the roles themselves. He would review the month's activities, describe developments and "challenges" in each of the divisions of his company. He would occasionally try a new idea out with me, and ask me whether the company had ever tried implementing the idea before. He always inquired about how I was doing—and meant it.

I functioned as something of an informal company historian since, as a long-time consultant, I had more of a sense of history and continuity than the many newer leaders, managers, and employees. He was very sensitive to not making the same mistake twice or "reinventing the wheel." Although when he had to be decisive, he could be and was, he also went to great lengths to be inclusive and in meetings to ask for honest appraisal of his ideas, or anyone's—which was usually forthcoming. He trusted those whom he led and they trusted him. Put differently, trust was the foundation of his work with leaders, managers, and employees. Sometimes as he reviewed the month—and back much further in time—he talked about "putting out fires" in various divisions, and about what was working well and what needed to be addressed.

On several occasions during our 10 or so years of monthly visits, he would reflect to me that one thing he especially valued about our visits was that he could take time out from a life of one meeting and problem after the other, to step back and think about the whole month (and further) and get a sense of the "big picture" of his company. It was a reprieve, a safe place in time where he was not "putting one fire out after another."

As he spoke I thought of his inevitable *fragmentation* from addressing so many different groups and issues, one after the other, and trying to forge a sense of community and common identity. By contrast, our "visits" were an opportunity for him not only to imagine the company as a whole, but also to achieve a greater sense of *personal integration*. He could better see "how the pieces of the puzzle fit together." I also inquired into his family life—or he would bring up the subject himself. The situation at home often weighed on his mind—for example, aging and ill parents and parents-in-law and their eventual deaths, marriage of a child. Discussion of "work" in relation to "family" and personal issues, such as his own aging and less energy than years before, also aided the process of integration and deepened our relationship. He often inquired about *my* life and health—as I often had illnesses to contend with. He was as concerned about others as he was about their task performance.

In addition to empathy, I could identify with him in many areas, since I was also in my 50s and 60s and lacked the stamina at work that I once had. He would often confide in me his inner conflicts and how they found expression in his leadership in the workplace—whether he still was fit to be the leader or whether he should step down to a company role with less responsibility.

In our relationship, he was mostly the storyteller and I the story listener. I would occasionally tell a story that resonated with his, make an observation, offer an interpretation, or ask a question, but my goal was to help him to put his own "Humpty Dumpty together again," that is, to integrate or defragment his life.

Almost each time we met, a significant shift would take place around halfway through the visit. Up to that point, we would sit facing each other in comfortable chairs with tall backs, and we would look at each other as we spoke. Often around the half-hour point, he would lean his head back, rest his head on the back of the chair, close his eyes, and continue speaking, but now on a deeper, more *emotionally* engaged level. Much of the earlier conversation had been about organizational facts and details, matters outside himself. Now he was in tune with feelings—often *feelings about the facts*. Some of what he would say was free association.

He would be in a kind of reverie. His tone of voice would change; he would speak much more softly now. I would often imagine him to be floating. He would speak of the company, of his hopes and fears and fantasies. I would feel it to be a privilege to be in his presence during these times. I would sense that these were moments of his own healing, of fragmentation, splits, and anxiety, and of reaching a deeper level of himself. I would sense great intimacy between us during these times.

At some point he would "awaken," so to speak, look at his wristwatch, and recognize that he needed to prepare for a lunch meeting. He would sincerely thank me as we shook hands and he patted me on the shoulder. He would personally usher me out the door. I would feel much better myself, and believe that through deep listening, I had helped him to heal and integrate at least a little, and for a little while, and to better address issues in his workplace.

Clearly, leaders and leadership are no simple matter. For one, leaders do not exist apart from followers. For another, their bond is largely regulated by the unconscious, often creating a tumultuous, even toxic, symbiosis. Sometimes, as in "good enough" leadership, the relationship is healing and is characterized by grace. Listening deeply allows the stories of leadership and followership to surface and be heard.

6. Organizational Change, Loss, and Grief

Introduction

The eminent organizational psychoanalytic theorist and consultant Harry Levinson was fond of saying that leaders must be the chief mourners to lead their workplaces through change. Yet as human history abundantly shows, leaders of all kinds or organizations—from workplaces to nations to empires to religions—rarely take on this role for their group, but instead often flamboyantly and violently force through change toward the future, often forbidding memory of the past (Doka, 1989). The "inability to mourn" and, in turn, failed adaptation (Mitscherlich & Mitscherlich, 1975; Pollock 1961, 1977; Volkan, 1981, 1988, 1997) describes the psychological reality of countless workplaces.

Since the 1980s through the present (2016), CEOs, provosts, presidents, and chairpersons have been brought on to rapidly "turn around" organizations that have experienced—or were perceived as experiencing—major losses. The magical answer has often been to downsize, reengineer, and restructure the organization, to outsource (offshore) unwanted functions, with little concern for those who were abruptly fired or for the survivors who had to assume the tasks and roles of those who were no longer there—and with no raise in salary.

Violent change took, and continues to take, an enormous psychological and physical as well as economic toll on those people who were metaphorically called "dead wood," "organizational fat," or "dead meat," who needed to be cut and sacrificed in order to create a "lean, mean, fighting machine." The casualties were not experienced as real people, but as "collateral damage." The organizational researcher or consultant who tries to understand or help people through these horrors is not "imagining things" when he or she "sees" blood on the floors and walls. Often the self of the researcher or consultant is a crucial key to recognizing

175

the emotional violence that underlies the supposedly rational logic of enhancing productivity, profitability, and instant increased shareholder value—though at best temporarily. The self—including the imagination—of the researcher or consultant becomes the key to seeing through the ritualistic "smoke and mirrors" that many leaders and quick-fix consultants use to revitalize the workplace. Things are not what they seem—and are made to seem.

This brings me to an issue of methodology in organizational research, consulting, and leadership. It is the central role of countertransference in all organizational work. Two of the most nagging methodological questions scientists and social scientists ask themselves (when they are being honest) are, "How much am I objectively reading nature, and how much am I reading into nature?" That is, how much am I *understanding*, and how much am I *projecting*? It is no different for organizational researchers and consultants who are trying to make sense out of their work and arrive at certain themes, patterns, and structures as they do their cross-organizational comparisons, especially during times of rapid, traumatic change. Over the past three and a half decades as I have conducted workshops and consultations, almost no matter where I have turned, *the triad of change, loss, and grief* has emerged as a central theme in the underlying, chronic distress organizations have suffered, especially in the throes of massive change.

It is tempting to read this triad as a universal given, almost a platonic form in human nature. At one level, all cultural change triggers responses of loss and mourning. Yet at another level, all changes are not psychologically equivalent, not interchangeable. Members of different organizations do not have the identical experience of change and loss. Part of a researcher and consultant's task, then, is to identify those feelings, values, and meanings that are unique to a specific organization and its era, as well as those that emerge from the very fact of being human. Here the dimension that psychoanalysis brings is of enormous help.

This chapter brings this triad to the center of organizational inquiry. Workplaces, not unlike ethnic groups and nations, are a vital, if fragile, part of who we are. Their stories and fantasies contain some of our most abiding meanings, deepest feelings, and deepest yearnings. Six diverse stories illustrate the role that change, loss, and grief play in shaping organizational stories and how access to this knowledge can help organizations heal. The first one is the occasion of a secretary's retirement.

A Story: The Secretary's Retirement

In one corporation's medical department, a 50-year-old secretary retired four months before she had originally planned to do so. In recent years, she had experienced a bout with lung cancer and had considerably slowed down on the job. She said to me that among her reasons for leaving several months ahead of schedule was that it had been hard for her to get used to saying good-bye to so many people all the time, and hard to get used to working continually with new people. She felt she could never settle into expectations and rhythms before they changed again. Furthermore, she felt others made decisions affecting her job without asking or consulting her. People's comings and goings had left her, she said, feeling abandoned, disoriented, and demoralized. She felt unappreciated for all her pitching in and going many an extra mile over the decade she had worked in the company. New managers thought only of their future, of the new history they would make, not of old-timers' past contributions as ongoing and valuable.

Moreover, her corporate leaders had declared a virtual ban on talking about those people who had left, saying anything good about them, or even grieving their loss. She felt as if she was expected to be highly productive while pretending nothing had happened to the organization, that people were no more than interchangeable parts of a machine. She decided this time not to persevere because she felt increasingly isolated and out of place. She felt displaced. The effects of her radiation therapy, of the cancer itself, and of recent conferences with upper management might well have been part of the picture. However, for her, change, loss, and personal grief triggered and made chronic her sense of anxiety. The grief and anxiety were compounded by the fact that they were worse than discountable: They were unspeakable, undiscussable. They were the organization's shame; they were its secret. She gave me the gift of her story and the organization's secret. Perhaps through my story listening, she felt less alone in her grief.

The second story begins as a seemingly typical account of corporate recruitment for a managerial position. The labyrinth eventually led to an innermost chamber of change, loss, and grief. The executive trusted me enough to make the undiscussable discussable. I had consulted many times with the corporation's medical department, so she and I were not strangers to each other. An ongoing but intermittent relationship set the stage for her telling his story to me, and my listening deeply to him.

A Story: She Is Gone

A midlevel executive of a large Great Plains corporation began a consultation at lunch by telling me about a series of interviews he and other members of his unit were conducting with several applicants for a managerial position within his division. The latest applicant, a man in his early 50s, had an impressive "ticket" of experience. A man from the Deep South who had spent many years as an officer in the armed services, the applicant impressed people as politically, economically, and clinically conservative—so much so that my client worried that this applicant might be all too susceptible to the influence of some of the junior managers and on-line workers and staff who were often outspokenly anti-black, anti-poor, and anti-Yankee.

All the other candidates had their pluses and minuses, so far as he and the other members of his unit were concerned, but this candidate had uniformly evoked the strongest negative reaction. Among some, it amounted even to revulsion—although they also conceded that by far he had the strongest "suit" of all the applicants. Moreover, a senior executive of the company was especially impressed by the applicant's credentials and attitude toward authority: namely, maintenance of a tight vertical "chain of command" style of leadership.

Although members of the unit appreciated having the opportunity to interview the candidates, they feared upper-level executives would preempt or ignore any recommendations they might make and choose whomever they wanted. Furthermore, the manager continued, several members of his unit reported a facet of their interview similar to what he experienced: namely, that the candidate asked little about what he could do for the unit and next to nothing about the interests and imagined futures of the managers and staff with whom he might serve as supervisor and/or coworker. They did not describe him as arrogant or boastful but as markedly one-sided in his interests during the conversation. Was he only interested in himself and not them? they wondered. My client, like his division members, felt left out and discounted in the conversation and speculated with misgivings about what it would be like to have this man around full-time.

As this medical manager spoke, my mind floated and teemed with various fantasies that could become hypotheses. There certainly were Oedipal ingredients, for example, conflicts between younger and older men for possession and dominance of the group. There were likewise dependency strivings as well as intimations of Oedipal revolt akin to siblings, male and female together, setting aside their internecine quarrels and competition for favoritism from the parents, in order to present a united front against an imagined "bad" parent and to care for one another. The uncertainty of the corporate situation, and of the members' future organizational roles, might have precipitated persecutory anxiety and paranoid defenses against it (Diamond, 1984; Diamond & Allcorn, 2009). The manager had begun his story in an almost indifferent, detached tone of voice. As he proceeded, his voice became more urgent and his eye contact with me more frequent.

When he paused at the end of the portion of the consultation just described, I said that the situation sounded difficult but that I still did not have a "handle" on it. I had the uneasy feeling that something was missing, that the story was incomplete. I reflected back to him his emotional involvement, different from his usually more laid-back, more distant, more matter-of-fact attitude toward corporate problems. I asked, "Is there some part of the story you've still not told? I feel that something is missing. Why now? Why *this* applicant?"

He continued, less in answering my barrage of questions than in free-associating. Not many months ago, he reminded me, one of the unit's favorite midlevel managers had been denied her bid for promotion by upper-level management. She subsequently left. The group still felt bitter about top management's decision and the peremptory way in which it appeared to have been made. Then a couple of months later, another midlevel manager who had worked there as a trainee (apprentice), and whom the unit had heavily "courted" to become a permanent employee, rejected the offer by the company and went to work elsewhere. The interviews with this military-style applicant, he continued, came right on the heels of these two disasters. As he recounted these two losses, his voice grew less urgent and slower.

I said I thought he knew where he was heading. I then interpreted somewhat as follows:

> You and your unit have suffered two great losses recently. One is a person to whom you were all very close. Suddenly she was taken away. The other was a person you wished would become a member of your group, and he decided to go somewhere else. There still is a lot of grief and bitterness and emptiness that has not been dealt with in your group. Suddenly, in comes this latest candidate, one you think will get along famously with the very upper-level management whom you mistrust, and your mistrust, or at least misgivings, escalate further. The main underlying feelings I am picking up are tremendous sadness at the loss and rage over your and others' helplessness to do anything about it. [I continued with a brief personal anecdote:] My mother's death, now three years ago, still affects me, and your own mother died not long thereafter. Do you think there could be any connection between your personal loss and grief and the parallel in your unit?

His eyes opened wider and became slightly tearful. He grew pensive, as his body seemed to relax. He corrected me:

> Not my mother, but my *daughter*. The manager we lost was like a daughter to me. I'm in my 50s, and she's in her 30s. I had taken her under my wing, so to speak. Everybody really liked her. I was just beginning to get to know her when she left because they wouldn't give her the promotion. And it's the same with my daughter. In her late teens, just when I was beginning to get to know her as a person and not just as a headache, she left home to go out

on her own. With this manager, it's like going through it all over again. It was like losing a daughter.

To stimulate any associations he might have, I had used my personal anecdote as a linking association between two disparate areas of life, personal and professional. I was wrong about the person ("object") who had been lost, but I had been on the right track to sense some additional, profound, overdetermined loss waiting in the wings.

Profound sadness and silence now characterized both the manager and the tone of our discussion. With a look of recognition and emotional exhaustion, he said, "Thanks." I then said briefly that I knew he wanted to be a good leader, and that since his authority in the larger corporation was limited, he might not be able or allowed to do all he wished for his own unit. There might well be realistic limits to his ideals and ambitions. I suggested that, important as the selection of a new manager was, from the emotional viewpoint the current applicant was a secondary concern. I interpreted the group members' preoccupation with the applicant and his real or imagined relationship with upper management to be a way of displacing attention from the deep grief that they felt about the two earlier group losses—together with the other, in his case familial, memories of loss these had in turn unearthed. I suggested his main role for now might best be as facilitator of his unit's grief work. I imagined aloud that as the members healed from these wounds, they would be able to be more realistic in their assessment of this and other candidates for the division. At that point the consultation concluded.

On the surface, I apparently "fell into" the information about this executive's recent losses. The question arises whether an organizational consultant might more systematically, efficiently, and deliberately inquire into possible links between a client's professional and personal, or present and past, realms of life. All meanings and behavior are overdetermined. That is, they are shaped by multiple, convergent "lines" of conscious and unconscious thought and feeling. In organizational consultations of any kind, we would thus do well to keep this principle in mind with respect not only to job-related losses but also to problems associated with any facet of work. However, such an approach must not be used mechanically ("canned"). Such questions are triggered by the consultant's own emotional response to the client. The timing of such a question or line of inquiry is crucial to its therapeutic efficacy. By closely following the client's chain of thoughts and affects, the consultant will know when the timing is emotionally right (ripe) for asking question(s).

I wish to add that, although my mother's then-recent death had heightened my awareness of loss, mortality, and grief, from the viewpoint of the consultation, this event was not the decisive factor in my inquiry into possible links among this manager's personal, family, and professional events together with their inner significance for him. If I had been able to fall into his world, it was at least in part because through listening carefully to his emotions via my own and to his verbal associations, and through attending closely to his gestures, I was able to let him fall into my own inner world. It was the fact of our shared humanity—despite the wide difference between our professional cultures and family backgrounds—that led me to reach into my own feelings and recent experiences as an "instrument" useful in facilitating his discovery of links among his own personal, family, and professional realms.

I conclude this example by underscoring the complexity of people's psychological realities in organizational groups. The principle of *overdetermination* applies here as in individual psychoanalytic therapy: that is, an event never merely means one thing; it can never be reduced to a single common denominator. The event means many things *simultaneously*—conscious and unconscious wishes, fantasies, anxieties, defenses, and so on. If I have emphasized the transferential dynamics (that is, the unconscious presence of the past in haunting the conscious present) of my client's experience of loss, this does not deny or lessen the intragroup reality of loss in his here and now. It does not imply that his coworker really meant nothing to him and that she merely or really meant something mistaken to him. The present is never only or merely the repository of the past.

The loss of a valued female colleague in an otherwise all-male medical department is the loss of a real colleague and friend, not only the echo of the loss of a daughter. If "she was like a daughter to me," she was also a living presence in the here and now to the group. My client missed her for herself and for her unconscious representation of his daughter. Because organizational group dynamics recapitulate earlier relationships, fantasies, and feelings, this does not mean that they consist *only* of these displaced, misplaced relationships. The sting is deeper, and hurts so much, because the loss means and feels so much at so many different levels. Group identity, history, feelings, and meanings are themselves psychological realities that can be lost as well as symbols that serve as vessels for other unacknowledged losses.

My next story relays an unconscious story embedded within the explicit story. It is about listening attentively to cues that allow the unconscious story to surface and be told. It is also a story about deep caring among coworkers, an increased rarity in our age.

A Story: "Be Very Careful Out There"

Listening is not only a matter of "ears." It is attentiveness with our whole body and being. It is deeper than even attentiveness to nonverbal as well as verbal cues. It thrives on—even as it dreads—serendipity, what we are not looking or listening for, what we do not even know to count as "data." During the winter of 1991,

I had driven 100 miles north of Oklahoma City before dawn one morning to consult with a medical clinic. I had driven there often, and in my nearly 35 years of doing clinical teaching and supervision in Oklahoma, I had thus far managed to outrun ice storms. That is, I had been able to do my teaching, supervision, or counseling and then head south again on the road before it iced over. On that day I was caught. What I had dreaded most had finally come to pass.

I decided to leave immediately after the noon conference, about 1:45 p.m. Several physicians and staff wished me well. I headed for the door of the clinic. The director of the laboratory, Zenka Miller, whom I had then known for twelve years, followed me to the door. With an intense, worried look, she said to me, "Be very careful out there." She looked me straight in the eyes; we held our gaze for what felt like several seconds. I felt her concern, even deep affection. As I drove home I witnessed many accidents, including a semitrailer jackknife dangerously and helplessly right in front of me. Luckily enough, I was not invovled in one of these accidents. Over the next couple of weeks, I could not rid myself of Zenka's look, the fact that she had even accompanied me to the door, which she had never done before. We had become good friends over the years, but never had she come so physically close to me. It felt eerie—as if for a few short seconds I had been her husband and she, my wife, at least in my fantasy.

Gradually, and vaguely, I remembered that, 15 or 20 years before, Zenka's husband, a commercial airline pilot and previously an air force jet pilot, had been tragically killed in an airplane crash somewhere in southwestern Pennsylvania during a snow—or ice—related accident. I started to understand the powerful emotional pull (transference) I felt that she had unconsciously directed toward me at the clinic door and my own emotional tidal wave (countertransference) directed back toward her. Feeling bewildered, I also felt deeply grateful for her affection and concern. I decided to find some way to talk with her, to acknowledge that there had been something profoundly special about that moment, and to say that I wondered whether it was linked somehow with her husband's death.

Several weeks later when I was next at work in her community clinic, I approached Zenka and said I wanted to thank her for that deeply affirming moment at the clinic entrance several weeks earlier. I said I felt as if something more than my own, individual leaving was taking place. I described aloud what my feelings and fantasies had been for that moment: I, her husband, and she, my wife. Her eyes became tearful, and she recounted having said good-bye to her husband the day that his plane iced over and crashed (the exact cause of the crash was never definitively determined). I said I felt that suddenly we were reliving something all over again, that my previous departure had possessed a special emotional bond that went further than my role as consultant and clinical supervisor in her organization and her formal role as laboratory director.

Both these interactions were tender, boundary-breaking moments for both of us. They affirmed for me not only how personal, marital, and family events can be played out in occupational or work roles, but also how my own response—bizarre feelings of suddenly being a colleague's husband, of being in mortal danger—can be data crucial for understanding and responding to another person in the workplace.

The beginning of this process, I emphasize, is that I was disturbed by something. Something felt eerie, uncanny. I made that disturbance central to my visceral, later more intellectual, comprehension of what was taking place. Taken a step further, this data included my own emotional response. Instead of my discounting as irrational, irrelevant, or extraneous my feelings and fantasies about my friend, I felt they were crucial to understanding her as a person with whom I worked and, in turn, for the organizational morale for which I had long labored.

Here my *subjective* response to her was an essential part of my eventual access to the *objective* data about her sudden, anxious juxtaposition of many worlds that crystallized for a moment in our workplace: past and present (and the anticipated, dreaded future that might play out the past), occupation and family, consultant and spouse, life and death. These all became players on the same, single, crowded stage. This was at once frightening to me in the boundaries it temporarily broke down and refreshingly liberating in what possibilities of a deeper work relationship it opened. A bridge had been built. A boundary between the professional and the personal had been crossed. It was as if we both lived, and could acknowledge that we lived, in the shadow of death, that part of our bond was a close familiarity with death. I was both person and metaphor.

In several subsequent visits she further reflected on how she had been feeling over the following weeks. She told me that on the afternoon of the ice storm, she had said to herself, "I've got to see Howard before he leaves today," albeit not knowing why or what the urgency was. She said that following our first visit about the moment in the doorway, she had talked with one of her daughters on the telephone and had realized that she had already felt "strange" for several weeks, that something else she could not name was going on in her life. Her daughter had reminded her it was *at this time of year* 20 years earlier that her husband had left for work for the last time and been killed in a plane crash. Zenka realized that her sense of eeriness or unreality (that something was missing in the story) was a kind of "anniversary reaction" or "post-traumatic stress reaction" (now virtually a folk-psychology term).

Not only did she discuss with me her phone call with her daughter, but we also used this renewed sense of kinship as a point of departure for talking about how clinic morale and communication between various units might improve generally. This illustrates how once acknowledged, unconscious influences in occupational groups can become profound sources of intimacy as well as productivity. We discussed impediments to interoffice communication within the organization and the sense of risk incurred with being known more at the core than at the periphery of our lives. To wait for everyone else in a clinic or corporation to break down barriers themselves would be to set them, and ourselves, up to fail. I said I did not believe that moments such as the one at the clinic doorway and our subsequent visit could be contrived or forced but that we could respond or fail to respond when they happened. Much as Searles (1975) discusses how patients come to serve as therapists to their analysts, Zenka Miller's transference served a similar therapeutic end for me. She urged me on to a higher level of development and reality testing.

Feelings, fantasies, and perceptions from the past not only distort but also nourish the present, but only when they are adequately processed (Tansey & Burke, 1989). They can doom the present when they "possess" it, that is, when they are enacted blindly and without reflection. But when they are mutually acknowledged, they add a poignancy to the present and give an additional sense of meaning and continuity to the lives of the participants. What prevented the interaction between Zenka and me from being a mere "repetition compulsion" of the past was that we could later acknowledge openly what was occurring unconsciously, out of awareness, and could transcend that past even as we were informed and nourished by it. What had started out as a momentary blurring of boundaries (between her husband and me, between husband role and coworker role) became a vehicle for affirming our separate realities and our friendship as coworkers.

This story shows how listening deeply in organizational work is not only about the emotional significance of large-scale events but also about attentiveness to small, although never minor, details of everyday relationships in the workplace. From the vantage point of the unconscious, "small" is often very "large." This is the essence of this book.

I now turn to a fourth and quite complex story about the role change, loss, and grief played in a city's large educational system. It turns out that the presenting problem sealed over a deeper and pervasive sense of loss and grief.

A Story: The Retreat

In the early 1990s, I was a member of a three-person "training team" (a widespread business and management term) for the three-day retreat of a city's approximately 26 school principals and superintendents and 7 school board members. For the first two days, the principals and superintendents, met as a group. On the third day, they were joined by the school board. An attempt was made to facilitate group morale both within the initial group of administrators and later within the combined group. A decade of animosity and mistrust existed between the two groups, now exacerbated by, among other events, the recent failure of a school bond issue and the resignation of a controversial superintendent. Thus, it would be a challenge at this retreat for an already embattled school board to join a group of administrators who had spent two days together developing a sense of boundaries and identity.

Historical Context: A Longitudinal View of the Present

Until 1980, Midwest City had been a largely Anglo—and German—American rural farming community of 18,000 people. As recently as 1950, an article in a school annual yearbook was in German. During the 1980s, the population increased to 25,000 with the building and expansion of the food-processing industry, founded on the heels of Reagan-era decentralization and deregulation. Hispanics, Turks, Laotians, Cambodians, and Vietnamese numbered high in the ethnic influx. Midwest City rapidly became a multiethnic, multioccupational community. A town once highly Methodist now had its Buddhist temple and Islamic mosque. At the food-processing plants there was high worker turnover. In the schools, there was considerable student turnover. At the retreat, several people noted that the teacher turnover rate in Midwest City was the highest in the state. Over the past decade, the district had lost three superintendents. Devastation from a tornado in the late 1960s persisted in townspeople's memories.

Throughout the Midwest City retreat and the planning sessions, my approach was to subordinate any content I might introduce to the relationship context in which it was taking place. I tried to make sure no information, interpretation, confrontation, or role play would intrude upon and threaten the nurturing, safe environment we had strived to create. I recognized that anything any of us, facilitator or not, might say to one another could be construed in terms of its relative truth value (reality), the ebb and flow of our relationships with one another, or, at some level, both. Worse, any preconceived theory or model could be used to prejudice or limit knowledge and feeling. (This defensive maneuver is as true for scientists as for any "laity.") Furthermore, since mistrust had become endemic to Midwest City, every sentence anyone uttered at the retreat would likely be carefully scrutinized for its ostensible, if not hidden, threat.

At the beginning of the retreat, there was considerable reservation, if not outright hostility, on the part of the administrators about getting together at all. Several raised the questions, "Whose idea was the workshop?" and "Why didn't they ask us principals what we thought about training?" They agreed to attend, but many felt it to be by command. Mistrust was in the air long before it became an obsessive theme during the retreat itself. Trust and mistrust were rooted not only in the present but also, as one principal put it, "in the land mines of history in Midwest City."

Having a sense of longitudinal history was crucial to understanding, and of being of any help, in the present. Past school district superintendents, the loyalties and rancor they inspired, and the town's inability to "let go" of that history haunted the retreat. Dr. John Hart had been a respected, even beloved, superintendent for the 16 years prior to 1980. Then came what many described as "the Frantz fiasco," a five-year period after which Dr. Paul Frantz was charged, tried, and imprisoned for financially exploiting the school district's money. His embarrassing era was followed by that of Dr. Jerry Rauschmann, who was brought in to be a kind of executive antidote to the humiliating, exploitative years of Dr. Frantz. Instead, Rauschmann took his mandate to turn the district around and became heavy-handed throughout the school district. He was seen as tyrannical, degrading, controlling, and intrusive.

He was supported politically by a fiercely loyal faction of principals, who came to be known as "Jerry's Kids." Sometime during 1990 he was asked to leave because of the chaos he had sown in Midwest City. Many thought his leaving constituted a crisis and felt abandoned and adrift. Others breathed a sigh of relief. Dr. Glenn Stuart had just been appointed the new interim superintendent. This administrators' and school board retreat seemed to be the first time the participants ever permitted themselves to speak about, and feel, their profound, subterranean grief. In short, the retreat was really a grief workshop: The objects lost were people's many selves and the envelope that was once the stable, eternal, agricultural Midwest City. Trying to emotionally "get my arms around" everything I had seen and heard thus far, I sensed that the community was mired in grief from so much loss.

Organizational and Community Grief

On the third day, I wondered aloud to the group, "How do organizations, communities grieve?" I also wondered what impediments to grief work there were in the educational system in Midwest City. From what I had heard earlier in the retreat, and from studies such as that of the history of National Socialism in Germany, I speculated that part of the *inability* to mourn, the retreat from mourning, came out as blaming, hating, aggression, fighting (including outright warfare), and scapegoating by projecting our own inner chaos onto villains and victims. One way to avoid grief is to find someone (a leader) or some other group (a pariah) to blame, and embody and personify our own evil so that we can maintain the illusion and hope that what was lost can be restored (Fornari, 1975; Volkan,

1997). Ironically, under these circumstances splitting feels like healing, although genuine healing is a process of integrating in one's self and one's group what has been split off and projected.

I said to the group that I had heard over the past three days numerous references to a feeling of "urgency" to *do* something, to have a plan of action or policy. I wondered whether, in addition to action being necessary to complete any task, the present sense of urgency to "do something" might not also be a response to grief: a kind of flight into relentless activity in order not to feel. If so, what, then, would grief work be? I suggested it would involve reviewing history rather than banning its mention; reviewing events, feelings, and images; and telling and retelling the story until it felt finished, exorcised, and worked through by being fully faced emotionally.

A Creative Moment in the Retreat

Around two or three o'clock in the afternoon, the principals and school board members were discussing the wish for trust, communication problems, and the fear of making mistakes. All this had been deftly facilitated by Janet Brown. Suddenly from the back of the room Dr. Stuart walked to the front while Janet Brown was talking. He stood politely to the side until Janet Brown finished a sentence. He then said something like:

> I realize I'm interrupting, but I'd like to do something with your permission. I'd like five people to come forward, and I want to charge you with something on behalf of the administrators and school board. [He then called five people by name; they walked to the front and faced him as the larger group watched, wondering what was going to happen. Shaking their hands, touching them on the shoulders, and patting their backs, as if in reassurance, he then said to them and to the larger convocation.] I want to publicly make a promise to you that, as your new superintendent, I will do my very best to listen to you, to be clear and straight with you, and to do my best for Midwest City. In turn, I want to charge you with the responsibility of making known the school administrators' and board's needs as clearly and directly as possible, that you trust me to tell me things you think I'll disagree with as much as agree with. I want you to come up with a list of priorities for your schools and for education in our district. I realize that I'm an interim superintendent, but I want to assure you I'm going to work very hard for Midwest City, and I ask the same of you. Will you give me your support in our common goal?

They movingly assented and shook hands. He touched them on the shoulder and back. Everyone returned to his or her place, and the group discussion of trust resumed, with a brief word of thanks from Janet Brown.

Dr. Stuart had just conducted a spontaneous ritual—complete with laying on of hands—within the overall retreat ritual. He must have felt safe and secure enough within this creative play space to dare violate the trainers' sequence. Yet he must have known that this was no violation at all but a *fulfillment* of the creative cultural space we had hoped to open for experiment. The role inversion (administrators and board members as students, trainers as teachers) had paradoxically reaffirmed and clarified the real community leaders' roles. The group process had begun to transcend the past and to open a window toward a future that would not merely repeat that past. Within the safe holding environment, Glenn Stuart and others had been willing to risk doing something out of the ordinary.

For the earlier part of this combined retreat, and for the prior administrative retreat, the three facilitators had led and been the focus of much of the group process (through didactic presentations and exercises). From this point, board members, administrators, and superintendents increasingly began to interact *with one another*, only occasionally mediated by one or more of the trainers. The facilitators had served as container (Bion 1959) of much of the group anguish over members' history and feelings. Now Midwest City participants were able to safely and compassionately contain one another in our presence.

The Crucible of Apology, Forgiveness, Grief, Reparation, and Reconciliation

Henry Ramirez, a school board member, said, "People were *abused* in this district. We're here today because people were abused." There was utter silence in the group. The mood change was palpable. Everyone's eyes were riveted on Ramirez. The chief trainer, Janet Brown, acknowledged his courage in saying this publicly.

Glenn Stuart said, "You and I can ask for trust, but it doesn't come automatically. You build trust by example. None of us lay out a plan to fail, to make mistakes. We can decide how long a person has to prove himself, but that's not the same thing as trusting or not trusting."

Henry Ramirez continued, "I saw certain administrators and board members treated with favor. I treated them with disfavor [strong] out of anger. Ill feelings were fostered outside."

A principal or board member said, "Part of the problem of trust is that I treated my colleagues wrong. Dishonesty, being a hypocrite, giving different messages to different people, giving more money to some people, less to others, favors of leave. If this were a store, we'd be out of business, with mispriced goods, and a dirty store. Only a clean store attracts customers and thrives."

Henry Ramirez added, "I've mistreated other persons on the *board*. We can come out of this workshop as a real team and leave some of this history behind us."

A few moments later, Nancy Wall, school board president, said, "Three years ago the superintendent asked board members to be in the schools 50 percent of the time. In the schools, everyone [teachers, principals] started looking over their shoulder. Yes, board members are [now] welcome in the schools. Everyone can [openly] disagree now [at the retreat]. Before, however, there was too much of people getting into little groups and disagreeing with other little groups. There was no trust."

Walter Smith, a principal and assistant superintendent (whose son-in-law, Bob Kaiser, age 30, had been killed in an auto accident the Saturday afternoon prior to the retreat), said, "We're all responsible for what happened here the last four years, not just Jerry Rauschmann or the board."

Janet Brown added, "People have been avoiding grieving and have a lot of pain."

Nancy Wall said, "There's a danger of blaming Jerry Rauschmann rather than taking responsibility, too." Jim Unruh, a principal, said he wished he could have been in a meeting like this last year, around the time of forced school busing.

Carl Shreck—who throughout the retreat had been an articulate and angry person, a group spokesperson—now spoke, his cracking voice finally giving way to flowing tears and sobbing:

We called ourselves "Jerry's Kids." There were people who were in and people who were out. [He struggled for words, speaking slowly, *very* differently from his previous machine-gun diction.] Lots of people assume that if you were in, you got treated better, that you had it easier. [Now he is even more emphatic, even slower.] If you were in, you *didn't* get certain things, contrary to belief. You wouldn't believe who he was hardest on. If you needed secretarial help [he gave other examples, specific situations, and needs], you didn't get it. If you were one of Jerry's Kids, you didn't get things other people could expect to get.

I didn't speak to him the last two months [bitter, enraged, tearful]. I know I'm getting emotional. I couldn't forgive. I was obsessed with the anger and the hatred I felt toward him. I had gone through an identical experience not long before in my personal life situation. Somebody had hurt me deeply and I couldn't let go of it. After I had fumed and held my grudge for months, a friend of mine said to me, "You need to forgive him." Only when I could forgive him did I quit being obsessed with it and let it go.

The same happened with Jerry. I couldn't call him. I couldn't bring myself to do that. I felt so angry, so humiliated, I couldn't bring myself to call him. One day I was driving my car and I just said out loud to myself, "I forgive him." I could feel the heavy weight lift from my shoulders. We need to forgive a lot of stuff and let it go so we can start.

Deeply moved by these words, group members were silent for minutes. Then Nancy Wall talked about how interrelated "personal" and "professional" selves or roles are and how the group was deeply affected by what had been said: "I try to put myself in the place of an administrator who disagrees with a board member."

During the ensuing break, many administrators and board members were openly in tears as they wandered around the room and approached one another, apologizing, asking for forgiveness, and beginning the process of making amends. It was a very moving moment in the life of the distressed groups and their members.

Metaphor of "Jerry's Kids"

The participants had moved from distraught distress and a frenzy of action, through confession and absolution, then toward greater integration and differentiation, and now toward a greater capacity to perform their respective tasks in the town's educational system. As I left, I kept returning to the image of Jerry's Kids. I thought this must refer not only to the faction around Jerry Rauschmann, visionary leader and hated autocrat, but also to Jerry Lewis, the comedian who championed the cause of children suffering from muscular dystrophy, children who are otherwise helpless, dependent victims in need of rescue by good parents. Behind the image of being favored (idealization) lurked an image of being abused (bitterness, outrage) by the administrative patriarch. This latter contrasted sharply with the initial impression of Jerry's Kids as designating people who presumably had benefited from his favors.

I wondered, too, whether part of the psychological plausibility of the notion of "Jerry's Kids" as a metaphor might have been attributable to administrators' identification with disabled children, which would exonerate them from their own, largely disavowed, aggressive, even murderous, impulses and wishes. It was as if they were saying, "There are no bad kids, only bad parents." The metaphor might also have condensed or fused the image of a wished-for protective, nurturing parent and an abusive, tormenting parent with whom one had unconsciously identified.

In the Midwest City retreat, there were many layers of parent–child transference-laden relationships: among the facilitators, the school principals, and the school board (each side alternately personifying parental [authority-menacing] and child [dependent-fearful] roles); between individual administrators themselves; between administrators and past superintendents; and between various professional educational groups and their town constituencies. What made the difference in Midwest City? What allowed people who had started out in an us-them, good-bad polarization of their social world end by recognizing and publicly confessing that everyone had done wrong, felt guilt, wished to make amends, and wanted to create a future that did not repeat the bitter, abusive past? Members of the board and administrators had reacted to the superintendents' abuse and abandonment (within the larger community historical context of change and loss) with greed, competition for scarce economic and emotional resources, and a fulminating sibling rivalry.

These were covered over by a social fiction of united administrators versus school board (us versus them) onto which much of the inner disorganization was displaced to manage the enormous anxiety. In the retreat groups and in the larger city, the wished-for family-fantasies of father-leader, the group-as-mother, or the group-as-family had failed utterly, and nothing or no one could contain these feelings and fantasies long enough for the people to sort them out and work them through. The sense of withering, isolation, and death was overwhelming, made flesh by the brutal car accident just preceding the retreat.

The retreat occurred in a time of deficient, absent, and punitive, if not abusive, parent-leaders and against a backdrop of a decade of massive community change. The group process of the three-day retreat suggested that the inability or unwillingness to mourn change and loss had led to cultural entrenchment, rigidified by myths of the past. Given the long history of sacrifice (victimization) as a problem-solving mode in Midwest City, I wondered whether communal renewal was possible without victimizing others. Into this context the three facilitators came and worked as (pre-Oedipal, maternal) nurturers and (Oedipal-level, paternal) benign authority figures, "transference" objects who were nonjudgmental; who listened and helped group members feel heard, acknowledged, and understood; and who in so doing facilitated both differentiation and integration. The retreat culminated in a painful but liberating grieving of many losses and of the self-protective, often destructive, narcissistic response to the changes. Only on Wednesday did the principals' and board members' anger, persecutory anxiety, mutual suspicion, and polarization begin to dissolve, tears flow, and admission of abuse and hard feelings emerge.

Group members identified with and internalized the functions of the facilitators, thereby becoming healthier parenting, nurturing, and authority figures with one another. Relationships came to be less dominated by paranoid suspiciousness and raw ambivalence. The facilitators did not accomplish this alone. The retreat was cocreated by all participants. If the facilitators "made" a safe space for the group to expand its emotional compass and sense of relatedness, the group increasingly created a safe, nurturing space for itself in which forgiveness and reconciliation could occur and love and hate could coexist in the mind. Attack and withdrawal, despair and isolation, gave way to guilt and repair, love and compassion.

A Healing Organization and Community

By mid-Wednesday, the retreat group ceased, if only for a few hours, being imprisoned in mistrustful, and projection-ridden *I-it* relationships and entered the realm of *I-thou* relationships, as Buber ([1923] 1958) terms them. Group members became real people, not wooden figures, to each other. The emergent sense of we-ness expanded to encompass the *combined* group. It was one without the need for an enemy. For at least a while, everyone could be both good and evil. Group members did not purchase their sense of self by finding or creating yet a third group to embody their own evil. The process that unfolded did not have the defensive, trancelike, reality-distorting nature of Bion-type dependency, fight/ flight, or pairing (the search for a group savior) "basic assumption" groups trapped in unconscious fantasy; nor did it have the magical thinking that Didier Anzieu (1984) characterizes as the unconscious, dreamlike core of much group process.

The retreat led me to wonder about the relationship between love and destructiveness (see Freud, [1920] 1955a). In the history of Midwest City's past decade, a cauldron filled with anger and resentment had long simmered. It had expelled the ability to love, to care, to repair injured relationships. With renewed ability to love came an ability to feel and accept guilt, and to repair relationships (Klein & Riviere, 1964). Destructiveness released its protective clutch.

We can begin to understand how inner pain is fended off by regression into the anger, divisiveness, aloofness, projection, and group fragmentation that had long characterized Midwest City. At the same time, the tender, vulnerable, loving feelings had not been given their due. They were buried by hate and the projection of guilt. It was as if to say: Why should I feel guilty toward them, when they are attacking me? What Freud says in concluding *Civilization and Its Discontents* ([1930] 1961b) has disturbing cogency for our time:

> The fateful question for the human species seems to me to be whether and to what extent their cultural development will succeed in mastering the disturbance of their communal life by the human instinct of aggression and self-destruction. It may be that in this respect precisely the present time

deserves a special interest. Men have gained control over the forces of nature to such an extent that with their help they would have no difficulty in exterminating one another to the last man. They know this, and hence comes a large part of their current unrest, their unhappiness and their mood of anxiety. And now it is to be expected that the other of the two "Heavenly Powers," eternal Eros, will make an effort to assert himself in the struggle with his equally immortal adversary. But who can foresee with what success and with what result? ([1930]1961b, p. 145)

At the end of the fourth day, I left Midwest City less a stranger to it and to myself. I was grateful not only for the healing grief through which retreat participants grew, but also for how much they had stretched me emotionally in so short a time (Searles, 1965, who discusses the unconscious role of the patient as therapist to his analyst). It was then my turn to mourn, for intimacies such as I experienced as a consultant are gifts rarely so freely bestowed in any human relationship. I left affirmed in my organizational consulting approach of deep listening and in my understanding of cultural processes. As Winnicott might say, I left with the sense that I was very much alive and that, through mourning, whole cultures can learn to play again.

Throughout the retreat, I, together with my cofacilitators, had listened deeply at least as much as we had spoken. We spoke from having first listened. The people we worked with were as much experts as we were. By the retreat's end, members of the school administrators and school board came to listen deeply *to one another*. Perhaps listening was our most important work.

I turn now to a fifth story, a culture-wide story of what I have come to call *inconsolable grief* that is an outcome of three and a half decades of many waves of organizational downsizing, reduction in force, reengineering, restructuring, outsourcing, offshoring, deskilling and other euphemisms of "managed social change." This cultural-wide organizational revolution, that nullified the "psychological contract" between employer and employee, has produced millions of economic, psychological, familial, and community casualties—and is far from over.

A Cultural Story: Inconsolable Organizations

In the United States, the era beginning in the early 1980s and persisting through the present (2016) has been characterized by endless waves of downsizing, restructuring, reengineering, outsourcing, deskilling, and similar forms of organizational destruction—all in the name of saving organizations through continuous sacrifice. The unilateral, monolithic style of much leadership during this era has the qualities we associate with totalitarianism (Stein 2006a, 2008).

Near the end of a paper on organizational totalitarianism (Stein, 2006b), I wrote:

> . . .[E]ven though American-style organizational totalitarianism has primarily symbolic casualties, they are casualties of terror nonetheless. One should never say that these are "only" the victims of psychological oppression. And even though most of those who have been disposed of [via downsizing and other forms of "managed social change"] are resilient and find other jobs (usually of lesser pay, benefits, and status), they carry the emotional scars of betrayal and of having been treated as inanimate "dead wood" or as "fat" to be trimmed. Once we recognize the official language of economics to be the smokescreen that it is, we have no trouble in discerning the brutality—even sadism—that it has obscured. Yiannis Gabriel (2005, 2006) has recently invoked the term "miasma" to characterize life in those organizations whose atmosphere is thick with loss, dread, and pollution. We have created inconsolable organizations. (p. 20)

For me, an inconsolable organization (corporation, factory, hospital, university, government agency, etc.) is one that is so engulfed and mired in loss, grief, and despair that no efforts on its members' or leaders' part can remove the spell. Before continuing, I wish to "immerse" the reader briefly in the kind of experience for which I have coined the term, "inconsolable organization."

Some of my earliest thinking on inconsolable mourning came from a brief consultation with a research and development unit of US West immediately after the merger/takeover by Qwest in June 2000, led by the charismatic and flamboyant executive Joseph Nacchio. To a person, the dozen or so demoralized employees I interviewed spoke of how Nacchio was only interested in grandiose plans for fiber-optic telecommunication networks and had dismissed the long-standing contribution of service-oriented telephone linesmen that had long been the basis for US West. They felt that they had just been deprived of their identity, and to make matters worse, that the historical identity of US West had now been ridiculed as virtually worthless and had been pulled out from under them. Members of the research and development group had a wait of many months before finding out what their fate was to be. They had lost their sense of purpose and direction, and engaged in busywork. There was a heavy emotional aura of dejection and demoralization, what I would later come to call inconsolable grief.

Some seven years later, in April 2007, I sent the paragraph immediately above to one of the persons with whom I had consulted at Qwest/US West. Her response adds additional emotional weight to the long-term oppressive effects of her experience. I quote with her permission:

This has been an interesting moment for me. First of all, let me say that I think your paragraph is accurate and you can go ahead with it without reservations. The other part of my comment has more to do with the effect that your paragraph has had on me. I haven't responded to you earlier simply because when I try to talk about that time, I still get blocked. I hadn't realized that I am still very sad and angry and feel betrayed by that whole experience. Even after all these years, I can't quite put into words what that was like. (from the letter of 24 May 2007, quoted with permission)

As discussed earlier, according to Yiannis Gabriel, organizational miasma (2005, 2006, 2008, 2012) is the group psychological response (adaptation) to organizational carnage. An organization that becomes chronically mired in miasma further becomes what Michael Diamond (1998) calls a "defective container." Unfelt and unresolved (unconscious) grief over change and loss at the group as well as individual level underlies the experience of miasma. Like the concept of organizational miasma, the notion of inconsolable grief has considerable explanatory value for many facets of organizational and wider cultural change. Specifically, inconsolable grief underlies (1) much of the sense of miasma's thick pollution, and (2) the inability of the organization or wider culture to contain anxiety.

In terms of process, the way I *learned* about organizational totalitarianism and inconsolable organizations was through listening deeply to people's stories of their workplace lives during this unspeakably difficult time. I listened at multiple levels to the emotional texture of their stories, trying to validate their suffering through bearing witness to their storytelling.

Listening deeply is a gift of the heart to people undergoing or who have undergone downsizing, restructuring, reengineering, and other euphemisms of "managed social change," or who have temporarily survived it. Under these grave circumstances, one works in—or has been fired ("terminated") from—a dispiriting workplace, one filled with despair, and little or no hope. The survivors who are supposed to feel "fortunate" in fact feel overwhelmed with work and grief. People go away, but the work stays. For those who remain behind, even more work is piled on them. They live with the fear that they are not doing a good enough job, that they are "next" in line to be fired. People are spiritually wounded, if they have not already suffered a spiritual death.

One woman in the midst of a massive reduction in force (RIF), spoke of "what it's like to work here" in terms of how the CEO "cut the heart out of the organization," as she gestured with an imaginary knife in her hand as if she were stabbing herself in her chest. There is the loss of the crucial fantasy that one is worthwhile and valuable; with it there is loss of personal integrity. One lives with the feeling that there is a target on one's back. From the loss of morale, there is in turn degradation in organizational performance. To add to the cruelty, the loss and sense of loss are unspeakable. The pain and suffering are undiscussable. Employees are admonished to "Get on with your job as if nothing happened, and be glad you still have a job."

Downsizing destroys all meaning, all dignity; it takes away everything that makes a human being feel worthwhile, an experiencing subject. People feel crushed and devastated. In the face of this miasma (Gabriel, 2005, 2006, 2008, 2012) of despair, listening deeply to the stories of people who have been terminated and those who "survived" (at least for a while), is spiritually as well as psychologically validating. It is a bearing witness to the death of the spirit in the workplace (Allcorn, 2001). It fosters at least a degree of spiritual healing in the person telling the story of his or her experience. Listening deeply helps people to live under the condition they cannot change. People feel heard instead of abandoned. The story listener gives to the storyteller the gift of presence, just as the storyteller bestows the gift of one's innermost soul.

From a recurrent organizational story (downsizing, restructuring, reengineering) that is as much a national disaster as it is a local one, I turn to a tale of the devastating tornado of May 3, 1999, in the Oklahoma City and surrounding area, a tornado that razed whole towns and sections of towns. It is a story of the ravage wrought on many kinds of social "units" from cities to organizations to families to ordinary people. It shows the emotional and unconscious reverberations of a natural disaster. It is also in part my own story, since I live here, only several miles from the path of the storm. Finally, it demonstrates the crucial role of deep listening in any kind of help offered.

Outer and Inner Catastrophes
A Story from the May 3, 1999, Great Plains Tornado

My sixth and final story comes from the area in and around Oklahoma City. It is a story at the conjunction of the personal, the organizational, and the community. It is about massive, traumatic change, loss, and grief on what is for many people an unimaginable scale. It is also about an accidental consultation. Two days after the May 3, 1999, tornado in the Oklahoma City region, I was in the process of leaving a meeting in a clinical department in a health sciences center. As everyone else was quickly leaving, a senior physician with whom I had worked for nearly two decades approached me. The meeting had been uneventful and had been like similar ones I had attended for years.

As my colleague came closer, I noticed that his eyes were very red. He looked exhausted. He said to me: "You're kind of in the psychological field. Is it normal for a man to get tearful after a tornado rips through your town? I'm teary all the time. Will they stop? What am I asking you for? I know what you'll say. But I've never had feelings as intense as this. I'm a physician and a specialist in workplace catastrophes, so there ain't much I haven't seen. I don't know why I keep getting tearful. It's embarrassing. It comes over me in waves."

I stumbled to say *something* to a man I deeply respected as a scientist, physician, pathologist, and toxicologist in medicine. My family and I had crouched low in our bathtub on the night of May 3. I think I just asked him to "Tell me what's going on. You look exhausted"—a look different from what I had ever seen of this spry, usually witty, wry man in his 60s.

He continued, saying something like:

> I spent all night down in Moore, Oklahoma [one of the heavily populated areas hardest hit by the F-5 tornado]. That was on top of my regular job [in the college of medicine]. I was trying to help people sort through the rubble of their homes, to help people fill out insurance forms and file insurance claims, trying to do anything that might be helpful. I saw all these people out in the streets looking back at heaps that had been their homes. It was unreal. I was spooked. This one fellow started pacing back and forth near the curb that had his house number on it. His house was completely gone. It looked almost like a vacant lot. What was someone supposed to do to help him? I put my arm around his shoulder and just stood there with him. The world had been taken away, and all I could do was paperwork to help folks remember what they had.

He continued speaking for several minutes, relating incident after incident from that night, as if he were trying to put together broken glass. He described the eerie sight at shelters where he had seen people standing vigil over their few possessions. They wouldn't let them out of their sight. He returned to the theme of not understanding why he is so *emotional* about this, why he can't get it out of his mind, why he can't let go of the images of the rubble. I thought to ask him about the rubble, what he "saw" in it, but I didn't want to bombard him with questions. Instead, I listened to him via listening to myself, so to speak. I sensed that he needed to tell someone who would listen, someone who would hold onto the story as it was coming to him, and to help him make sense of it. I listened and tried to stay with him emotionally as he was sharing his overwhelming experiences and feelings.

As he spoke, my thoughts and feelings drifted, and I entered a surreal "twilight zone" that collapsed space and time. I imagined a possible link between 1999 and 1995, between his inner and external worlds over time (Volkan & Hawkins, 1971; Giovanchini, 1969). I remembered that he had been an early "responder" at the scene of the bombing of the Murrah Federal Building in downtown

Oklahoma City four years earlier. I wondered aloud whether there might be some connection between the tornado and the bombing. He said that it was an interesting idea, one that he'd never thought of. We visited for a few more minutes. As we parted, I told him that I appreciated that he was comfortable talking with me about this difficult subject, and that I wanted him to know that I was available to talk with him anytime—even by phone at night if he needed it. He thanked me.

About a week later, we were at a similar clinical meeting. After it was over, my friend approached me. He looked tired, but very much like himself rather than someone haunted. I asked him how he was doing. He said:

> I'm doing much better. I want to tell you how much I appreciate our visit last week, and to tell you that something you said helped me to figure out what was going on that had made me so emotional, so volatile. You provided the trigger, the missing piece: the *bombing* [of the Murrah Federal Building on April 19, 1995]. You asked me whether there was any connection between the tornado and the bombing. It got me to thinking: What bothered me *most* about all the devastation after the tornado was that I kept seeing all this *blackened stuff* in the rubble. I tried to avoid looking. [He was speaking now in a different "voice," as if in a kind of trance, reliving something.] I got to thinking: I remember where I saw this before. I was one of the people the authorities had go through what was left of the Murrah Building less than 24 hours after the bombing to determine where it was safe to go. This was even before a lot of the rescuers and recovery personnel were inside. The police wanted to know what we were dealing with toxicologically. What kinds of solvents or explosives were around that the rescuers and fireman might be exposed to? So they had me walk around in stuff where no one had been yet.

He paused, then continued:

> As I was looking for possible exposures, I kept seeing *blackened body parts, blackened blood on body parts*. I don't remember looking directly at them. It's like I didn't want to see it, but I saw it anyway. I couldn't help but see them. Nobody should have to see sights like that, burned bones poking through metal and stone. *That's* what was so overwhelming when I was helping out after the tornado. It was a *flashback*! I'd never had them before. I thought I saw the same thing again. I couldn't be sure, just as I didn't look closely enough in the Murrah Building to say for positive that charred flesh and bones are what I saw. But I didn't want to see it again.

As he told the latter part of the story, my abdomen tightened; I began to feel nausea. I trust my countertransference, my emotional response, to have conveyed the revulsion he had experienced. I do not know whether there was in him a forbidden wish behind the revulsion, but I sensed the disgust and horror. He thanked me for helping him to "piece together" what had happened and to help him understand why the tornado had had such an emotional effect on him. If he felt understood, I also felt understood, capable of understanding, capable—at least then—of *bearing* to hold on to not-knowing, able to accompany him in discovering more of the story in such terrible circumstances. He became reconnected to the "more" of the story that overwhelmed him. One could speculate that he had dissociated the experience into an alter-self or ego-alien fragment, but what is most crucial is the phenomenology, his description of his *experience*, and the relationship between us that permits the description and feelings to emerge, and for healing to *begin* to occur.

My colleague and friend can be considered to have been a "direct" helper and early responder following both the April 1995 Oklahoma City bombing *and* the May 1999 central Oklahoma tornado. Although a health professional, he was also twice an emotionally traumatized casualty. My role was more indirect, more unofficial. I brought to our visit multiple conceptual viewpoints, ranging from a psychoanalytic developmental one to a cross-cultural comparison of trauma. Most of all, I sought to suspend these and listen to *him*, and not listen primarily through the defensive use of theory and method. I felt that I was bearing witness to him, the horror he had been through, the waves of feelings he was experiencing, and the grief in which he felt he might drown. He, together with the emotions, fantasies, and body sensations that our discussion engendered in me by projective identification, led me to "provide" what he needed (Boyer, 1999). I stayed with him, both physically and emotionally as long as he needed.

I want to end this story by saying what has come to be obvious in light of the recurrent devastating hurricanes, tornadoes, mass shootings, and bombings that have become an everyday part of our modern world. Increasingly, we are all "participant observers"—organizational researchers, consultants, and leaders included—in a world where massive psychic as well as physical trauma is always a possibility (Krystal, 1968; Brenner, 2004). Nowhere is immune to catastrophe. Nowhere is immutably safe. Vulnerability—and personal and group defenses against vulnerability—is now taken for granted. Even our planet Earth is endangered.

In the long and heavy shadow of the attacks on the World Trade Center and the Pentagon on September 11, 2001, the ability to stand still and listen was, and remains, perhaps the most precious virtue and gift. Countless people were too overwhelmed to mourn. Perhaps the rapidly ensuing, long War on Terror and the fatal invasion of Iraq were at least in part a refusal to grieve and an inability to mourn (Mitscherlich & Mitscherlich, 1975), and instead represented a flight into violent action. Workplace organizations and nation-states alike are vulnerable to the lure of "doing something" decisive to avoid feeling out of control and helpless. Under these circumstances, deep listening is essential to any possibility of working through the enormous trauma and loss.

Conclusion

Recapitulation

This book has brought listening deeply to the center of all organizational research and consulting—and far beyond. I have argued that genuine listening is never "mere" listening on the road to *doing* something important. *Listening is doing.* I began this book by addressing an imaginary companion, the reader, whom I would accompany on this journey through the book. I wish to conclude by returning to my companion. "You have made a sincere effort," this reader might say to me, with a sigh. "But the world you portray isn't the *real* world of power, politics, outcome measures, economic bottom lines, corporate and national greed. In this real world, your psychodynamics and idealism have little or no place."

Clearly, groups can be ugly lynch mobs, vast social instruments of perversity. Nationalism, wars, and more recently terrorism have shown us this. So have great novels, such as Walter Van Tilburg Clark's grim 1940 novel *The Ox-Bow Incident* or William Golding's 1954 novel *The Lord of the Flies*. Groups can also be places of forgiveness, of affirmation of our deepest, most authentic selves—and at the same time be places where tasks can be accomplished. Writers such as Freud, Bion, Volkan, Kernberg, Anzieu, and Turquet have grippingly shown how in groups we can regress to the search for dependency, fight/flight murderousness, messianic rejuvenation, or symbiotic fusion into oneness (Turquet, 1974). Nevertheless, groups can serve also as emotionally healing, integrative, differentiating forces. Task and relationship, instrumental (purposive, realistic, goal-oriented) and expressive (symbolic, metaphoric, intrinsically meaningful) cultural forms, can be allies as well as foes.

Empathy, identification, and intimacy can help instrumental tasks be better performed. They can also nourish a creative, playful attitude toward the task itself and improve morale. If in groups we can collude in the sense of participating in

201

sinister, tacit, unconscious destructiveness, we can also learn to play together. Just as leaders can be autocratic and brutal, they can also be open, inclusive, and listen deeply to those whom they lead. And just as leaders and groups can flee from mourning in the throes of change, they can also go through the painful yet liberating process of mourning and come out the other side renewed.

In allowing a genuinely therapeutic regression, listening deeply enables people to regain access to parts of themselves that have been split off, projected, and repressed. In becoming more whole, more tolerant of inner conflict, they can permit others to be more whole. In organizations, as in other cultural groups, deep listening offers the potential not only of helping group members acknowledge and feel the backward pulls, but also of freeing them toward more differentiated, integrated, inclusive, whole lives.

Listening Deeply, Feeling Alive, and Recovering the Spirit of Play

Listening deeply uncovers massive personal and institutional inhibitions to playfulness and, when allowed to go to the heart of the matter, liberates this very playfulness so that it can more fully serve life and its works. The question arises: What sort of human being, what view of the nature of being human, does this approach commend? Human inner conflict remains: That is the great lesson of the psychodynamic revolution. It is not magically banished. The essence of being human, however, becomes more than conflict and compromise among the mental structural agencies of id-ego-superego, between ego and reality, between ambition and possibility, between the pleasure principle and the reality principle. Although we never leave our bodily, our biological, experience and foundation, that very foundation is itself redefined. There is a sense of being alive, being real, being whole. Winnicott (1967) writes:

> Psycho-analysts who have rightly emphasized the significance of instinctual experience and of reactions to frustration have failed to state with comparable clearness or conviction the tremendous intensity of these non-climactic experiences that are called playing. Starting as we do from psycho-neurotic illness and with ego defences related to anxiety that arises from the instinctual life, we tend to think of health in terms of the state of ego defences— we say it is more healthy when these defences are not rigid, etc. But when we have reached this point we have not started to describe what life is like apart from illness or absence of illness. That is to say, we have yet to tackle the question of *what life is about*. Our psychotic patients force us to give attention to this sort of basic problem. We now see that it is not instinctual satisfaction that makes a baby begin to be, to feel that life is real, to find life is worth living. In fact, instinctual gratifications start off as part-functions

and they become *seductions* unless based on a well-established capacity in the individual person for total experience in the area of transitional phenomena. It is the self that must precede the self's use of instinct; the rider must ride the horse, not be run away with. (p. 370)

In all organizations, trust and open communication in groups are required if we are to look critically at ourselves and our work and thereby creatively further our efforts. Yet throughout modern organizational life, such trust and dialogue are often lacking. Listening to everyone, not engaging in frenetic busy-ness to flee from listening, is the heart of group morale, task performance, and productivity, I try to tell myself. Yet that ideal has been eclipsed by the compulsion toward action, the illusion of total control, the pursuit of short-term profit, and retreat into the technological desolation that masks as connection. Through emotion-numbing corporate bureaucracy, technocracy, and autocratic leadership, organizations have become close to lifeless in order to "do the job." "Where in organizations can we go with the 'stuff' that bothers us?" clients repeatedly ask me. To whom can we dare talk about our lives as they intertwine with those of coworkers, supervisors, employees, leaders, and others? Mere compartmentalization of function into occasional support groups or employee assistance programs ("safety valves") are not and must not become the solution.

What, then, is our implicit task as internal or external consultants, as organizational development specialists, as researchers, and as leaders? Drawing from Bion, I describe our task as a composed image of a DNA-like double helix: helping create a situation (1) in which a real task (that of instrumental work) can be accomplished, and (2) in which creative, developmental learning (the expressive side of culture, emotional as well as cognitive) takes place. This task is one in which the human tendency toward transference is *consciously recognized* and thereby needs less to be compulsively acted out. It is one in which the consultant or researcher realizes that key data about the organization come from the consultant's own experience, not only from what is observed, heard, or read in formal organizational charts or spreadsheets. Further, the implicit task includes the process of providing a holding environment that is successor to the originally maternal—more widely, paternal—caregiving role: absorbing and not retaliating, integrating, asking, waiting, withstanding the anxiety of being lost, of not knowing. It is to relinquish the drivenness of ambition ("to fix it quickly"), and to give generously of self and time in the service of working out an answer together.

This perspective points, in turn, to the *prerequisites* of an organizational culture supportive of listening deeply, where listening deeply is not only widely valued, but is also part of the organizational ethos. The virtues or principles that characterize "good enough" leaders (-ship) constitute a "good enough" foundation of an organizational atmosphere in which listening deeply occupies the core: openness, inclusiveness, transparency, mutual trust, and mutual respect. It is an emotional climate set by the example of the leaders, in which there are no "black boxes" of secrecy, unilateral control, and inaccessibility.

Resistances to Listening Deeply

I have often heard consulting colleagues place an unquestioning primacy on the formal structure and tasks designated by the organization's leadership, and insist that any subjective intervention must serve the formal work, not question it. For instance, at one organizational conference I attended, a consultant said, "Our task is to help people in organizations to do their work, not be angels of relatedness to the benighted." I do not accept this cultural divide between "work" (often seen as male) and "relatedness" (often seen as female), for we should not only take that work as a given but also question that very work, improve on it, ask what the work is for and if it is worthwhile. Neither social structure nor tasks are to be unexamined givens. Reality is and must be regarded as analyzable. If the consultant is empathic, he or she is implicitly critical.

The "work" of the SS guards at the Nazi death camps was to manufacture death after first having manufactured nonpersons. The "work" of steel mill workers from the late nineteenth through the early twentieth centuries in the industrial valleys of the North American Northeast was to make the United States an "industrial giant," to produce metal from ore, to generate profits for ambitious entrepreneurs, and to think little of their own safety or of the endless billowing of pollution into the atmosphere. A psychodynamically rooted organizational consultant does not automatically take the work and workplace as an unquestioned, fixed, and independent variable. Instead, he or she fosters a compassionate but self-critical attitude toward both the interpersonal relationships and the task(s). Authentic organizational consultation is also culture criticism from within. The "eye of the outsider" helps people see themselves.

In medical meetings and organizational conferences of all types, it is difficult to create an atmosphere in which talking about matters not immediately connected to the "nuts and bolts" of administration, finance, production, or curriculum construction—what we call real work—is welcomed or even possible. Nonetheless, such matters press for a hearing. A rather ordinary experience prompts me to wonder anew about the purpose and possibility of our organizational groups. The following story illustrates how listening deeply allows underlying group purposes and issues to surface and, at least to a degree, be worked through.

A Story: What *Weren't* We Talking About?

In 1989, I participated as a visitor in the six-hour July meeting of the Michigan Behavioral Science Teachers of Family Medicine. In keeping with the printed agenda, the group formally began with a lengthy, systematic philosophical and intellectual exposition and analysis of Dr. G. Gayle Stephens's republished essay "Family Medicine as Counterculture" (1989; see also Frey, 1989), a clarion call that had been first published a decade earlier. Starkly punctuating the abstract conversation, one participant poignantly reminded the group that "it isn't 1967 any longer," an idea no one pursued. The implication was that the 1960s days of idealism are long over, and that we should "get real," so to speak, in the era over two decades later. Several participants later briefly alluded to "family medicine and the role of the prophet," to "flowers," and to "flower children."

I felt uneasy, as if something was missing from all these erudite words. I wondered what we were *avoiding* talking about. I began thinking about the passage of time, its irreversibility despite our dreams, the fate of our ideals and of idealism. I felt that these issues were the unstated parts of the current reassessment of family medicine as counterculture.

The group later discussed at length how Balint groups were conducted in members' respective residencies. Recurrent words and phrases during this phase were "fear that Balint will become 'therapy' . . . need for defenses . . . fear of vulnerability . . . need for control, fear of going out of control . . . abortion . . . abortive. . . . aborted [as in efforts] . . . safety . . . ground rules . . . [and near the end:] time . . . doors . . . doors closing." Although Balint groups were the focus or object of the discussion, I sensed that some other unidentified issue was using Balint as its vehicle. The multitude of variations had still not stated the main theme. A mood of rootlessness prevailed amid a firm agenda.

At around three o'clock, group members began to introduce many new topics. Speech became more urgent and faster. Participants interrupted one another more than earlier. I could hardly keep up with the flow of issues raised. Looking at the large wall clock, I said:

> This group will end at 4:00 p.m. The discussion of Balint groups is certainly legitimate, but we are not only talking about Balint groups which you and I lead. We are also talking about ourselves, about time and not enough time, about beginnings and endings, not only of Balint groups, but also of this [monthly] group. I think that the sudden use of words [metaphors] such as "doors," "abortive," "closing doors," "time," "endings," "vulnerability," and "defense" are about us right here.

The group's mood changed profoundly. One member immediately, and tearfully, testified to how much this group meant to her, how she drew strength from it to take back to her institution. A sharing of feelings—hope, loss, sadness, gratitude for the group—replaced many of the earlier philosophical abstractions and debate over do's and don'ts in Balint groups. Many people now talked of former participants who no longer attended, of repeated endings and beginnings in their group. Several members spoke with regret of the group's fluidity and boundary-lessness. "We've never had a core group," one participant lamented wistfully. The group slowly disbanded long after the four o'clock hour had passed.

In my view, the underlying group themes all along had been of closeness, intimacy, death, dissolution, boundaries, loss, and separation. Yet even in a group that convened regularly for mutual support, these very themes eluded participants' consciousness, while at the same time heavily influenced group agendas and discussion. This group ultimately succeeded in coming to terms with its own issues. Many professional groups, however, become bastions in which members fend off the very thing they need in order to heal themselves and perform their task with vitality. Medical case conferences, for instance, are frequently devoted exclusively to the quest for the exact diagnosis (diseases) and procedures (treatments) and are often devoid of a patient or the patient's story at all. Sometimes we do not even say the patient's name, only the disease. The only acceptable story is the medical account. At the same time, the often unstated "patient" under treatment is the practitioner group itself—its members' own anxieties—through the "real" patient into whom the anxieties are projected.

From Competition to Empathy and Identification

The competitive mood in American medical organizations and other workplaces such as corporations, together with identification with "the competitive spirit" as a means of giving vent to otherwise unacceptable aggressiveness, contributes to the cultural resistance to candid disclosure of personal issues in Balint and other supportive practitioner groups. Following a Balint group in the late 1980s, a family physician said to me that he was increasingly reluctant to speak freely of personal weaknesses and uncertainties about physician–patient relationships or clinical decisions because there were physicians present in the groups from *other* corporate health maintenance organizations, preferred provider organizations, and possibly even a member of a peer review organization. He felt afraid of *exposing* himself, and instead felt the need to *protect* himself. He said that he felt uncomfortable revealing too much lest a physician from another corporation "get the competitive edge" or "get something" on him that could be used against him outside the group. His was a witchcraft fear in modern, corporate dress. He could have been speaking today, in 2016.

Witchcraft anxiety, common in small-scale preliterate societies, is often tinged with paranoia. In corporate life, however, the cycle of hostility and projected hostility refers directly to disturbed interpersonal relations rather than to their displacement onto the supernatural. The result—increased anxiety, defensiveness, obsession with boundaries, and withdrawal from intimacy—is, however, identical. In the relentless strategy to achieve, to out-produce last year's goals, and to get the dirt on another group or person, groups come to mistrust themselves as well as others. Intimacy and growth in such groups become increasingly difficult because they conflict emotionally with the more vigilantly defended, although unspoken, regressive goal of self-protection and the gaining of advantage over others.

We fear to talk directly and openly about our own humanness within professional and corporate groups of colleagues. We imagine doing so would reveal our weaknesses and vulnerability. We perceive that it would detract from our power and position of strength, from our need to appear untroubled, unflappable, tough, and indomitable. Paradoxically, we foster fragile, illusory safety in groups by first *creating* a sense of endangerment. The professional group meeting, with its often rigidly formalized agenda and ritualized process, serves as a massive group or social defense against the recognition and emergence of deeper concerns and feelings. Even the best strategic plans, mission statements, and explicit performance appraisal systems will not save us from ourselves.

Why are we doing this? Much as we complain about the sterility of our endless meetings, they also serve the purpose of keeping at bay large, often frightening and vulnerable portions of ourselves. How can we enthusiastically create, design, produce, market, and sell if we act as if we must despair of ever being whole? In the profession of medicine, for instance, how can we inquire into a patient's personal, family, occupational, and social history, or situate the patient within a community, if we do not have access to our own worlds?

In "Countertransference in [Psychiatric] Hospital Treatment," Stamm (1987) observes:

> According to Bion, the work group is continually buffeted by three kinds of unconscious forces or needs that may influence it at any point in time: security, self-preservation, and salvation. . . . Other factors also complicate the task of facilitating the "work ego" of the group. These factors may include ongoing interdisciplinary or interpersonal tensions, anxiety created by uncertainty about insurance payments, or even larger organizational issues such as the appointment of a new hospital director. These issues notwithstanding, the therapeutic task of the treatment team and its leader is . . . to provide Winnicott's stable and secure "holding environment" where optimal psychological work can take place.

The sine qua non of teamwork is to create a climate where staff members feel comfortable enough to risk self-disclosure, not so much to use the group as a forum for personal psychotherapy, but to use it for understanding one's personal reactions and thus for helping the patient. (p. 2)

Let me offer a brief story of a group's journey from defensive sarcasm to empathy via identification.

A Story: Back Pain and Empathy

At one medical case conference, a group of physician faculty and resident trainees discussed a patient with back pain, a complaint that, when they see it on a medical chart, generally makes physicians cringe even before they enter the exam room and meet the patient. They are certain that the patient is an addict who is going to try to dupe them into prescribing narcotic pain pills. As the discussion continued, participants gave consideration, in sequence, to hospitalization versus outpatient treatment, to Medicare and medicolegal issues, and to treatment approaches ranging from oral medications to subsequently resorting to "the game book" of outwitting the patient.

They then had a humbling realization that most treatment modalities now in use are unproven, and still later realized that back pain patients are doctors' and workers' compensation's nemesis. Finally, they considered various techniques of patient education and inquiry into the details of job performance as it affects the spine. Scathing gallows humor punctuated the search for answers. Several participants jeeringly imitated in exaggerated vocalizations their back patients' complaints. "Pain patients," as physicians call them, are the kind of patients many physicians "love to hate."

Finally, one physician personalized the discussion by saying, "*I've* had lower back pain, and I sat on the floor five days in misery." Another soon added, "These people *hurt.*" What had thus far been a wide-ranging clinical discussion of a *category of stigmatized patients* who were universally disliked and held suspect (for example, for harboring ulterior, economic motives) suddenly became *humanized via empathy and identification*. In discussions such as this, practitioners often use their topic or case to defend against acknowledging a common humanity and destiny shared with patients. This group was able to bridge that barrier—if only momentarily. Several group members in different ways had said, "Many people use back pain to try conning you, but a lot of people really hurt; and I know about that because *I've* really hurt before, too."

The path to more humane care of patients with back pain occurred via acknowledgment in a group setting of the physician's own suffering. Patients ceased being an objectified "it" dissociated from the physicians' own steely ideal self-image and became more humanized. Specifically, many physicians in the group could afford to see the patients in themselves and themselves in the patients—rather than to brand them as a separate, despised category of subhuman beings.

The Heart of Listening Deeply

In my experience from over four decades of work with organizational groups of all kinds, some profound, shared, unconscious agenda frequently serves as the immense sea upon which floats, and upon which is cast about, the ostensible and official corporate, clinical, curricular, or administrative tasks for which the group has assembled. Biomedical physicians often consciously recognize that not only are no two patients alike, but also that a physician never sees the same patient twice. This is equally true for all types of organizational groups. Tasks (work) are inseparable from the people who perform them.

What we do is part of who we are, and who we are is part of what we do. It is our faulty thinking that fractures them, makes persons mechanically subservient to a task-role, and converts people into inanimate machines. Yet we try to enforce the illusion of sameness, uniformity by protocol, through the ritualistic regimentation of limiting what is allowed to happen and what is allowed to be spoken—and even thought. We pretend the sea's great depths are not there at all.

Martin Buber (1965) writes, "At the opposite pole from compulsion there stands not freedom but communion. Compulsion is a negative reality; communion is the positive reality; freedom is a possibility, possibility regained. At the opposite pole of being compelled by destiny or nature or men there does not stand being free of destiny or nature or men but to commune and to covenant with them" (p. 91). In groups the purpose of the banal and the bureaucratic is to protect us from the profound. Under their spell, we "think," cleansed of "feeling." Group "reason" and obsession with "technique" keeps at bay the painful and the joyful, which would burst open our cultural prison doors. We often use groups to flee from the very feelings and insights we require to liberate us.

If massive social and organizational change makes moral strangers of us, and estranges us from selves we had thought secure, then empathy, identification, and compassion are a "road less traveled by" that can restore a sense of moral community and communion. If we each can listen to one another, can tolerate and then take an interest in people who have *outwardly* different, exotic language and style—between companies and countries alike—then we will be able to enter other people's worlds and allow ourselves to be permeable to theirs. We may even find common ground and common humanity. Failure of moral consensus is failure of imagination, of listening, of love.

In this book, I have suggested that a way out of reactionary narcissism, post-modernist and nativist alike, is through listening deeply to one another via empathy, identification, and compassion. As Friedrich von Schiller and Ludwig van Beethoven say jointly in the final movement of Beethoven's *Ninth Symphony*, in joy's magic lies the binding of what custom has harshly torn asunder. Beneath all formal text is the unheard voice of our shared, as yet unrealized, humanity (Spiro, 1986).

In *The Future of an Illusion*, Freud ([1927] 1961a) offers hope through the quiet, persistent voice of reason in the face of our wish to find comfort in illusion. The chief instrument of science's advance is the "primacy of the intellect," which counters wish-fulfilling belief systems with reality testing. Nevertheless, as many psychoanalysts after Freud have come to emphasize, the intellect (reason) can be informed as well as distorted by the heart. It all depends, as we say in the vernacular, upon what is in the heart.

To my reader, who has persevered with me over these many pages, I emphasize that just as feelings can muddle and inflame thinking, they can also help us think more clearly, more compassionately. Disembodied reason was not Freud's goal, nor is it mine; rather it is thinking integrated with feeling, with both able to reflect upon themselves instead of acting compulsively to avoid painful thought or affect.

To listen is to unearth rather than to bury. It is to feel as we think rather than to be compelled to act. It gives us all greater liberty and responsibility in our actions. It gives us a wider compass for our thinking because our own imagination has been enlarged. Listening deeply bestows upon us increased inner space and greater interpersonal space. It allows us to be creative rather than compulsive. To have been listened to gives us subtle power and a wiser will. From having been acknowledged, from having been heard, we are capable of being present to others, of bestowing on them what we have received.

The stories described in this book show the profound human potential living beneath masks of organizational and other social forms. Listening deeply shows promise in a wide variety of organizational settings. It suggests that whatever trade we ply and whatever tasks we perform, our relationships are—and ought to be—superordinate to the content, skills, or organizational ideologies we advocate. An organizational anthropology or other social science that "applies" some content or other skill, but does not base *everything* it does on the depths and breadth of relationship is, to borrow from Saint Paul, but the sound of a clanging cymbal (1 *Corinthians* 13:1).

The heart of listening deeply, of any organizational consultation, is attentiveness to others' voices and to one's own as a tool of hearing others. It is the capacity for surprise in the face of any and all planning. Serendipity is readiness for playfulness in the face of surprise. It is the incorporation of the astonishing into the ordinary, the refusal to hide behind a shield of routine. It is a willingness to be moved, changed, by the very people whom one, as consultant or trainer, is brought in to change. It is a letting go of control and a letting in of creativity. The approach of listening deeply has taught me how profoundly humane, compassionate, renewing, generous, and healing groups can be.

Groups are often a land of missed opportunity where false, compliant selves mask and subjugate the real self that languishes underneath (Winnicott 1965c). Only as we can realize and acknowledge that the purpose of the group is ultimately the group itself—that is, ourselves—can we begin to address all levels of agendas and nurture the humanity of the participants and their organizations.

Catching One Another When We Fall

At one corporate meeting I facilitated many years ago, one midlevel manager asked, "Can you trust people to catch you when you fall? Sometimes I can; sometimes I can't. We need to learn to take care of each other better." Another manager added, "We need to do something to nurture *new* members of the company." Yet another said, "Caretaking and nurturing are inseparable from trust. If we can't trust each other, we won't take care of each other."

The person who had spoken second was in charge of orienting recent recruits. She hoped to improve organizational morale by nurturing the newcomers, not leaving them dangling, stranded, or isolated, as she herself had once felt. She had adapted passively to the depressed morale and high turnover to which the organization had long been accustomed. She wanted to do better by the next generation in the company.

In this book, a common thread uniting the numerous stories and chapters has been the approach of listening deeply as a way to help people "catch" one another and themselves (symbolically, metaphorically, every day, not in enforced, ritualized morale-building exercises such as Ropes Courses and Outward Bound), to allow themselves the vulnerability of falling into not knowing, and learn to trust that they will not fall forever or smash into pieces. Catching provides a holding environment. Behind the metaphor of catching and being caught is the universal fear and fantasy—and for many, real experience—of being dropped, abandoned, allowed to fall in space or out of the eye's loving glance, shattered to pieces and death at the bottom of the abyss.

Listening deeply helps people in organizations *understand and thereby withstand* the temptation to push other people off the ledge into the vast ravine so that they themselves will not perish, the temptation to sacrifice others so that one might survive. It helps people in organizations recognize falls and setups for such precipices, provide a safety net of empathy for others who are falling, and develop sufficient trust in working relationships that when, not if, they fall, they can count on others to be there and vice versa.

In my work as a consultant, I am repeatedly astonished by how generously people try to catch one another when they fall, and how they help one another to stand firmly again. That is what listening deeply is about. It can never be about completeness or perfection. It is about being present with our whole being. And that very ordinary place is where we fall and stand, start and end, and begin again.

The Compass of Deep Listening

Listening deeply has, I believe, very practical implications and relevance *far beyond organizational consulting*. From time to time in this book, I have already addressed organizational researchers and leaders as well as consultants. In fact, all the "listening professions"—and further, all people who should listen deeply to others—could benefit from what I have written here. This would include physicians, nurses, PAs, nurse practitioners, social workers, case managers, psychologists, psychiatrists, psychoanalysts, school teachers and administrators, police, firefighters, politicians and government workers, diplomats, employers and employees, and so on. As a matter of fact, parents and couples need to listen well to each other and to their children.

A reader of this book need only to substitute any of the above professions and roles for the term *organizational consultant* to see how obvious the content and perspective of this book applies to them. Likewise, the settings to which this book applies extend far beyond conventionally understood *workplace organizations*. These include families, couples, churches, mosques, synagogues, medical offices, schools, embassies—all of which are, after all, places in which work is performed.

A Few Suggestions for Listening Deeply

What, then, does this book imply for the *process* of deep listening? Put another way, what does listening deeply look and sound like? Drawing together the insights of previous chapters, let me offer some succinct suggestions—not "magic bullets"—on how one might listen deeply:

1. Trust the process.
2. Do not hurry; you need time; time is on your and your client's side.
3. Don't expect a conversation to make sense for a while.
4. Take your pulse, not only the client's.
5. Make listening your chief agenda, an end in itself as well as a means.

6. Listening is your most important work.
7. Do not try to cover or fill in the silences with your own words to quell your anxiety.
8. Breathe slowly.
9. Do not switch off to another topic when what you hear troubles you.
10. Continue listening even when you feel you have lost the plot or lost your place.
11. Observe your own reactions (emotions, physical sensations, thoughts, fantasies) when you hear particular words or phrases (e.g., metaphors, words uttered with more than usual emotion).
12. Speak from having listened; don't make up your response while your client is still speaking.
13. Keep listening after the conversation has officially ended; what your client says then might be the most important thing that he or she says.
14. Don't try to make sense of it all in a single visit; there is always a next time for learning and feeling more.

Taken together, these recommendations serve as *reminders* for skills that are part of listening deeply. They are like PowerPoint bullets or lists in many training presentations. Taken too literally and mechanistically, they are antithetical to the spirit of this book. It is important to appreciate that the message and spirit of this book are not represented by the list itself. If anything, the succinct suggestions should serve as a shorthand to *remind* the readers of the complexity at the heart of listening deeply.

The Need for Deep Listening

In our times when no one has the time to listen, deep listening is more, not less, urgently needed. Further, to paraphrase one of the reviewers of the manuscript of this book for the University of Missouri Press (2016): Although organizational research and consultation typically occur in the wake of seemingly irreparable conflict, discord, hostilities, emotional abuse, leadership failure, and the like, there are many success stories to be told. At the same time, I have not sugarcoated the dark, destructive side of human nature and of organizational life. This book has offered both kinds of stories, united by the process of listening. Often success is defined and experienced in terms of enhanced processes of inner and group integration, inclusiveness, compassion, resilience, and reparation between groups and individuals previously frozen in opposition, mistrust, and hate.

These outcomes result in large part from participants learning to listen deeply themselves by modeling their experience with and observation of psychodynamically oriented consultants. In this way, empathy, identification, and compassion, the heart of listening deeply, are transmitted from consultant to client(s) and organization. From having been attentively listened to, clients and client organizations are better capable of listening to others and to themselves.

Michael Diamond observes (personal communication, e-mail July 25, 2016, quoted with permission):

> In our present day public arena, it is my observation and experience that we do not listen deeply. We do not listen to each other. We do not listen to ourselves. It is more frequently the case that we engage in competitive speeches where it becomes more about who wins and who loses and who can shout the loudest. Advocating a point of view, striving to be the one who is right, proving oneself to be the smartest person in the room, have nothing whatsoever to do with listening or for that matter nothing to do with communicating, and certainly have nothing whatsoever to do with acquiring understanding between fellow human beings. In sum, I have to ask: how do we evolve as a species where there is an absence of this critical human potential.

In recent decades, the tone of much American organizational, community, and political life has become divisive, rancorous, vile, and vicious. If ever were more listening than speaking needed, it is now. If there is to be a return to civility, it will come from listening empathically to other people as individuals and groups. By its very nature, listening deeply is inclusive—a much-needed antidote to the prevailing angry exclusionary rhetoric and behavior. Speaking from listening is of a far softer and humane quality than hard-hearted speaking without listening.

Democracy requires attentive listening. So does understanding groups, their metaphors and leaders, and the ability to mourn in the face of great change and loss. This necessity extends far beyond the boundaries of the United States. The future of the Earth depends on the inclusiveness only listening deeply can bring.

References

Abse, D. W. (1988). Kriegman's "nonentitlement" and Ibsen's *Rosmersholm*. In V. D. Volkan and T. C. Rodgers (Eds.), *Attitudes of entitlement: Theoretical and clinical issues* (pp. 79–92). Charlottesville: University Press of Virginia.

Alanen, Y. (1990). Comments on current international relations. *Mind and Human Interaction, 1*(4) (April), 7–9.

Alexander, L. (1981). The double-bind between dialysis patients and their health practitioners. In L. Eisenberg and A. Kleinman, (Eds.), *The relevance of social science for medicine* (pp. 307–329). Boston: D. Reidel.

Alford, C. F. (1988). Mastery and retreat: Psychological sources of the appeal of Ronald Reagan. *Political Psychology, 9*(4), 571–589.

Alford, C. F. (1990). The organization of evil. *Political Psychology, 11*(1), 5–27.

Allcorn, S. (2001). *Death of the spirit in the American workplace.* Westport, CT: Quorum/ Praeger.

———, & Baum, H.S., Diamond, M.A., & Stein, H.F. (1996). *The HUMAN cost of a management failure: Organizational downsizing at general hospital.* Westport, CT: Quorum Books.

———, & Diamond, M. A. (1997). *Managing people during stressful times: The psychologically defensive workplace.* Westport, CT: Quorum.

———, & Stein, H. F. (2012). What me worry: Deregulation and its discontents, In Susan Long and Burkard Sievers, (Eds.), *Towards a Socioanalysis of Money, Finance and Capitalism: Beneath the Surface of the Financial Industry* (pp. 120–134). Oxford, UK: Routledge.

———, & Stein, H. F. (2015). *The dysfunctional workplace: Theory, stories, and practice.* Columbia, MO: University of Missouri Press.

———, & Stein, H. F. (2016). Storytelling: An approach to knowing organisations and their people. *Organisational & Social Dynamics, 16*(1), 19–38.

Anzieu, D. (1984). *The group and the unconscious.* B. Kilborne, Trans. Boston: Routledge and Kegan Paul.

Apprey, M. (1986). Discussion: A prefatory note on motives and projective identification. *International Journal of Psychoanalytic Psychotherapy, 11*, 111–116.

———, & Stein, H. F. (1993). *Intersubjectivity, projective identification and otherness.* Pittsburgh. Duquesne University Press.

Arendt, H. (1963). *Eichmann in Jerusalem: A report on the banality of evil.* New York: Penguin.

Argyris, C. (1990). *Overcoming organizational defenses.* Boston: Allyn and Bacon.

Asch, S. (1952). *Social psychology.* New York: Holt.

Aschheim, S. (2014). In a *New York Times* essay, "SS-Obersturmbannführer (Retired)," reviewing Bettina Stangneth's book, *Eichmann Before Jerusalem.* Retrieved September 4, 2014, http://www.nytimes.com/2014/09/07/books/review/eichmann-before-jerusalem-by-bettina-stangneth accessed 24 January 2015

Back, L. (2007). *The art of Listening* Oxford, UK: Berg.

Balint, M. [1957] (1964). *The doctor, his patient, and the illness.* New York: International Universities Press.

———. (1968). *The basic fault.* London: Tavistock.

Baum, H. S. (1986). Response to commentary by Cynthia McSwain. *Political Psychology, 7*(1): 159–162.

Bauman, Z. (1989). *Modernity and the holocaust.* Malden, MA: Polity Press.

———. (1987). *The invisible bureaucracy: The unconscious in organizational problem solving.* New York: Oxford University Press.

Becker, E. [1973] (1997). *The denial of death.* New York: Free Press.

———. (1985). *Escape from evil.* New York: Free Press.

Berger, P. L., & Luckmann, T. (1966). *The social construction of reality: A treatise in the sociology of knowledge.* New York: Doubleday.

Bion, W. R. (1959). *Experiences in groups.* New York: Basic Books.

———. (1962). *Learning from experience.* New York: Basic Books.

———. (1963). *Elements of psycho-analysis.* New York: Basic Books.

———. (1970). *Attention and interpretation.* New York: Basic Books.

Borbely, A. (1998). A psychoanalytic concept of metaphor. *International Journal of Psychoanalysis, 79*, 923–936.

Boyer, L. B. (1983). *The regressed patient.* New York: Jason Aronson.

———. (1989). Countertransference and technique in working with the regressed patient: Further remarks. *International Journal of Psycho-Analysis, 70*: 701–714.

———. (1993). Countertransference: Brief history and clinical issues. In L. B. Boyer & P. L. Giovacchini (Eds.), *Master Clinicians on Treating Regressed Patients*, (Vol. 2, pp. 1–24). Northvale, NJ: Jason Aronson.

———. (1999). *Countertransference and regression.* Northvale, NJ: Jason Aronson.

Brenner, I. (2004). *Psychic trauma: Dynamics, symptoms, and treatment.* Northvale, NJ: Jason Aronson.

Buber, M. [1923] (1958). *I and thou.* R. G. Smith, Trans. (2nd ed.). New York: Charles Scribner's Sons.

———. (1965). *Between man and man.* R. G. Smith, Trans. New York: Macmillan.

Castro, J. (1993, March 29). Disposable workers. *Time*, 43–47.

Clark, W. Van Tilburg. (1940/1989). *The ox-bow incident.* New York: Random House.

Colson, D. B., Allen, J. G., Coyne, L., Dexter, N., Jehl, N., Mayer, C. A., & Spohn, H. (1986). An anatomy of countertransference: Staff reactions to difficult psychiatric hospital patients. *Hospital and Community Psychiatry, 37*(9): 923–938.

Czander, W. (1993). *The psychodynamics of work and organizations.* New York: Guilford Press.

deMause, L. (1982). *Foundations of psychohistory.* New York: Creative Roots.

———, & Ebel, H. (Eds.). (1977). *Jimmy Carter and American fantasy: Psychohistorical Explorations.* New York: Two Continents/Psychohistory Press.

De Vos, G. A. (1966). Toward a cross-cultural psychology of caste behavior. In G. De Vos and H. Wagatsuma, (Eds.), *Japan's Invisible Race* (pp. 353–384). Berkeley and Los Angeles: University of California Press.

Devereux, G. (1955). Charismatic leadership and crisis. *Psychoanalysis and the Social Sciences, 4*, pp. 145–157.

———. (1967). *From anxiety to method in the behavioral sciences.* The Hague: Mouton.

———. (1980). *Basic problems of ethno-psychiatry.* B. M. Gulati and G. Devereux, Trans. Chicago: University of Chicago Press.

Diamond, M. A. (1984). Bureaucracy as externalized self-system: A view from the psychological interior. *Administration and Society, 16*(2), 195–214.

———. (1988). Organizational identity: A psychoanalytic exploration of organizational meaning. *Administration and Society, 20*(2): 166–190.

———. (1993). *The unconscious life of organizations: Interpreting organizational identity.* Westport, CT: Quorum/Greenwood Press.

———. (1998). The symbiotic lure: Organizations as defective containers. *Administrative Theory and Praxis, 20*(3), 315–325.

———. (2014). Metaphoric processes and organisational change: A contemporary psychoanalytic perspective," *Organisational and Social Dynamics, 14*(1), 104–129.

———. (2017). *Discovering Organizational Identity: Dynamics of Rational Attachment.* Columbia: University of Missouri Press.

———, & Allcorn, S. (1985). Psychological responses to stress in complex organizations. *Administration and Society, 17*(2), 217–239.

———, & Allcorn, S. (1986). Role formation as defensive activity in bureaucratic organizations. *Political Psychology 7*(4): 709-732

———, & Allcorn, S. (2003). The cornerstone of psychoanalytic organizational analysis: Psychological reality, transference and counter-transference in the workplace. *Human Relations, 56*(4), 491–514.

———, & Allcorn, S. (2009). Private selves in public organizations: The psychodynamics of organizational diagnosis and change. New York: Palgrave Macmillan.

———, Stein, H. F. & Allcorn, S. (2002). Organizational silos: Horizontal fragmentation in organizations. *Journal for the Psychoanalysis of Culture and Society, 7*(2), 280–296.

———, Allcorn, S., & Stein, H. F. (2004). The surface of organizational boundaries: A view from psychoanalytic object relations theory. *Human Relations, 57*(1), 31–53.

————, & Allcorn, S. (2009). *Private selves in public organizations*. New York: Palgrave Macmillan.

Doka, K. J. (1989). *Disenfranchised grief: Recognizing hidden sorrow*. Lanham, MA: Lexington Books.

Duncan, C. M. & Diamond, M.A. (2011). One foot in, one foot out: The paradox of participant observation. 6th International Conference on Interdisciplinary Social Sciences. July 11–13, 2011. Center for the Study of Organizational Change, University of Missouri, Columbia.

Drucker, P. F. (1954). *The practice of management*. New York: Harper.

Dundes, A. (1980). *Interpreting folklore*. Bloomington: Indiana University Press.

————. (1984). *Life is like a chicken coop ladder: A portrait of German culture through folklore*. New York: Columbia University Press.

Ebel, H. (1990). *Confessions: 1982–1990*. West Hartford, CT: Unpublished manuscript.

Encyclopedia of Business, 2nd ed. Retrieved June 16, 2014, http://www.referenceforbusi ness.com/management/Int-Loc/Leadership-Theories-and-Studies.html

Erikson, E. H. (1964). *Insight and responsibility*. New York: Norton.

————. (1968). *Identity: Youth and crisis*. New York: Norton.

Erikson, K., & Wallas, S. P., (Eds.) (1990). *The nature of work: Sociological perspectives*. New Haven: American Sociological Association/Yale University Press.

Evans-Pritchard, E. E. [1948] (1964). The divine kingship of the Shilluk of the Nilotic Sudan. In *Social Anthropology and Other Essays* (pp. 192–212). New York: Free Press.

Ewing, K. P. (1991). Can psychoanalytic theories explain the Pakistani woman? Intrapsychic autonomy and interpersonal engagement in the extended family. *Ethos*, *19*(2): 131–160.

Fornari, F. [1966] (1975). *The psychoanalysis of war*. A. Pfeifer, Trans. Bloomington: University of Indiana Press.

Frank, A. W. (1998). Just listening: Narrative and deep illness. *Families, Systems and Health*, *16*: 197–216.

————. (2013). *The Wounded Storyteller. Body, Illness, and Ethics* (2nd ed.) Chicago: University of Chicago Press. (1997)

French, R. (2001). "Negative capability": Managing the confusing uncertainties of change, *Journal of Organizational Change Management*, *14*(5), 480–492.

————, & Simpson, P. (1999). "Our best work happens when we don't know what we're doing." *Socio-Analysis*, *1*(2), 216–230.

————, & Simpson, P. (2014). *Attention cooperation, purpose: An approach to working in groups using insights from Wilfred Bion*. London: Karnac.

Friedman, L. J. (1971). Michael Balint—in memoriam. *Psychiatry in Medicine*, *2*, 95–7.

Freud, A. (1966). *Normality and pathology in childhood*. New York: International Universities Press.

Freud, S. [1912] (1958). Recommendations to physicians practicing psycho-analysis. In *Standard Edition of the Complete Psychological Works of Sigmund Freud* (*SE*) (Vol. 12, pp. 109–120). London: Hogarth Press.

————. [1917] (1957). Mourning and melancholia. In *SE*, (Vol. 14, pp. 239–258). London: Hogarth Press.

————. [1920] (1955a). Beyond the pleasure principle. In *SE* (Vol. 18, pp. 7–64). London: Hogarth Press.

———. [1921] (1955a). Group psychology and the analysis of the ego. In *SE* (Vol. 18, pp. 69–143). London: Hogarth Press.

———. [1921] (1955b). Identification. In *SE* (Vol. 18, pp. 105–110). London: Hogarth Press.

———. [1927] (196la). The future of an illusion. In *SE* (Vol. 21, pp. 3–56). London: Hogarth Press.

———. [1930] (196lb). Civilization and its discontents. In *SE* (Vol. 21, pp. 64–145). London: Hogarth Press.

———. [1937] (1964). Constructions in analysis. In *SE* (Vol. 23, pp. 257–269). London: Hogarth Press.

Frey, J. J. (1989). Church or sect? The counterculture 10 years later. *Family Medicine*, *21*(2): 100.

Friedman, L. J. (1971). Michael Balint—in memoriam. *Psychiatry in Medicine*, *2*: 95–97.

Friedman, M. (1985). *The healing dialogue in psychotherapy*. New York: Jason Aronson.

Fry, A. (1970). *How a people die*. Toronto: Doubleday.

Gabriel, Y. (1999). *Organizations in depth*. Thousand Oaks, CA: Sage.

———. (2000). *Storytelling in organizations: Facts, fictions, and fantasies*. New York, Oxford University Press.

———. (2005, July 4–5). Organizations and their discontents: Miasma, toxicity and violation. Paper presented at Critical Management Studies 4 Conference. Cambridge, England.

———. (2006, June 29–30). "Miasma, polluted identities, paralysed selves." Keynote Presentation for the 8th Storytelling Seminar, University of East Anglia.

———. (2008). Organizational miasma, purification and cleansing. In Ahlers-Niemann, A., Beumer, U., Redding Mersky, R., & Sievers, B., (Eds.), *Organisationslandschaften: Sozioanalytische Gedanken und Interventionen zur normalen Verrüchtheit in Organisationen* [*The Normal madness in organizations: Socioanalytic thoughts and interventions*] (ppp. 53–74). Bergische Glädbach, Germany: EHP Publishers, Verlag Andreas Kohlhage.

———. (2012). Organizations in a state of darkness: Towards a theory of organizational miasma. *Organization Studies*, *33*, 1137–1152.

GAP Committee on International Relations, & Stein, H. F. (1987). *Us and them: The psychology ethnonationalism*. Group for the Advancement of Psychiatry (GAP) (Report No. 123). New York: Brunner/Mazel.

Giovacchini, P. L. (1969). The influence of interpretation upon schizophrenic patients. *International Journal of Psycho-Analysis*, *50*, 179–186.

Glenn, M. L. (1983). Balint revisited: On the 25th anniversary of the publication of *The doctor, his patient, and the illness*. *Family Systems Medicine*, *1*(1), 75–81.

Golding, W. (1954). *The lord of the flies*. New York: Putnam.

Grieco, M. S. (1988). Birth-marked? A critical view on analyzing organizational culture. *Human Organization*, *47*(1), 84–87.

Grolnick, S. (1987). Reflections on psychoanalytic subjectivity and objectivity as applied to anthropology. *Ethos, 15*(1), 136–143.

Grotstein, J. S. (1981). *Splitting and projective identification*. New York: Jason Aronson.

Hammer, M., & Champy, J. A. (1993). *Reengineering the corporation: A manifesto for business*. New York: HarperBusiness.

Heschel, A. J. (1965). *Who is man?* Stanford: Stanford University Press.

Hirschhorn, L. (1988). *The workplace within: Psychodynamics of organizational life*. Cambridge, MA: MIT Press.

Hoffer, E. (1955). *The passionate state of mind and other aphorisms*. New York: Harper and Row.

Hunt, J. C. (1989). *Psychoanalytic aspects of fieldwork*. Sage University Paper Series on Qualitative Research Methods (Vol. 18). Newbury Park, CA: Sage.

Janis, I. L. (1971). Groupthink. *Psychology Today, 5*(6), 43–44, 46, 74–76.

———. (1982). *Groupthink*. Boston: Houghton Mifflin.

Jaques, E. (1955). Social systems as a defense against persecutory and depressive anxiety. In M. Klein, P. Heimann, and R. Money-Kyrle (Eds.), *New Directions in Psycho-Analysis: The Significance of Infant Conflict in the Pattern of Adult Behavior* (pp. 478–498). New York: Basic Books.

Jilek, W. C. (1974). *Salish Indian mental health and culture change: Psychohygienic and therapeutic aspects of the Guardian Spirit Ceremonial*. Toronto: Holt, Rinehart and Winston.

Jilek-Aall, L. (1986). Review of *A poison stronger than love: The destruction of an Ojibwa community*, by A. M. Shkilnyk. *Transcultural Psychiatric Research Review, 23*, 241–244.

Johnson, A. (2001). The Balint movement in America. *Family Medicine, 33*(3), 171–177.

Johnson, T. M. (1987). Consultation psychiatry as applied medical anthropology. In H. A. Baer (Ed.), *Encounters with Biomedicine: Case Studies in Medical Anthropology* (pp. 269–294). New York: Gordon and Breach.

Jones, E. (1953). *The life and work of Sigmund Freud* (Vol. 1). New York: Basic Books.

Keats, J. [1817] (1974). Letter to George and Thomas Keats, December. In *The Norton Anthology of English Literature* (Vol. 2, 3rd ed., pp. 704–706). New York: Norton.

Kernberg, O. F. (1965). Notes on countertransference. *Journal of the American Psychoanalytic Association, 13*, 38–56.

———. (1976). *Object relations theory and clinical psychoanalysis*. New York: Jason Aronson.

———. (1998). *Ideology, conflict, and leadership in groups and organizations*. New Haven: Yale University Press.

Kets de Vries, M. F. R. (Ed.). (1984). *The irrational executive: Psychoanalytic explorations of management*. New York, NY: International University Press.

Kets de Vries, M. F. R. (1991). *Organizations on the couch: Clinical perspectives on organizational behavior and change* [Jossey Bass Business and Management Series]. San Francisco: Jossey-Bass.

———. (2003). *Leaders, fools and impostors: Essays on the psychology of leadership* (Rev. ed.). Bloomington, IN: iUniverse.

———. (2006). *The leader on the couch: A clinical approach to changing people and organizations*. San Francisco: Jossey-Bass.

———, & Miller, D. (1984). *The neurotic organization: Diagnosing and changing counterproductive styles of management*. San Francisco: Jossey-Bass.

Kirshner, L. A. (2010). Paradoxes of the self: The contrapuntal style of Arnold Modell. *Journal of the American Psychoanalytic Association, 58*, 327–345.

Klein, M. (1946). Notes on some schizoid mechanisms. *International Journal of Psycho-Analysis, 27*, 99–110.

———. (1955). On identification. In M. Klein, P. Heimann, and R. Money-Kyrle (Eds.), *New directions in psychoanalysis: The significance of infant conflict in the pattern of adult behavior* (pp. 309–345). New York: Basic Books.

———, & Riviere, J. (1964). *Love, hate and reparation*. New York: Norton.

Kluckhohn, F. R., and Strodtbeck, F. (1961). *Variations in value orientations*. Evanston, IL: Row Peterson.

Koenigsberg, R. A. (1975). *Hitler's ideology: A study in psychoanalytic sociology*. New York: Library of Social Science.

———. (1989). *Symbiosis and separation: Towards a psychology of culture*. New York: Library of Art and Social Science.

———. (2016). Ideology and metaphor. *Library of Social Science*. Retrieved December 27, 2016, https://www.libraryofsocialscience.com/newsletter/posts/2016/2016 -04-06-Ideology_Metaphor.html

Symbiosis and separation: Towards a psychology of culture. New York: Library of Art and Social Science.

Kohut, H. (1971). *The analysis of the self*. New York: International Universities Press.

———. (1972). Thoughts on narcissism and narcissistic rage.In R. S. Eissler (Ed.), *The Psychoanalytic Study of the Child* (Vol. 27, pp. 360–400). New York: Quadrangle/ New York Times Press.

———. (1984). *How does analysis cure?* Chicago: University of Chicago Press.

Kormos, H. R. (1984). The industrialization of medicine. In J. L. Ruffini (Ed.), *Advances in medical social science* (Vol. 2, pp. 323–339). New York: Gordon and Breach.

Krystal, H. (1968). *Massive psychic trauma*. New York: International Universities Press.

La Barre, W. (1971). Materials for a history of studies of crisis cults: A bibliographic essay. *Current Anthropology, 12*(1), 3–44.

———. (1972). *The ghost dance: The origins of religion*. New York: Dell.

———. (1978). The clinic and the field. In G. D. Spindler (Ed.), *The Making of Psychological Anthropology* (pp. 259–299). Berkeley and Los Angeles: University of California Press.

La Farge, O. [1945] (1967). Archaeology on the hoof. In L. Deuel (Ed.), *Conquistadors without swords: Archaeologists in the Americas* (pp. 347–356). New York: St. Martin's Press.

Lakoff, G. & Johnson, M. (1980). *Metaphors we live by*. Chicago: University of Chicago Press.

———, & Johnson, M. (1999). *Philosophy in the Flesh: The embodied mind & its challenge to Western thought*. New York: Basic Books.

Laplanche, J., & Pontalis, J.-B. (1973). D. Nicholson-Smith, Trans. *The Language of psycho-analysis*. New York: Norton.

Larçon, J-P., & Reitter, R. (1984). Corporate imagery and corporate identity. In M. F. R. Kets DeVries (Ed.), *The irrational executive: Psychoanalytic studies in management* (pp. 344–355). New York: International Universities Press.

Larsen, K. S. (1986). Social psychological factors in military technology and strategy. *Journal of Peace Studies, 23*(4), 391–398.

Lazarus, R. S. (1961). *Adjustment and personality*. New York: McGraw-Hill.

"Lean/Six Sigma" (2016, February 1). The Human Resources Department of the University of Oklahoma Health Sciences Center sent an e-mail flyer to all employees, announcing forthcoming "Lean/Six Sigma Certification Workshops." It was sent on behalf of Dr. B. M. Pulat, Lean/Six Sigma Black Belt. To be offered were workshops on "Lean Six Fundamentals," "Lean Processes/Office," and "Six Sigma" skills.

Levine, H. B., Jacobs, D., & Rubin, L. J. (Eds.). (1988). *Psychoanalysis and the nuclear threat: Clinical and theoretical studies*. Hillsdale, NJ: Analytic Press.

Levinson, H. (1984). Reciprocation: The relationship between man and organization. In M. F. R. Kets deVries (Ed.), *The irrational executive: Psychoanalytic studies in management* (pp. 264–285). New York: International Universities Press.

———, Price, C. R., Munden, K. J. Mandl, H. J., & Solley, C. M. (1962). *Men, management, and mental health*. Cambridge, MA: Harvard University Press.

Lifton, R. J. (1979). *The broken connection: On death and the continuity of life*. New York: Simon and Schuster.

———. (1986). *Nazi doctors: Medical killing and the psychology of genocide*. New York: Basic Books.

Lindsmith, A. R., & Strauss, A.L. (1968). *Social psychology* (3d ed.). New York: Holt, Rinehart and Winston.

Luel, S. A., & Marcus, P. (Eds.). (1984). *Psychoanalytic reflections on the Holocaust: Selected essays*. New York: KTAV Publishing.

Luthans, F. (2005). *Organizational behavior*. New York: McGraw-Hill.

Mack, J. E. (Ed.). (1986). Aggression and its alternatives in the conduct of international relations [Special issue]. *Psychoanalytic Inquiry, 6*(2).

Martinette, C. (2002). *Learning organizations and leadership style*. Retrieved June 16, 2014, http://www.usfa.fema.gov/downloads/pdf/tr02cm.pdf

Masterson, J. F. (1983). *Countertransference and psychotherapeutic technique*. New York: Brunner/Mazel.

———. (1985). *The real self: A developmental, self, and object relations approach*. New York: Brunner/Mazel.

McCully, R.S. (1980). A Commentary on Adolf Eichmann's Rorschach, *Journal of Personality Assessment, 4*(3): 311-318.

McDermott, J. (1991). *Corporate society: Class, property, and contemporary capitalism*. Boulder: Westview Press.

McDougall, W. [1920] (1927). *The group mind* (2nd ed.). London: Cambridge University Press.

McGoldrick, M., & Gerson, R. (1985). *Genograms in family assessment.* New York: Norton.

Meltzer, D. (1967). *The psycho-analytical process.* London: Heinemann.

Merenstein, J. H, & Chillag, K. (1999). Balint seminar leaders: What do they do? *Family Medicine, 31*(3), 182–186.

Mitscherlich, A., & Mitscherlich, M. (1975). *The inability to mourn: Principles of collective behavior.* New York: Grove Press.

Modell, A. H. (1984). *Psychoanalysis in a new context.* Madison, CT: International Universities Press.

———. (2006). *Imagination and the meaningful brain.* Cambridge: MIT Press.

———. (2009). Metaphor: The bridge between feelings and knowledge. *Psychoanalytic Inquiry, 29,* 6–11.

Montville, J. V. (1989). Psychoanalytic enlightenment and the greening of diplomacy. *Journal of the American Psychoanalytic Association, 37*(2), 297–318.

Morrow, L. (1993, March 29). The temping of America. *Time,* 40–41.

Nacht, S. (1962). The curative factor in psycho-analysis. *International Journal of Psycho-Analysis, 43,* 206–211.

Nedelmann, C. (1986). A psychoanalytical view of the nuclear threat—from the angle of the German sense of political inferiority. *Psychoanalytic Inquiry, 6*(2), 287–302.

Niederland, W. G. (1961). The problem of the survivor. *Journal of the Hillside Hospital 10,* 233–247.

Ogden, T. H. (1989a). *The primitive edge of experience.* Northvale, NJ: Jason Aronson.

———. (1989b). On the concept of an autistic-contiguous position. *International Journal of Psychoanalysis, 70*(1), 127–140.

———. (1993). *The matrix of the mind: Object relations and the psychoanalytic dialogue.* Northvale, NJ: Jason Aronson.

———. (1999). The analytic third: working with intersubjective facts. In S. A. Mitchell & L. Aron (Eds.), *Relational psychoanalysis: Vol. 1. The Emergence of a Tradition* (pp. 459–492). Hillsdale, NJ: Analytic Press.

Orwell, G. (1949). *1984.* New York: Harcourt, Brace.

Owen, H. (1986). Griefwork in organizations. *Foresight Journal, 1*(1), 1–14.

———. (1987). *Spirit: Transformation and development in organizations.* Potomac, MD: Abbott.

Owen. W. [1920] (1963). Futility. In *The collected poems of Wilfred Owen* (p. 58). New York: New Directions.

Pascal, B. (1670). *Pensée.* [Section 4, no. 227]. Paris: Ernest Flammarion.

Paul, R. A. (1987). The question of applied psychoanalysis and the interpretation of cultural symbolism. *Ethos, 15*(1), 82–103.

Pelled, E. (2007). Learning from experience: Bion's concept of reverie and Buddhist meditation. A comparative study. *International Journal of Psychoanalysis, 88,* 1507–1526.

Pendagast, E. G., & Sherman, C. O. (1977). A guide to the genogram family systems training. *The Family, 5*(1), 3–14.

Piaget, J., & Inhelder, B. (1969). *The psychology of the child.* H. Weaver, Trans. New York: Basic Books.

Pollock, G. H. (1961). Mourning and adaptation. *International Journal of Psycho-Analysis*, *42*, 341–461.

———. (1977). The mourning process and creative organizational change. *Journal of the American Psychoanalytic Association*, *25*(1), 3–34.

Reciniello, S. (2014). *The conscious leader: Nine principles and practices to a create wide-awake and productive workplace*. London: LID Publishing 2014.

Reik, T. (1948). *Listening with the third ear: The inner experience of a psychoanalyst*. New York: Grove Press.

Rhodes, L. A. (1986). The anthropologist as institutional analyst. *Ethos*, *14*(2), 204–217.

Rothschild, F. A. (1959). Introduction. Abraham J. Heschel. *Between God and man* (pp. 7–32). New York: Free Press.

Rutter, K. A. (2003). From measuring clouds to active listening. *Management Learning*, *34*(4), 465–480.

Saffo, P. (2005, September/October). The ghost dances: Half the world is rushing toward the future and the other toward the past. Both have weapons. *California Monthly* (Vol. 116, no. 3). Retrieved December 20, 2011, from http://www.mind fully.org/Technology/2005/Ghost-Dances-Saffor1sep05.htm

Safran, J. D. (2011). Theodor Reik's *Listening with the third ear* and the role of self-analysis in contemporary psychoanalytic thinking. *Psychoanalytic Review*, *98*(2), 205–216.

Schein, E. (1985). *Organizational culture and leadership*. San Francisco: Jossey-Bass.

Schwartz, H. (1990). *Narcissistic process and corporate decay: The theory of the organizational ideal*. New York: New York University Press.

Schwartzman, H. B. (1989). *The meeting: Gatherings in organizations and communities*. New York: Plenum Press.

Scott-Stevens, S. (1988). The holistic anthropologist: A case study of a consultancy at a western New Mexico uranium mine. *High Plains Applied Anthropologist*, *8*(1), 3–32.

Searles, H. F. (1965). *Collected papers on schizophrenia and related subjects*. New York: International Universities Press.

———. (1975). The patient as therapist to his analyst. In P. L. Giovacchini (Ed.) in collaboration with A. Flarsheim and L. B. Boyer, *Tactics and techniques in psychoanalytic therapy: Countertransference*, (Vol. 2, pp. 95–151). New York: Jason Aronson.

Shapiro, W. (1989). Thanatophobic man. *Anthropology Today*, *5*(2), 11–14.

Shkilnyk, A. M. (1985). *A poison stronger than love: The destruction of an Ojibwa community*. New Haven: Yale University Press.

Spence, D. P. (1984). *Narrative truth and historical truth: Meaning and interpretation in psychoanalysis*. New York: Norton.

Spiro, M. E. (1986). Cultural relativism and the future of anthropology. *Cultural Anthropology*, *1*(3), 259–286.

Stamm, I. (1987). Countertransference in hospital treatment: Basic concepts and paradigms [Paper series, no. 2]. Topeka, KS: Menninger Foundation.

Stapley, L. (2006). *Individuals, groups, and organizations: Beneath the surface*. London: Karnac.

Stein, H. F. (1980). *An ethno-historic study of Slovak-American identity*. New York: Arno Press/New York Times Press.

———. (1982a). The ethnographic mode of teaching clinical behavioral science, In N. Chrisman & T. Maretzki, (Eds.), *Clinically applied anthropology: Anthropologists in health science settings* (pp. 61–82). Boston, MA: D. Reidel.

———. (1982b). "Health" and "wellness" as euphemism: The cultural context of insidious draconian health policy. *Continuing Education for the Family Physician, 16*(3), 33–44.

———. (1982c). Neo-Darwinism and survival through fitness. *Journal of Psychohistory, 10*(2), 163–187.

———. (1982d). Wellness as illusion. *Delaware Medical Journal, 54*(11), 637–641.

———. (1982e). Autism and architecture: A tale of inner landscapes. *Continuing Education for the Family Physician, 16*(6), 115–116, 19.

———. (1983a). Lessons of the revolution: A critical event and the contexts of family systems medicine. *Family Systems Medicine, 1*(3), 31–36.

———. (1983b). The money taboo in American medicine. *Medical Anthropology, 7*(4), 1–15.

———. (1984). "Misplaced persons": The crisis of emotional separation in geographical mobility and uprootedness. *Journal of Psychoanalytic Anthropology, 7*(3), 269–292.

———. (1985a). Culture change, symbolic object loss, and restitutional process. *Psychoanalysis and Contemporary Thought, 8*(3), 301–332.

———. (1985b). *The psychoanthopology of American culture.* New York: Psychohistory Press.

———. (1985c). Psychological complementarity in Soviet-American relations. *Political Psychology, 6*(2), 249–261.

———. (1985d). Therapist and family values in cultural context. *Counseling and Values, 30*(1), 35–46.

———. (1986). Social role and unconscious complementarity. *Journal of Psychoanalytic Anthropology, 9*(3), 235–268.

———. (1987a). *Developmental time, cultural space: Studies in psychogeography.* Norman: University of Oklahoma Press.

———. (1987b). Encompassing systems: Implications for citizen diplomacy. *Journal of Humanistic Psychology, 27*(3), 364–384.

———. (1987c). An ethnographic model for clinical teaching: Implications for applied anthropology. *High Plains Applied Anthropologist, 7*(2), 20–35.

———. (1987d). Farmer and cowboy: The duality of the midwestern/southwestern male ethos—a study in ethnicity, regionalism, and national identity. In *From metaphor to meaning: Papers in psychoanalytic anthropology,* by H. F. Stein and M. Apprey (pp. 178–227). Charlottesville: University Press of Virginia.

———. (1987e). The problem of cultural persistence, and the differentiation of self in one's culture. In *From metaphor to meaning: Papers in psychoanalytic anthropology,* by H. F. Stein and M. Apprey (pp. 302–320). Charlottesville: University Press of Virginia.

———. (1988). Uncomfortable knowledge: An ethnographic clinical training model. *Family Systems Medicine, 6*(1), 117–128.

———. (1990a). *American medicine as culture.* Boulder: Westview Press.

———. (1990b). The story behind the clinical story: An inquiry into biomedical narrative. *Family Systems Medicine, 8*(2), 213–227.

———. (1998). *Euphemism, spin, and the crisis in organizational life.* Westport. CT: Quorum Books.

———. (2001). *Nothing personal, just business: A guided journey into organizational darkness.* Westport, CT: Quorum Books.

———. (2005). *Beneath the crust of culture.* New York and Amsterdam: Rodopi.

———. (2006a). The inconsolable organization: Toward a theory of organizational and cultural change. *Psychoanalysis, Culture and Society, 12,* 349–368.

———. (2006b, October 7). *Organizational totalitarianism and the voices of dissent.* Paper presented at the 2006 Annual Colloquium, Center for the Study of Organizational Change, University of Missouri–Columbia. 7 October 2006.

———. (2007). *Insight and imagination.* Lanham, MD: University Press of America/ Rowman and Littlefield.

———. (2008). Organizational totalitarianism and the voices of dissent. In S. P. Banks, (Ed.), *Dissent and the Failure of Leadership.* (pp. 75–96). Cheltenham Glos, UK: Edward Elgar Publishing Ltd. New Horizons in Leadership Studies.

———, & Allcorn, S. (2010a). The unreality principle and deregulation: A psychocultural exploration. *The Journal of Psychohistory, 38*(1), 27–48.

———, & Allcorn. S. (2010b). The unreality of deregulation: The cultural sychodynamics of an enduring myth. In L. Cherubini (Ed.), *The study of identity as a concept and social construct in behavioral and social science research: Inter-disciplinary and global perspectives,* (pp. 9–38). Lampeter, Wales, UK: The Edwin Mellen Press.

———, & Allcorn, S. (2010c). The unreality behind the ideology of deregulation, *Psychology and Education Journal: An Interdisciplinary Journal. 48*(1–2)2011: 1-15.

———, & Allcorn, S. (2011). The unreality behind the ideology of deregulation. *Psychology and Education Journal: An Interdisciplinary Journal, 48*(1–2), 1–15.

———, & Allcorn, S. (2014). Good enough leadership: A model of leadership. *Organisational and Social Dynamics, 14*(2), 342–366.

———, & Apprey, M. (1985). *Context and dynamics in clinical knowledge.* Charlottesville: University Press of Virginia.

———, & Apprey, M. (1987). *From metaphor to meaning.* Charlottesville, VA: University Press of Virginia.

———, & Apprey, M. (1990). *Clinical stories and their translations.* Charlottesville, VA: University Press of Virginia.

———, & Fox, D. P. (1985). Work as family: Occupational relationships and social transference. In *Context and Dynamics in Cinical Knowledge,* by H. F. Stein and M. Apprey, (pp. 182–197). Charlottesville, VA: University Press of Virginia.

———, & Grant, W. D. (1993). *Behavioral science in family medicine: A program for second and third year family medicine residents* (Rev. ed.). Kansas City, MO: Society of Teachers of Family Medicine.

————, & Hill, R. F. (1979). Adaptive modalities among Slovak- and Polish-Americans: Some issues in cultural continuity and change. *Anthropology, 3*(1–2), 95–107.

————, & Hill, R. F. (1988). The dogma of technology. In L. B. Boyer and S. Grolnick (Eds.), *The Psychoanalytic Study of Society*, (Vol. 13, pp. 149–179). Hillsdale, NJ: Analytic Press.

————, & Niederland, W. G. (Eds.) (1989). *Maps from the mind: Readings in psycho geography*. Norman, OK: University of Oklahoma Press.

Stephens, G. G. (1989). Family medicine as counterculture. *Family Medicine, 21*(2), 103–109.

————. (2012, May 3). *Give a damn about patients*. Presentation at the 2012 American Academy of Family Physicians National Conference of Special Constituencies meeting in Kansas City, Missouri. Retrieved from https://www.youtube.com /watch?v=-BAnEkK3T_M).

Stierlin, H. (1973). Group fantasies and family myths: Some theoretical and practical aspects. *Family Process, 12*, 111–125.

Stokes, P., & Gabriel, Y. (2010). Engaging with genocide: The challenge for organization and management studies. *Organization, 17*(4), 461–480.

Sutherland, J. D. (1980). British object relations theorists: Balint, Winnicott, Fairbairn, Guntrip. *Journal of the American Psychoanalytic Association, 28*(4), 829–860.

————. (1990). Bion revisited: Group dynamics and group psychotherapy. In E. Trist and H. Murray (Eds.), *The Social Engagement of Social Science: A Tavistock Anthology* (pp. 119–140). Philadelphia: University of Pennsylvania Press.

't Hart, P. (1991). Irving L. Janis' victims of groupthink. *Political Psychology, 12*(2), 247–278.

Tansey, M. J., & Burke, W. F. (1989). *Understanding countertransference: From projective identification to empathy*. Hillsdale, NJ: Analytic Press.

Taylor, F. W. (1911). *Principles of scientific management*. New York: Harper and Brothers.

Theodorson, G. A., & Theodorson, A. G. (1969). *A modern dictionary of sociology*. New York: Barnes and Noble Books.

Thompson, N. (Guest ed.). (2007). Loss and Grief in the Workplace [Special Issue]. *Illness, Crisis, and Loss, 15*(3).

Tillich, P. (1955). *The courage to be*. London: Nisbet.

Tombaugh, J. R., and White, L. P. (1990). Downsizing: An empirical assessment of survivors' perceptions in a postlayoff environment. *Organization Development Journal, 8*(2), 32–34.

Turkle, S. (2011). *Alone together: Why we expect more from technology and less from each other*. New York: Basic Books.

————. (2015). *Reclaiming conversation: The power of talk in a digital age*. New York: Penguin.

Turquet, P.M. (1974). Leadership: The individual and the group. In G. S. Gibbard, et al. (Eds.), *The Large Group: Therapy and Dynamics*. San Francisco and London: Jossey Bass.

Vivian, P., & Hormann, S. (2002). Trauma and healing in organizations. *OD Practitioner*, *34*(4): 37–42.

———, & Hormann, S. (2013). *Organizational trauma and healing*. Seattle: CreateSpace Independent Publishing Platform/Amazon.

Volkan, V. D. (1979). *Cyprus—war and adaptation: A psychoanalytic history of two ethnic groups in conflict*. Charlottesville, VA: University Press of Virginia.

———. (1980). Narcissistic personality organization and "reparative" leadership. *International Journal of Group Psychotherapy*, *30*(2), 131–152.

———. (1981). *Linking objects and linking phenomena: A study of the forms, symptoms, metapsychology, and therapy of complicated mourning*. New York: International Universities Press.

———. (1987). Psychological concepts useful in the building of political foundations between nations: Track II diplomacy. *Journal of the American Psychoanalytic Association*, *35*(4), 903–935.

———. (1988). *The need to have enemies and allies: From clinical practice to international relationships*. Northvale, NJ: Jason Aronson.

———. (1990). Change, mourning and reorganization in Moscow. *Mind and Human Interaction*, *2*(1), 3–4, 19–20.

———. (1991). On "chosen trauma." *Mind and Human Interaction*, *3*(1), 13.

———. (1997). *Blood lines: From ethnic pride to ethnic terrorism*. New York: Farrar Straus & Giroux.

———. (2004). *Blind trust: Large groups and their leaders in times of crisis and terror*. Charlottesville, VA: Pitchstone.

———, & Hawkins, D. R. (1971). The "fieldwork" method of teaching and learning clinical psychiatry. *Comprehensive Psychiatry*, *12*(2), 103–115.

———, & Itzkowitz, N. (1984). *The immortal Atatürk: A psychobiography*. Chicago: University of Chicago Press.

Voon, M.L., Lo, M.C., Ngui, K.S. and Ayob, N.B. (2011). "The influence of leadership styles on employees' job satisfaction in public sector organizations in Malaysia." *International Journal of Business, Management and Social Sciences* (Vol. 2, No. 1), pp. 24-32.

Waxler, N. E. (1981). The social labeling perspective on illness. In L. Eisenberg and A. Kleinman (Eds.), *The Relevance of Social Science for Medicine* (pp. 283–306). Boston: D. Reidel.

Winnicott, D. W. [1949] (1964). *The child, the family and the outside world*. Baltimore: Penguin Books.

———. (1953). Transitional objects and transitional phenomena: A study of the first not-me possession. *International Journal of Psycho-Analysis*, *34*(2), 89–97.

———. [1954] (1958). Metapsychological and clinical aspects of regression within the psycho-analytical set-up. In *Collected Papers* (pp. 278–294). New York: Basic Books.

———. (1958). *Collected papers, through paediatrics to psychoanalysis* (pp. 229–242). London: Tavistock.

———. [1960] (1965a). The theory of the parent-infant relationship. In *The Maturational Processes and the Facilitating Environment* (pp. 37–55). New York: International Universities Press.

———. [1963] (1965b). Psychiatric disorders in terms of infantile maturational process-es. In *The Maturational Processes and the Facilitating Environment* (pp. 230–241). New York: International Universities Press.

———. (1965c). *The maturational processes and the facilitating environment.* New York: International Universities Press.

———. (1967). The location of cultural experience. *International Journal of Psycho-Analysis, 48,* 368–372.

———. (1971). *Playing and reality.* London: Tavistock.

Yalom, I. D. (1970). *The theory and practice of group psychotherapy.* New York: Basic Books.

Zaleznick, A. (1989). *The managerial mystique: Restoring leadership in business.* New York: Harper and Row.

Zinner, J, & Shapiro, R. (1972). Projective identification as a mode of perception and behavior in families of adolescents. *International Journal of Psycho-Analysis, 53,* 523–530.

Index